Triangulating Methodological Approaches in Corpus-Linguistic Research

Contemporary corpus linguists use a wide variety of methods to study discourse patterns. This volume provides a systematic comparison of various methodological approaches in corpus linguistics through a series of parallel empirical studies that use a single corpus dataset to answer the same overarching research question. Ten contributing experts each use a different method to address the same broadly framed research question: In what ways does language use in online Q+A forum responses differ across four world English varieties (India, Philippines, UK, and US)? Contributions are based on analysis of the same 400,000 word corpus from online Q+A forums, and contributors employ methodologies including corpus-based discourse analysis, audience perceptions, multi-dimensional analysis, pragmatic analysis, and keyword analysis.

In their introductory and concluding chapters, the volume editors compare and contrast the findings from each method and assess the degree to which 'triangulating' multiple approaches may provide a more nuanced understanding of a research question, with the aim of identifying a set of complementary approaches which could arguably take into account analytical blind spots. Baker and Egbert also consider the importance of issues such as researcher subjectivity, type of annotation, the limitations and affordances of different corpus tools, the relative strengths of qualitative and quantitative approaches, and the value of considering data or information beyond the corpus. Rather than attempting to find the 'best' approach, the focus of the volume is on how different corpus-linguistic methodologies may complement one another and raises suggestions for further methodological studies which use triangulation to enrich corpus-related research.

Paul Baker is Professor of English Language at Lancaster University. His research involves applications of corpus linguistics, and his recent books include *Using Corpora to Analyze Gender* (2014), *Discourse Analysis and Media Attitudes* (2013), and *Sociolinguistics and Corpus Linguistics* (2010). He is the commissioning editor of the journal *Corpora*.

Jesse Egbert is Assistant Professor of Linguistics and English Language at Brigham Young University. His research focuses on register variation and methodological issues in corpus linguistics. His research has been published in journals such as *Corpora*, *International Journal of Corpus Linguistics*, *Applied Linguistics*, and *Journal of English Linguistics*.

Routledge Advances in Corpus Linguistics

Edited by
Tony McEnery,
Lancaster University, UK
Michael Hoey,
Liverpool University, UK

For a full list of titles in this series, please visit www.routledge.com

8 Public Discourses of Gay Men
Paul Baker

9 Semantic Prosody
A Critical Evaluation
Dominic Stewart

10 Corpus-Assisted Discourse Studies on the Iraq Conflict
Wording the War
Edited by John Morley and Paul Bayley

11 Corpus-Based Contrastive Studies of English and Chinese
Richard Xiao and Tony McEnery

12 The Discourse of Teaching Practice Feedback
A Corpus-Based Investigation of Spoken and Written Modes
Fiona Farr

13 Corpus Approaches to Evaluation
Susan Hunston

14 Corpus Stylistics and Dickens's Fiction
Michaela Mahlberg

15 Spoken Corpus Linguistics
From Monomodal to Multimodal
Svenja Adolphs and Ronald Carter

16 Digital Literary Studies
Corpus Approaches to Poetry, Prose, and Drama
David L. Hoover, Jonathan Culpeper, and Kieran O'Halloran

17 Triangulating Methodological Approaches in Corpus-Linguistic Research
Edited by Paul Baker and Jesse Egbert

Triangulating Methodological Approaches in Corpus-Linguistic Research

Edited by Paul Baker and Jesse Egbert

Routledge
Taylor & Francis Group
New York London

First published 2016
by Routledge
711 Third Avenue, New York, NY 10017
2 Park Square, Milton Park, Abingdon, Oxfordshire OX14 4RN

Routledge is an imprint of the Taylor & Francis Group, an informa business

First issued in paperback 2018

Library of Congress Cataloging-in-Publication Data
Names: Baker, Paul, 1972– editor. | Egbert, Jesse, 1985– editor.
Title: Triangulating methodological approaches in corpus linguistic research / Edited by Paul Baker and Jesse Egbert.
Description: New York : Routledge, [2016] | Series: Routledge Advances in Corpus Linguistics ; 17 | Includes bibliographical references and index.
Identifiers: LCCN 2016003274 | ISBN 9781138850255 (hardback : alk. paper) | ISBN 9781315724812 (ebk.)
Subjects: LCSH: Corpora (Linguistics)—Technological innovations. | Corpora (Linguistics)—Methodology. | Computational linguistics.
Classification: LCC P128.C68 T75 2016 | DDC 410.1/88—dc23
LC record available at http://lccn.loc.gov/2016003274

ISBN: 978-1-138-85025-5 (hbk)
ISBN: 978-0-367-02433-8 (pbk)

Typeset in Sabon
by Apex CoVantage, LLC

The research presented here was supported by the ESRC Centre for Corpus Approaches to Social Science, ESRC grant reference ES/K002155/1.

Contents

Tables

Figures

1 Introduction

Paul Baker and Jesse Egbert

Introduction

This chapter serves as an introduction to the aims and structure of the book. It begins with an outline of the aim of the project we undertook, as well as a brief discussion of the concepts and central tenets of corpus linguistics and triangulation. This is followed by a survey of the small amount of triangulation-related research in corpus linguistics. Next, we outline how the project was conceived, giving a description of the corpus used in the project, how analysts were contacted, and how they were asked to carry out an analysis. The corpus-driven versus corpus-based distinction is used as a starting point for explaining how the analyses were grouped and ordered in the book. The chapter ends with a short overview of the ten analysis chapters.

All Roads Lead to Rome?

Around 20 BC, Emperor Caesar Augustus erected the Golden Milestone, a monument in the central forum of Ancient Rome. Such was the power of the Empire that all roads were considered to begin from it and distances were measured from that point, resulting in the still-used phrase (or variations upon it) 'All roads lead to Rome'. Today the phrase is not used literally, but more colloquially it means 'it doesn't matter how you do it, you'll get the same result'.

In this book, we set out to test the applicability of the phrase to corpus linguistics, a method (or collection of principles and procedures) which uses large collections of naturally occurring language texts (written, spoken, or computer mediated) that are sampled and balanced in order to represent a particular variety (e.g. nineteenth century fiction, twentieth century news articles, twenty-first century tweets). In dealing with real, often unpredictable and linguistically 'messy' texts, corpus linguistics differs from introspective methods of analysis which can rely on neater but somewhat artificial-looking cases of language such as 'the duke gave my aunt this teapot' (Halliday & Matthiessen 2004: 53).[1] It also differs from more traditionally human-based qualitative research in that extremely large numbers of texts are analysed with the help of computers which process data and carry out statistical tests in order to identify unexpectedly frequent or salient language patterns. However, it would be unfair to cast corpus linguistics as a merely quantitative form of analysis—the patterns need to be interpreted and explained by human researchers, and this involves close reading of the texts in a corpus, often abetted again by corpus tools which can present the texts or sections of them in ways that make it easier for human eyes to process. As Biber (1998: 4) points out, 'Association patterns represent quantitative relations, measuring the extent to which features and variants are associated with contextual factors. However functional (qualitative) interpretation is also an essential step in any corpus-based analysis'.

Corpus linguists are thus able to make fairly confident generalisations about the varieties of language they are examining based on the combination of automated and human elements to the analysis. The automated side helps to direct the human researcher to aspects of the corpus that he or she may not have thought interesting to look at (a form of analysis which Tognini-Bonelli (2001) called corpus driven), but it can also help to confirm or refute existing researcher hypotheses (referred to as corpus-based analysis). Partington, Duguid, and Taylor (2013: 9) refer to the serendipity of corpus research as

> the chancing upon hitherto unforeseen phenomena or connections . . . Evidence-driven research is highly likely to take the researcher into uncharted waters because the observations arising from the data will inevitably dictate to a considerable degree which next steps are taken.

Does an uncharted corpus contain a set of discoverable 'findings', possibly a finite number, or at least a smallish subset which most people would concur are particularly notable or even unexpected (the opposite of so-called 'so what' findings (Baker & McEnery 2015: 9)). And if so, is it the case that, assuming the analyst has a reasonably high degree of experience and expertise, the procedures of corpus linguistics will direct everybody to the same set of salient findings, the same serendipities? In other words, if we vary the procedure and analyst, but keep the research question and the corpus the same, are we likely to obtain similar outcomes? For corpus linguists, do all roads really lead to Rome?

Why would it matter if they don't? A key advantage of corpus linguistics over other forms of analysis is that the computational procedures are thought to remove human cognitive, social, or political biases which may skew analysis in certain directions or even lead to faulty conclusions. Unlike humans, computers do not care about what they study, so there is no chance that their findings are misguided by conviction ('I know it's true; it must be true!'). Nor do computers make errors due to fatigue or boredom. It is tempting to view corpus linguistics in a similar light to 'hard' sciences such as biology or chemistry, where phenomena can be objectively measured.

Potassium placed in water will always result in potassium hydroxide and hydrogen gas. There is a sense of reassurance about the replicability of that kind of research—facts are facts. And with its reliance on scientific, empirical notions of sampling, balance and representativeness in corpus construction, along with the certainty that our tools and procedures of analysis will not mislead us, corpus linguists might not be blamed if they experience a robust feeling of confidence about the validity of their findings.

But what if this is not the case? What if say, ten people, all with their own favourite way of doing corpus linguistics, all good at what they do, were given the same corpus and research question and asked to produce an analysis. What if they all found different things? Even worse, what if their findings disagreed? Would that render the method unworkable? Or would it tell us something interesting in itself? These are the issues which inspired this edited collection, and we explore them by carrying out a comparison of ten analyses of the same corpus in order to see the extent to which all roads actually do lead to Rome. Such a meta-analysis hopefully provides a clearer picture around questions of analytical objectivity and also should give insight into what individual techniques can achieve and how they may complement one another. A different way of looking at this collection of chapters, though, is that they also work as analyses in themselves of a corpus of an 'emerging' register of language. They tell many interesting things about how people who have learnt different varieties of English use this form of language in ways that reflect aspects of their identity and culture.

Triangulation

Triangulation is a term taken from land surveying which uses distance from and direction to two landmarks in order to elicit bearings on the location of a third point (hence completing one triangle). According to Layder (1993: 128), methodological triangulation facilitates validity checks of hypotheses, anchors findings in more robust interpretations and explanations, and allows the researcher to respond flexibly to unforeseen problems and aspects of the research. Such triangulation can involve using multiple methods, analysts, or datasets, and it has been used for decades by social scientists as a means of explaining behaviour by studying it from two or more perspectives (Webb, Campbell, Schwartz & Sechrest, 1966, Glaser & Strauss 1967, Newby 1977, Layder 1993, Cohen & Manion 2000). Most contemporary corpus linguists employ triangulation to an extent in their own research by, for example, using different techniques on their corpora. However, the potential benefits of triangulating the results of two or more corpus-linguistic methods have been largely unexplored.

This book is not the first study of this kind, although it is the largest study of triangulation in corpus linguistics that we are aware of. Prior to our study, there existed a collection by van Dijk and Petofi (1977) which contained multiple analyses of a short story called "The Lover and His Lass" by James Thurber. Grimshaw (1994) contains a collection of analyses of a transcript of a thesis defence, while another collection by van den Berg, Wetherell, and Houtkoop-Steenstra (2004) involves 12 chapters which each analyse the same transcript of interview data about race. Grimshaw's book is the only one which attempts to synthesize the analyses in a concluding chapter called 'What Have We Learnt?', but all three collections consist of qualitative analyses of relatively short texts and do not involve corpus-based methods.

It is worth describing two related pieces of research in more detail before moving further on, as they function as unintended pilot studies to this one, both involving corpus-based critical discourse analysis of newspapers. First, Marchi and Taylor (2009) separately carried out critical analyses of a newspaper corpus, asking the question 'how do journalists talk about themselves/each other and their profession in a corpus of British media texts?' In comparing their results, they noted a range of convergent (broadly similar), complementary (different but not contradictory), and dissonant (contradictory) findings. An example of a dissonant finding was that one analyst concluded that journalists tend to talk about themselves, while the other noted that they do not talk about themselves but instead refer to other newsmakers. Both journalists had convergent findings relating to notions of good and bad journalism, while complementary findings were cases where analysts focused on related but different aspects of the corpus data. For example, one analyst noted a number of metaphors which constructed journalists as beasts, e.g. *press pack*, *feeding frenzy*, while the other pointed out that journalism is a highly reflexive activity, talking about and to itself. These two findings function together as pieces of a larger picture. Marchi and Taylor (2009: 18) conclude that 'the implementation of triangulation within a research study in no way guarantees greater validity, nor can it be used to make claims for "scientific" neutrality'.

Second, one of the authors of this chapter carried out a slightly larger pilot study (Baker 2015), giving five analysts a newspaper corpus about foreign doctors and asking 'How are foreign doctors represented in this corpus?' While Marchi and Taylor's meta-analysis was more qualitative and reflective, this study attempted to impose an element of quantification onto the analysis by counting and comparing findings. Of the 26 separate findings identified across the reports, all five analysts agreed on only one: the finding that foreign doctors were criticized (and thus seen as unwanted) for having poor language skills. A further five findings were shared by at least three out of the five analysts, but the majority (17) were only made by a single analyst. While this meta-analysis did not point to a great deal of shared discovery, unlike Marchi and Taylor, no cases were found where the analysts had completely divergent results. Instead, the results were mainly different but complementary. A conclusion from this research was that a productive analysis would be one where either multiple techniques were used or where a single technique was carried out exhaustively (e.g., a close reading of all concordance lines of a relevant search term rather than a sample). Reflecting back on this study, it could be argued that the analysts were perhaps restricted in terms of having quite a narrow research question to answer—based on how foreign doctors were represented in the corpus, but at the same time they were given a great deal of freedom in terms of how they approached the analysis—with the result that some people carried out multiple methods while others only undertook one procedure, possibly making comparisons somewhat unreasonable.

Pilot studies are most useful if we can take lessons from them, and the aforementioned study by Baker (2015) helped in the design of the larger study which takes up this book. We used a wider research question along with a more general corpus which did not contain a single overarching finding (such as the British press are hostile towards foreign doctors). We also discussed the intended methods that we wished the analysts to carry out to ensure that each one used a single main technique rather than some of them carrying out their own triangulatory methods. Finally, while at least one chapter in the book takes a critical perspective towards the corpus, unlike the two studies described earlier, we did not aim to restrict the current project to only critical corpus analyses of discourse. Instead, analysts were given a wider scope to carry out any form of linguistic research on the corpus.

Question-and-Answer Forums

In this section, we describe the rationale behind the creation of the Q+A corpus which the analysts used.

A Q+A forum is a website that allows users to post questions and contribute answers on a variety of topics. After selecting a relevant topic strand, users can post a question to request information, advice, or opinions from others. The requester then waits for other users to read their question and post responses. The question strand typically closes once the requester has selected the best answer. Then the question and the entire strand of answers remains online for others to view. Users do not usually receive any money for contributing answers. However, an incentive, such as earning points, is often offered for contributing answers.

It is estimated that interactive discussion websites, such as Q+A forums, make up more than 6% of the web pages on the Internet (Biber, Egbert, & Davies, 2015: 23). This is a staggering number considering the vast array of text types (see Biber et al. 2015) and the huge number of web pages online.[2] In 2012, Yahoo! reported that over 300 million questions had been asked since the service began in 2005.[3]

Despite the prominence of Q+A forums in the online community, there has been surprisingly little research on the linguistic features of this register. There has been some linguistic research on the more general domain of computer-mediated communication (CMC) (see, e.g., Herring 1996). A study by Knight (2015) compared modal verb use in the CANCELC corpus of emails, blogs, discussion boards, text messages, and tweets with the spoken and written sections of the British National Corpus. Hypothesising that as CMC contains both features of speech and writing, modal verb use in CANCELC would fall somewhere in between the two, Knight was surprised to find that in fact some of the highest use of modals occurred in CANCELC, especially in emails, texts, and discussion boards. Knight concludes that for these three forms, modal verb use acts as a relationship maintenance device, marking connectedness between sender and sendee.

In another corpus-based study, Titak and Roberson (2013) investigated the linguistic features of reader comments, finding that they frequently use features associated with a more personal, narrative focus and direct statements of opinion. Some researchers have explored the use of online forums for foreign language learning (Hanna & de Nooy 2003; Mazzolini & Maddison 2007). However, it should be noted that there are clear situational differences between Q+A forums and other CMC registers.

Some computational linguists have taken an interest in classifying Q+A forum responses into categories such as 'conversational' and 'informational' (Harper, Moy, & Konstan, 2009). Others have developed computational models designed to predict answer quality (Adamic, Zhang, Bakshy, & Ackerman, 2008; Shah & Pomerantz 2010), requester satisfaction (Liu, Bian, & Agichtein, 2008), and user participation (Shah, Oh, & Oh, 2008).

In one of the only linguistic studies that included Q+A forums, Biber & Egbert (forthcoming) showed that these forums use high frequencies of linguistic features typically associated with oral registers (e.g., personal pronouns and adverbs) and low frequencies of features associated with written registers (e.g., nominalizations, attributive adjectives). This study showed that Q+A forums tend to use more features of narrative (e.g., past tense, third-person pronouns) and fewer features associated with informational prose (e.g., pre-modifying nouns). However, Biber and Egbert's study was a comprehensive linguistic analysis of more than 30 web registers, and Q+A forums were mentioned only briefly.

We believe the Q+A forum is an ideal register to focus this book around as it (a) is an emerging register that enables examination of linguistic innovation, (b) is largely unexplored by corpus linguists, and (c) lends itself to comparisons with spoken and written registers. Also, the Q+A forums often involve discussion of topics such as current events, relationships, religion, language, family, society, and culture, which are pertinent to discourse analytical approaches.

The Q+A Corpus

As the focus of the book, we have compiled a 400,000 word corpus consisting of web pages from online Q+A forums. We designed the Q+A corpus to be balanced across two strata: country and topic. We collected data from four countries where English is widely spoken, UK, US, India, and the

Philippines, allowing the potential for comparison between different Englishes. Two of the countries (UK and US) could be viewed as containing a majority of native speakers of English, while India and the Philippines have English as a nonindigenous 'imported' variety. In India, 10.35% of the population uses English, although only 0.1% have English as their first language (Census of India 2003; Tropf 2004). The Government of India uses both Hindi and English with the latter viewed as an associate or assistant official language. In the Philippines, 63.71% of the population aged over five speak English (Philippines National Statistic Office 2005), although 0.4% have English as a first language (Gonzalez 1998). English is taught in schools as one of the two official languages of the country (the other is Filipino).

As we mentioned in the previous section, very little research has been done on the language of Q+A forums. However, there has been a great deal of previous corpus research on English in India and the Philippines. The Kolaphur Corpus is a corpus of Indian English created in 1978 that has been widely used in studies of this world English variety (e.g., Leitner 1991; Devyani 2001; Wilson 2005). The International Corpus of English (ICE) has subcorpora for both Indian English (ICE-IND) and Philippine English (ICE-PHI). These have been used extensively in previous research. For example, Collins (2009) investigated the frequencies of modals across nine varieties of English, including data from the ICE-IND and ICE-PHI. Zipp and Bernaisch (2012) also included the ICE-IND and ICE-PHI in a comparative study of particle verbs. Friginal (2007) investigated the use of a large set of linguistic features in a corpus of outsourced call centers in the Philippines.

Within each of the four countries, we sampled roughly equal numbers of texts from three topic areas: Society & Culture, Family & Relationships, and Politics & Government. We established several criteria that determined whether a question was considered a candidate for inclusion in the corpus. Our sampling procedures were simple: we began with the most recent question and worked through the questions in reverse chronological order, including each question that met the following criteria until we achieved our target corpus size. First, each question was required to have 'resolved' status, meaning that the requester had selected a 'best answer' and the question was no longer accepting responses. Second, we required each question to have at least five answers that included at least one complete sentence in an effort to collect enough running text for the corpus analyses in this book. Third, in order to achieve a variety of topics, we required that each question must be distinct from other questions in the corpus, e.g., if there were two questions which used a different wording but essentially asked the same question, we only selected one of them for inclusion. Finally, some of the questions had more than 100 answers. In these cases, we only included the first 50 answers in an effort to minimize the influence of a single text on the overall corpus. Before doing this, we sorted the answers from oldest to newest and sampled chronologically beginning with the oldest text. This was done to retain the original order of the answers. For each question, we always included the best answer in the corpus text. Using this design and these principles, we collected the corpus manually in a cyclical fashion in order to achieve balance and representativeness of each country and topic.

Each question and its associated answers were stored in plain text format. This process eliminated all graphics and images. However, these were actually quite rare. Additionally, any non-ASCII characters were also eliminated. The texts were annotated with tags marking the start and end of (a) the question, (b) any additional details included by the requester, (c) each answer, and (d) the best answer. We also included header information at the beginning of each text that included

1 Complete URL
2 Country
3 Topic
4 Total number of answers
5 Word count

Each text file was then saved using a filename that contained a two-digit country code, a two-digit topic code, and a unique two-digit ID number. For example, UK_PG_01 was the filename for the first Q+A text from the Politics & Government topic in the UK variety. Finally, a copy of each text was tagged using the CLAWS 7 part of speech tagger (Garside 1987), resulting in an untagged and a tagged version of the Q+A corpus. Table 1.1 contains a description of the corpus.

Table 1.1 Composition of the Q+A corpus with total text counts, total word counts, and mean word counts across varieties

	Word count	*Text count*	*Mean word count*
IN_FR	34089	23	1482
IN_PG	33939	24	1414
IN_SC	34036	22	1547
IN Subtotal	102064	69	1479
PH_FR	33891	23	1474
PH_PG	34076	22	1549
PH_SC	33763	21	1608
PH Subtotal	101730	66	1541
UK_FR	33136	21	1578
UK_PG	33819	22	1537
UK_SC	33433	20	1672
UK Subtotal	100388	63	1593
US_FR	34146	22	1552
US_PG	33989	21	1619
US_SC	34090	24	1420
US Subtotal	102225	67	1526
Overall Total	406407	265	1534

Study Procedures

As discussed in previous sections, the overarching purpose of this book is to carry out a grand experiment that will help us determine the potential of methodological triangulation in corpus-linguistic research. We began by developing the following two-part research question:

> In what ways does language use in online Q+A forum responses differ across
>
> - four world English varieties (India, Philippines, UK, and US)
> - and/or among topic (Society & Culture, Family & Relationships, and Politics & Government)?

We believed that this research question was broad enough to be addressed using a wide variety of corpus methods while still being narrow enough to produce answers that could be compared across methods. The question thus contains two parts, allowing analysts to choose to focus on either difference between language variety or between topic or both. The wording of the question perhaps indicates that we placed a higher premium on the first part involving language varieties, and, indeed, this part of the question tended to receive the most focus overall. However, some analysts addressed the second part of the question involving variation around topic and, in particular, this part of the question functioned as a useful 'backup' if analysts did not find that their approach resulted in much to say about differences among the language varieties. A pertinent point to make here is that within many kinds of research, it is differences that tend to be seen as more interesting and worthy of reporting than similarities (which can be perceived as a *lack* of difference), although see Baker (2010) and Taylor (2013) who argue for greater consideration of similarity in corpus research.

As the two editors of this volume and the creators of the corpus, we decided that we would contribute a chapter each. We both proposed a particular type of analysis and then worked on our own chapters at the same time and independently. This ensured that our engagement with the corpus was not influenced by reading findings from other researchers and also gave us the opportunity to iron out any problems (e.g., tagging inconsistencies) with the corpus that might have arisen. Once we had finished our own chapters, we exchanged them and made comments. Unlike other edited collections we have had experience working on, we have tried as much as possible to enable the authors to have as much freedom as possible in terms of the analysis that they carried out and the way that they communicated their findings. Indeed, a pleasurable aspect of editing this book was embracing the different writing styles of the analysts rather than trying to impose a flattened, standardized style across them. Where we did give notes they were concerned with issues such as typographical errors, unclear passages, or keeping to the word count (we asked authors to aim for 4,000–6,000 words that introduced their study aims, described their study methods, and outlined their results). In a couple of cases, we discussed the authors' focus on the Research Questions or asked them to consider explanations for their findings.

Once we had ascertained that we were able to conduct different analyses that produced something interesting, we next created a list of names of potential analysts to recruit. We chose potential analysts whose work we were familiar with, who were active researchers, and were experts in a particular method. Each analyst was sent the same email, where we detailed the project along with the corpus and the method of analysis we thought the analyst might consider using. We were aware that asking authors to be involved in such a project is potentially face threatening, and in order to make it clear that we were not aiming to show that any one method was better than the others, we included the following text as part of the letter we wrote to them:

> The book will be structured around the analysis chapters, with introduction sections written by the two editors which will outline the aims of the book and describe the corpus. The latter part of the book will involve a comparative analysis of the methods, along with discussion of different findings. We should stress that we don't intend to frame this as a competition to find the 'best' approach, but instead want to focus on the extent that different approaches can present findings that are unique or complementary.

The authors were provided with the research question introduced earlier, the corpus in tagged and untagged format, and some instructions regarding their task. We aimed for ten analyses in total, so with the two we had done ourselves, we decided to contact nine additional analysts (allowing for the possibility that one author might withdraw). Two of the authors recruited a colleague to help them, so two of the chapters are co-authored. This raises a potential issue with regard to the extent to which each chapter was produced under the same circumstances, but we acknowledge that it is impossible to account for all the variables that could have influenced how authors approached the chapter. The two joint contributions should be viewed as differing in one significant way from the other analyses, and the number of authors is certainly a factor that we do not wish to brush over.

As the project continued, three of the authors wrote to us that they were not able to complete their analysis. One author noted that they felt their approach to the corpus had not yielded anything interesting, another had a change of mind after receiving the corpus, and a third had to withdraw due to other commitments. Two additional authors were found to act as replacements, giving us the target of ten chapters. Although the two additional authors were recruited later in the project, they were given the same amount of time as the earlier authors to submit their chapters. Three out of an initial nine withdrawals was rather more than we had been expecting. This may be coincidence, or it could reflect how such meta-analyses can be daunting due to their comparative nature (unlike Baker's pilot study, the identities of all the analysts are made clear). In any case, we feel a sense of pride and gratitude towards the authors who contributed towards the collection, without whom the project would not have been possible.

After receiving revised drafts from each of the authors, the two co-editors independently carried out a comprehensive synthesis of the results from each of the ten chapters. Individual findings were recorded in an Excel spreadsheet. Any differences between our lists of findings was discussed until we reached agreement on the complete list of research findings from each chapter. We then grouped these findings into categories and noted any contradictions between findings from different chapters. Finally, we sent an email to each of the authors with the results of our research synthesis. We offered them the opportunity to review the findings from other authors and to write a brief (no more than 1,000 word) postscript for their chapter commenting on similarities and differences between their findings and the findings from other chapters. Six authors produced a postscript (Tony McEnery, Amanda Potts, Bethany Gray, Stefan Gries, Paul Baker, and Jesse Egbert).

The Ten Approaches

A useful distinction to cite here is one made by Tognini-Bonelli (2001: 65) between corpus-driven and corpus-based approaches. Broadly speaking, the former involve forms of analysis which do not start with a hypothesis or a predetermined set of features to examine. Instead the analysis is driven by corpus procedures which help to identify frequent or salient features. Corpus-driven approaches tend not to make any distinction between pre-corpus concepts such as lexis, syntax, or semantics, so they should avoid using tagged corpora which impose preconceived theories onto the data. On the other hand, corpus-based approaches involve a more targeted analysis on a (usually pre-selected) set of features in the corpus, sometimes to test an existing hypothesis. McEnery, Xiao, and Tono (2006: 11) argue that in fact 'the sharp distinction between the corpus-based vs. corpus-driven approaches to language studies is in reality fuzzy'. We agree, noting that it is very difficult to carry out a truly 'naïve' corpus-driven analysis and that most forms of analysis appear somewhere on a cline between the two extremes. We have tried to place the ten analysis chapters on this cline, and they are ordered in the book from what we feel is the most to the least corpus driven. We would characterize the first four analysis chapters (by Tony McEnery, Bethany Gray, Amanda Potts, and Eric Friginal and Doug Biber) as more towards the corpus-driven end of the cline, in that these four chapters consider the corpus in its entirety rather than looking for a smaller selection of features within it. The next four chapters (Vaclav Brezina, Stefan Gries, Jonathan Culpeper and Claire Hardaker, and Paul Baker) are more corpus-based in that a smaller

Table 1.2 The ten approaches

Framework	*Chapter*	*Approach*	*Author*
Roughly corpus driven (analysis of whole corpus)	2	Keywords	Tony McEnery
	3	Lexical bundles	Bethany Gray
	4	Semantic annotation	Amanda Potts
	5	Multi-dimensional analysis	Eric Friginal and Doug Biber
Roughly corpus-based (selecting smaller number of features)	6	Collocational networks	Vaclav Brezina
	7	Variationist analysis	Stefan Gries
	8	Pragmatic features	Jonathan Culpeper and Claire Hardaker
	9	Gendered discourses	Paul Baker
Close analysis of a sample from the corpus	10	Qualitative analysis of stance	Erez Levon
	11	Stylistic perception analysis	Jesse Egbert

set of phenomena within the corpus forms the basis of the interrogation. Finally, there are two chapters (Erez Levon and Jesse Egbert) that could be argued as not properly incorporating a corpus-driven or corpus-based form of analysis but instead involve a close analysis of a smaller sample of the corpus texts. Both of these chapters could be conceived as 'qualitative' analyses, although in different ways they both involve quantitative elements too. The approaches are summarized in Table 1.2.

Next we present a brief overview of each of the ten approaches, noting any pertinent points that were unique to an individual chapter or author.

Keywords: Tony McEnery

Tony McEnery's chapter could be considered the most 'corpus driven' of the ten approaches in that the starting unit of analysis was an unannotated word. Keywords are words which are statistically significantly more frequent in one corpus (or subset of a corpus) when compared against another corpus (or subset thereof), and Tony derives a set of keywords for each of the four language varieties by comparing each variety against the 'remainder' of the corpus (in this case, a combination of the other three subcorpora). The keywords technique is almost purely corpus driven in that every word in the corpus is considered potentially of interest, so the procedure drives what will be analysed. This is not the only chapter to use the keyness technique—it is also carried out by Amanda Potts in Chapter 4, although she implemented it on semantic categories rather than words. A potential issue with keywords is that they can produce too many words to adequately do justice to (Tony's procedure generated 234 keywords), and altering settings such as minimum frequency, dispersion, or keyness value can result in different numbers of keywords. Indeed, an entire book on triangulation could have been devoted to ten keyword studies of the same corpus, each using different settings.

Lexical Bundles: Bethany Gray

While Tony McEnery's chapter considers single words, Bethany Gray looks at fixed sequences of words. As lexical bundles tend to be less frequent than words, applying keyness techniques to bundles does not always result in much to analyse, unless extremely liberal settings are applied. Bethany does not use keyness then to identify bundles of interest but instead bases her analysis around four-word bundles which occur at least ten times across at least five files in the corpus, resulting in a working set of 82 bundles. While Tony's classification of keywords was a bottom-up process, based on assigning words to semantic fields by hand and thus requiring the creation of semantic fields as an ongoing process, existing research on lexical bundles has resulted in a pre-existing categorization scheme based on structural type and discourse function. Therefore, once the bundles were identified, the analysis was of the top-down variety, with different bundles assigned into the pre-set functional categories. Bethany's chapter is distinctive from the others in the book in that most of the analysts focused on the first part of the research question, which involved comparing the four language varieties. However, Bethany did not find that there was much variation when she addressed this question. While a conclusion of 'there is hardly any difference' constitutes a finding in itself and is worth reporting, Bethany's analysis, perhaps understandably, moves to the second part of the research question, which involves a comparison of the topic groups.

Semantic Annotation: Amanda Potts

We have placed Amanda Potts's chapter third, as it incorporates an existing annotation scheme from the outset onto the corpus data, although it could still be conceived as corpus driven in that a keyness approach is taken which allows for any feature of the corpus to emerge as interesting. Amanda's analysis fits neatly alongside the previous two chapters then, in that it uses keyness like Tony McEnery's but also employs a pre-existing categorisation scheme like Bethany Gray's. As with Tony's chapter, the four varieties are each compared in turn against the 'remainder' of the corpus to result in a list of key items (in this case, groups of words which have received the same semantic tag). The rationale behind such a procedure is that single words may not be frequent enough to be key, but if words of similar meaning are grouped together, then the concept they refer to may emerge as key, something which could be overlooked by a qualitative analyst or even a traditional keywords approach. It is worth noting that this chapter was one where we engaged in some discussion with the author in regard to the measure used to calculate key categories, and it was eventually decided to use the log-likelihood measure in order to enable a clearer comparison with Tony's chapter. Clearly though, choice of measure is likely to impact on the key items elicited.

Multi-dimensional Analysis: Eric Friginal and Doug Biber

Chapter 5 is perhaps the last chapter that we could argue as taking a more corpus driven than corpus-based approach in terms of it using an automated technique to see what emerges as interesting. As with the previous chapter, the corpus is subjected to a pre-existing annotation scheme, although unlike semantic annotation, where every word receives a tag (and is thus considered as potentially interesting), the multi-dimensional analysis approach is based on the tagging and counting of over 100 grammatical, syntactic, and semantic features which are then subjected to multivariate analysis to identify how features co-occur. Therefore, not every word in the corpus is tagged or counted. Rather than extracting linguistic dimensions from a new multi-dimensional analysis, Eric Friginal and Doug Biber relied on Dimension 1 from Biber's (1988) study, which constitutes a linear scale from involved to informational language production as eliciting the greatest amount of difference between the four subcorpora, and while all the texts were fairly 'involved', there were contrasts between native and non-native varieties, as well as differences around topic. Eric and Doug offer some explanations for their findings based on a discussion around the education status and potential homogeneity of non-native posters and the influence of British and American culture.

Collocational Networks: Vaclav Brezina

Vaclav Brezina's analysis is based on collocational networks around three high-frequency words in the corpus: *god*, *love*, and *president*, as well as a set of predetermined words (*wh-* question words) which were deemed to be a relevant indicator of the nature of the corpus. The use of frequency list comparisons to determine some the words to analyse suggests a corpus-driven approach similar to the previous four chapters, although the smaller number of words examined, along with some of the words being decided in advance, is perhaps more indicative of the corpus-based chapters which follow. Both Vaclav's chapter and Eric Friginal and Doug Biber's offer visual representations of the corpus data, with the former showing how collocates link together in the various subcorpora and the latter indicating where the subcorpora fit along the involved versus informational dimension. The collocational networks show how concepts are linked together more closely in some of the subcorpora. Such links (or lack of links) are thus revealing of different cultural attitudes.

Variationist Analysis: Stefan Gries

We now come to the more clearly corpus-based approaches as Stefan Gries undertakes an analysis of future choice in the corpus. Initially taking a 'traditional' approach, Stefan calculates the proportion of times writers use *will* as opposed to *going to* in each of the four language varieties, indicating that the two native speaker varieties rely on *will* rather less than the non-native speaker varieties. However, Stefan argues that it is important to try to take into account the wide number of factors which could have played a role in the frequencies of the different forms. His following analysis examines individual speaker variability, noting that speakers show variability in their use of *will* and that there is more variability between speakers of the language varieties than for the different topics. A second factor which Stefan tries to account for is lexically specific variation, indicating that use of *will*, *going to*, or *shall* can be dependent on the verb lemma they occur with. A third factor which Stefan considers is structural priming. Is it the case that speakers exhibit priming effects, i.e., they will repeat the same linguistic choices over time? In considering a wider range of factors that may contribute towards linguistic variation, this chapter acts as an insightful critique, warning us not to over-interpret differences between language varieties as due to culture alone, offering a unique perspective in the book.

Pragmatics: Jonathan Culpeper and Claire Hardaker

Addressing the fact that the examination of pragmatic features would appear to be a 'non-starter' for corpus linguistics, this chapter demonstrates some novel techniques for identifying a relevant subset of features to examine. Like the chapter by Amanda Potts, the chapter uses the semantic tagger Wmatrix. In this case though, it is to identify metapragmatic labels relating to speech acts, leading to an analysis of two speech acts that were chosen because they were both frequent and interpersonally sensitive: *blame* and *apologise*. Wmatrix is also utilized in the second part of the analysis, which focusses on words that have been tagged as 'Discourse Bin' and function as pragmatic noise. This led to a focus on two further words: *hey* and *wow*, again due to their frequency. The analysis thus tends towards being corpus-based in that a particular type of linguistic phenomena (pragmatic features) has been chosen in advance, although corpus-driven procedures based on frequency help to narrow that focus down to just four linguistic items. The third part of the analysis carries out a categorization of question-response patterns across the four language varieties and three topics. The chapter thus indicates how corpus methods can be fruitfully applied to research projects of a pragmatic nature.

Gendered Discourses: Paul Baker

Paul Baker's chapter takes a more socially critical approach to the corpus by considering whether there are differences between the four language varieties in terms of how gender is conceptualized. Beginning with a comparison of simple frequencies of gendered nouns and pronouns, Paul then moves to a second, more qualitative form of analysis, involving examination and categorization of concordance lines that contained the following gendered nouns: *men*, *women*, *girls*, *boys*, *guys*, *gentlemen*, and *ladies*. These concordance lines were categorized into sets of gendered discourses, depending on the ways that gender was conceptualized by the writers. The gendered discourses tended to discuss 'common-sense' characteristics about typical characteristics of men and women and how they relate to one another. Returning to a qualitative analysis, Paul then compared instances of these discourses across the four language varieties and ends his chapter by discussing how the discourses relate to different cultural contexts.

Qualitative Analysis of Stance: Erez Levon

The final two analysis chapters of the book offer somewhat different methodological approaches, making it difficult to classify them as either corpus driven or corpus based, demonstrating how a corpus can lend itself to a wide range of perhaps unexpected forms of inquiry. Both of these chapters involve analysis of smaller samples of the corpus. Erez Levon uses a corpus tool called ProtAnt (Anthony & Baker 2015) to carry out a qualitative analysis of stance on a principled, representative set of texts. ProtAnt calculates keywords in individual texts and then ranks texts in order of prototypicality based on the number of keywords they have. The 12 most prototypical texts (one from each combination of language variety and topic) amounted to around 15,000 words. Having identified a representative sample, Erez uses a number of analytical tools to identify stance-taking within it: overt politeness mechanisms, structural resonance, and inter-textuality. As with Bethany Gray's chapter, which worked with lexical bundles, Erez found that the most fruitful way of carrying out the comparison was by topic rather than by language variety, with the Politics & Government texts having questions that contained evaluations and the Society & Culture ones being more information-seeking. However, some differences at the level of language variety did emerge. While taking a very different route and using a much smaller dataset, it is notable that Erez's analysis came to quite similar conclusions as the more corpus-lexical approach taken by Jonathan Culpeper and Claire Hardaker.

Stylistic Perception: Jesse Egbert

Jesse Egbert's chapter also works with a sample of the corpus, using a random sampling method to elicit 60 questions and 300 answers. The first part of the analysis involves asking paid volunteers to rate the answers in terms of the extent that they perceived them to be readable, biased, effective, relevant, and informative. Jesse's approach is initially statistical, carrying out multivariate analyses of variance, factorial ANOVAs (Analysis of Variance), and correlations to identify significant differences in reader perceptions between the language varieties and topics. This is followed up with a qualitative component which considers specific uses of language in some of the questions that received particular ratings in order to attach explanations for the differences found. Jesse's chapter is perhaps the most distinct of the ten sets of analysis, although in its use of a sample of the data, it shares some commonalities with the previous chapter.

Conclusion

We hope that this volume demonstrates the wide variety of corpus-linguistic approaches that are available to the analysis of language data, and in the final chapter of the book, we focus on exploring their potential complementarity by carrying out a qualitative meta-analysis which compares the findings from the different chapters. Ultimately, we assess the degree to which the various methods can complement each other through triangulation of multiple methods, as well as offering some reflective insights into the ways that corpus linguistics employ methods and the extent to which they can be confident in their claims.

The next section of this volume contains the ten analysis chapters, organized according to the research goal categories described earlier. Finally, in Chapter 12, we offer a detailed report on the results of the comprehensive research synthesis. We identify systematic patterns in the findings, comment on the contributions of the various methods, and assess the usefulness of methodological triangulation in corpus linguistics. We then conclude the book by reflecting on the experimental process we carried out and discuss the implications of this experiment for corpus linguistics research.

Notes

1 To be fair, this excellent book on functional grammar takes the vast majority of its examples from real texts.
2 https://www.google.com/insidesearch/howsearchworks/thestory/
3 http://searchengineland.com/yahoo-answers-hits-300-million-questions-but-qa-activity-is-declining-127314

References

Adamic, L., Zhang, J., Bakshy, E. & Ackerman, M. (2008). Knowledge Sharing and Yahoo Answers: Everyone Knows Something. In *Proceedings of WWW.*

Anthony, L. & Baker, P. (2015). ProtAnt: A tool for analysing the prototypicality of texts. *International Journal of Corpus Linguistics*, 20, 273–293.

Baker, P. (2010). *Sociolinguistics and Corpus Linguistics*. Edinburgh: Edinburgh University Press.

Baker, P. (2015). Does Britain need any more foreign doctors? Inter-analyst consistency and corpus-assisted (critical) discourse analysis. In N. Groom, M. Charles & J. Suganthi (Eds.), *Corpora, Grammar and Discourse: In Honour of Susan Hunston* (pp. 283–300). Amsterdam/Atlanta: John Benjamins.

Baker, P. & McEnery, T. (Eds.) (2015). *Corpora and Discourse. Integrating Discourse and Corpora*. London: Palgrave MacMillan.

Biber, D. (1988). *Variation Across Speech and Writing*. Cambridge: Cambridge University Press.
Biber, D., Conrad, S. & Reppen, R. (1998). *Corpus Linguistics: Investigating Language Structure and Use*. Cambridge: Cambridge University Press.
Biber, D. & Egbert, J. (forthcoming). Register variation on the searchable web: A multi-dimensional analysis. *Journal of English Linguistics*. doi: 10.1177/0075424216628955.
Biber, D., Egbert, J. & Davies, M. (2015). Exploring the composition of the searchable web: A corpus-based taxonomy of web registers. *Corpora*, 10(1), 11–45.
Census of India (2003). *Languages of West Bengal in Census and Surveys, Bilingualism and Trilingualism*. New Delhi: Government of India.
Cohen, L. & Manion, L. (2000). *Research Methods in Education*. London: Routledge.
Collins, P. (2009). Modals and quasi-modals in world Englishes. *World Englishes*, 28(3), 281–292.
Devyani, S. (2001). The pluperfect in native and non-native English: A comparative corpus study. *Language Variation and Change*, 13, 343–373.
Friginal, E. (2007). Outsourced call centers and English in the Philippines. *World Englishes*, 26(3), 331–345.
Garside, R. (1987). The CLAWS word-tagging System. In R. Garside, G. Leech & G. Sampson (Eds.), *The Computational Analysis of English: A Corpus-Based Approach*. London: Longman. (pp. 30–41).
Glaser, B. G. & Strauss, A. L. (1967). *The Discovery of Grounded Theory: Strategies for Qualitative Research*. Chicago: Aldine.
Gonzalez, A. (1998). The language planning situation in the Philippines. *Journal of Multilingual and Multicultural Development*, 19(5&6), 478–525.
Grimshaw, A. D. (Ed.) (1994). *What's Going on Here: Complementary Studies of Professional Talk* (Vol. XLIII). Norwood, NJ: Ablex.
Halliday, M.A.K., and Matthiessen C.M.I.M. (2004). *An introduction to functional grammar*, 3rd ed. London: Arnold.
Hanna, B. E. & de Nooy, J. (2003). A funny thing happened on the way to the forum: Electronic discussion and foreign language teaching. *Language Learning & Technology*, 7(1), 71–85.
Harper, F. M., Moy, D. & Konstan, J. A. (2009). Facts or friends? Distinguishing informational and conversational questions in social Q&A sites. In *Proceedings of SIGCHI Conference on Human Factors in Computing Systems, New York: Association for Computer Machinery* (pp. 759–768).
Herring, S. C. (Ed.). (1996). *Computer-Mediated Communication: Linguistic, Social and Cross-Cultural Perspectives*. Amsterdam: John Benjamins.
Knight, D. (2015). e-Langauge: Communication in the Digital Age. In P. Baker & T. McEnery (Eds.), *Corpora and Discourse. Integrating Discourse and Corpora* (pp. 20–40). London: Palgrave MacMillan.
Layder, D. (1993). *New Strategies in Social Research*. Cambridge: Polity Press.
Leitner, G. (1991). The Kolhapur corpus of Indian English–intravarietal description and/or intervarietal comparison. In S. Johansson & A.-B. Stenström (Eds.), *English Computer Corpora: Selected Papers and Research Guide* (pp. 215–232). New York: Mouton de Gruyter.
Liu, Y., Bian, J. & Agichtein, E. (2008). Predicting information seeker satisfaction in community question answering. In *Proceedings of the ACM SIGIR International Conference on Research Development in Information Retrieval* (pp. 483–490). New York: Association for Computer Machinery.
Marchi, A. & Taylor, C. (2009). If on a winter's night two researchers . . . a challenge to assumptions of soundness of interpretation. *Critical Approaches to Discourse Analysis across Disciplines*, 3(1), 1–20.
Mazzolini, M. & Maddison, S. (2007). When to jump in: The role of the instructor in online discussion forums. *Computers and Education*, 49, 193–213.

McEnery, T., Xiao, R. & Tono, Y. (2006). *Corpus-Based Language Studies*. London: Routledge.
Newby, H. (1977). In the field: Reflections on the study of Suffolk farm workers. In C. Bell & H. Newby (Eds.), *Doing Sociological Research* (pp. 108–209). London: Allen and Unwin.
Partington, A., Duguid, A. & Taylor, C. (2013). *Patterns and Meanings in Discourse: Theory and Practice in Corpus-Assisted Discourse Studies (CADS)*. Studies in Corpus Linguistics. Amsterdam/Atlanta: John Benjamins.
Philippines National Statistics Office (2005). Educational characteristics of the Filiponos. Special Release 153. Accessed online at: https://psa.gov.ph/old/data/sectordata/sr05153tx.html
Shah, C., Oh, J. & Oh, S. (2008). Exploring characteristics and effects of user participation in online social Q&A sites. *First Monday*, 13(9): 18.
Shah, C. & Pomerantz, J. (2010). Evaluating and predicting answer quality in community QA. In *Proceedings of the ACM SIGIR International Conference on Research Development in Information Retrieval*, Geneva, Switzerland.
Taylor, C. (2013). Searching for similarity using corpus-assisted discourse studies. *Corpora*, 8(1), 81–113.
Titak, A. & Roberson, A. (2013). Dimensions of web registers: An exploratory multi-dimensional comparison. *Corpora*, 8(2), 239–271.
Tognini-Bonelli, E. (2001). *Corpus Linguistics at Work*. Studies in Corpus Linguistics: 6. Amsterdam/Atlanta: John Benjamins.
Tropf, H. S. (2004). *India and Its Languages*. Munich: Siemens AG.
van den Berg, H., Wetherell, M. & Houtkoop-Steenstra, H. (Eds.) (2004). *Analyzing Race Talk: Multidisciplinary Perspectives on the Research Interview*. Cambridge: Cambridge University Press.
van Dijk, T. A. & Petofi, J. (Eds.) (1977). *Grammars and Descriptions: Studies in Text Theory and Text Analysis*. Berlin: Walter de Gruyter.
Webb, E. J., Campbell, D. T., Schwartz, R. D. & Sechrest, L. (1966). *Unobtrusive Measures*. Chicago: Rand McNally.
Wilson, A. (2005). Modal verbs in written Indian English: A quantitative and comparative analysis of the Kolhapur corpus using correspondence analysis. *ICAME Journal*, 29, 151–169.
Zipp, L. & Bernaisch, T. (2012). Particle verbs across first and second language varieties of English. In M. Hundt & U. Gut (Eds.), *Mapping Unity and Diversity World-Wide* (pp 167–196). Amsterdam: John Benjamins.

2 Keywords

Tony McEnery

Introduction

In this chapter, I will use the keywords approach pioneered by Scott (1997) to explore the data provided. In the keywords approach, two corpora are compared to reveal words which have unusually high or low frequencies and point to salient uses of language. A standard approach to comparing two corpora is to take the data you are interested in and then compare it to a larger general reference corpus. That is a useful procedure to follow if you are interested in what makes your data distinct by comparison to general language usage. In the case of the data used in this study, such a comparison is most likely to reveal information about the register that the material was written in. Unless each comparison was done against a corpus reflecting the variety of English used in the data (Indian English, Philippine English, UK English, US English), then in addition we would find differences between the variety used in the corpus and the variety compared. So, for example, if I used the BNC (Aston & Burnard 1997) as a reference corpus, comparing each of the four corpora to it, then the UK material might reasonably show much about the Q+A register, while the other corpora would reflect the Q+A register for that variety of English and features that make that variety of English distinct from British English. The register variation could, in principle, have been factored out by gathering a Q+A corpus. However, to pursue that path would have been time consuming because one would have needed to gather a Q+A corpus for each variety of English being explored. Rather than do this, I decided that it would be better to see what made the discussions distinct from one another directly—not how they were distinct from a reference corpus in a different register or with a chat corpus. This approach, where data under investigation is divided in a meaningful fashion and the subparts of it are compared to one another to generate keywords, has been used by others (Baker 2006, Chapter 6; Culpeper 2009) and is useful at presenting what is important in the subdivisions of the corpus relative to other parts of the corpus.

In this study, the principled division of the data is into presumed varieties of English—I take the four subcorpora of data drawn from India, the Philippines, the UK and the US. We should be duly cautious about assuming that these represent entirely homogenous groups and be mindful of this when analysing the results—for example, there are many speakers of Indian heritage or nationality in the UK, and the Indian variety of English may thus be present in the UK material. With this note of caution in mind, I have compared each of the four subcorpora against the other three subcorpora in each case to produce a keyword list for that subcorpus. In doing so, I made two other decisions. First, I was not interested in keywords that were not well dispersed—my goal was not to find out what particularly vociferous individuals or lengthy discussions did to the data. My aim was to try to characterise the data as a whole. Hence a keyword in this study had to occur in at least five files. If any keyword was only key because of a majority of examples being drawn from one of the files in the corpus, i.e., from one discussion, I discarded it.

My second decision relates to frequency—I was not interested in low-frequency events. I did not wish to find words which were keywords in spite of being relatively infrequent. This was motivated by a desire, once again, to characterise what was typical in the dataset, i.e., keywords which characterised the data in general, not the rare and exceptional. Consequently a minimum frequency threshold of 20 occurrences in the corpus was set for the keyword procedure.

The keyword procedure uses a statistical test to determine whether a word is significantly more frequent or not. In this study, I used the log-likelihood procedure in WordSmith Tools to generate the wordlist. In doing so, given my desire to characterise the usual but relatively exceptional in the dataset, I adopted a (relatively inclusive) p value for the determination of keyness of 0.001.[1]

Keywords Found

The procedure outlined earlier generated 83 keywords for the Indian English material, 48 keywords for Philippine English, 46 keywords for UK English, and 57 keywords for US English. These are shown in Table 2.1 (note that WordSmith does not distinguish between upper- and lower-case letters when calculating keywords, so all the keywords have been written as lower case in the table).

This table is interesting in a very simple way—it shows how the tokenization procedures within the tool used determines what a word is. We shall not change that here, but note, for example, that this means one must concordance the original data to make any sense of certain keywords. So, for example, in Indian English *e* is a keyword largely because it is part of *i.e.*, which has an elevated frequency in that corpus. By default, WordSmith does not treat full stops as occurring within words, so it reads *i.e.* as two separate tokens. Similarly, *p* is a keyword in UK English in part because of a slight preference of contributors to the UK data to add a last note in the form of *p.s.* to their messages.

Table 2.1 The keywords in the four subcorpora

Variety	*Keywords*
Indian	*action, also, any, are, be, become, between, body, bush, by, can, communication, countries, country, culture, dear, e, each, educated, enjoy, every, evil, faith, focus, follow, god, govt, hands, happiness, human, important, in, india, indian, iran, iraq, is, islam, israel, knowledge, life, love, marriage, marry, mind, muslim, must, nation, national, necessary, of, others, our, peace, person, political, politicians, power, powerful, r, reason, religion, religions, religious, self, sex, should, society, terrorist, terrorists, thinking, thoughts, u, ur, us, very, we, which, wife, will, without, world, yourself*
Philippines	*and, ang, aquino, cant, christian, christians, constitution, doesnt, dont, during, election, filipino, filipinos, for, he, heart, her, hes, high, his, home, its, jesus, lets, liberal, married, na, obama, ones, parents, philippine, philippines, power, president, ready, respect, right, sacrifice, said, sin, things, times, truth, try, use, vote, will, world*
UK	*advice, american, americans, ask, at, been, bit, britain, british, dont, eat, england, english, eye, george, get, he, hear, http, ignore, i'm, it's, just, lol, look, looking, loved, m, me, my, p, probably, quite, read, say, side, sorry, them, they, think, two, uk, was, wedding, would, www*
US	*best, bill, care, city, considered, couple, difference, doesnt, dont, driving, facts, friends, friendship, girls, go, going, guy, had, her, hillary, i, its, job, keep, know, knows, lie, lies, like, lost, male, might, military, mom, money, obama, ones, out, parents, police, republican, republicans, right, running, said, she, she's, story, taxes, tell, trust, use, was, work, you, young, you're*

A further, very obvious, finding can be taken from Table 2.1. The register is clearly apparent in all of the keyword lists. Features of CMC—computer-mediated communication—(as noted by Ooi 2002, for example) are instantly visible; notably, non-standard orthography in the form of common abbreviations are present, such as the keyword *lol*, which are typical of the register, as are the use of speed-writing devices such as the keywords *u* or *ur* (used in place of *you* and *your*).

Of course the fact that some of these features are key in certain parts of the table indicates that the use of some of these devices by writers in the subcorpora may vary—so note, for example, that the speed-writing keywords *r*, *u*, and *ur* are key in the Indian subcorpus but not in any of the other subcorpora, indicating that this is a key feature of the Indian subcorpus relative to the other corpora. So while speed-writing devices of this sort may be a general feature of CMC, these specific examples seem to be used unusually frequently by the writers in one of the four subcorpora. The same applies to other CMC-related keywords, e.g., *lol* is key in the UK subcorpus, though it occurs with lower frequencies in the other corpora. So as well as finding that some of the subcorpora have preferences for specific examples of CMC usage, the general impression is of the CMC register being used across the corpora.

Setting register aside, I carried out a further analysis to explore the keyword table in more depth. This consisted of categorizing each word into a semantic field based on the most salient meaning that the keyword expresses. So, for example, a keyword such as *obama* may be put into the category Politician.[2] This can, on occasion, be done automatically using tools such as the UCREL Semantic Annotation System (USAS) (see Potts, Chapter 4). However, that tool is trained on British English and, for the purposes of this brief experiment, it was less time consuming for me to manually code the keywords rather than to hand correct the output from USAS. My purpose in making this categorization was to group together keywords so that key semantic fields that they are drawn from were highlighted. For example, the keywords *aquino*, *bill*, *bush*, *george*, and *hillary* were added to *obama* in the Politician semantic field, as they are used in the corpus to refer to specific politicians by name. The resulting analysis produced 91 semantic fields into which the 233 keywords were categorized. Note that this analysis may be called corpus driven—in each case the keyword arose from the corpus and was categorized according to a reading of the concordances of the keyword in the relevant subcorpus. Note also that a word may be placed in two semantic fields where it has a broadly balanced split between two meanings, as will be discussed shortly.

The analysis itself, if discussed completely, would clearly be too lengthy for the purposes of this chapter. So rather than introducing all of the semantic fields and analysing each of them in depth, I am going to focus on demonstrating how semantic fields may show similarities and differences between the four subcorpora. By means of this brief, illustrative analysis, I will show the type of findings that a keyword approach may provide.

Findings

The first point I would like to make is how keywords can show specific subcorpora to be quite distinctive. Fifty-eight of the 91 semantic fields—the majority—are only attested in one of the subcorpora. An exploration of the semantic fields in the Philippine subcorpus indicates how keywords may allow us to begin to see the distinctiveness of that discourse community. One field alone shows that point very well: the code-switching field. This is composed of just two keywords, *ang* and *na*. Both are frequent words in Tagalog and indicate that code-switching occurs in the subcorpus between English and Tagalog as in the following example from the Philippine subcorpus:

> 'the problem with most believers.. ang practice ng faith ay seasonal'. [PH_SC_01]

This is a good reminder that the note of caution sounded at the beginning of this chapter—that UK material, for example, did not simply mean data from an homogeneous language community—was a wise one. However, the absence of non-English keywords in the other three subcorpora indicates that, at the very least, code-switching is more frequent, or at least more systematically related to a singly non-English language, in the Philippine data. Another feature of the Philippine data is a series of keywords which generate semantic fields which relate to what one may characterise as conservative social values with keywords focussing around the home (*home*), direction (*lets*), restraint (*respect*), and a judgement of what is right (*right*). The keywords *lets* and *respect* require some exploration. With *lets*, there is a direction to agree on a particular position or action, such as

> 'Lets go to school and try to talk to your adviser', [PH_FR_08]
> 'lets just followed the catholic tradition', [PH_SC_01]
> 'lets just desensitize young people as much as we can'. [PH_SC_04]

With regards to restraint, in the Philippine data, there is a close link between respect and abstaining from sex before marriage, as in examples such as

> 'You will respect and appreciate one another much more knowing they are commited enough to wait'. [PH_FR_01]
> 'Practice pre-marital respect and consideration, and the sex question will answer itself'. [PH_FR_01]
> 'a man and woman build trust and respect for one another when they both survive the struggles of self-control'. [PH_FR_01]

This direction and restraint are clearly moral in nature and mesh with the moral overtones of *right*. Before discussing the word *right*, however, *lets* deserves a little more discussion. A possible explanation for this keyword not being explored so far is that it does not indicate a preference for direction; it may simply indicate one of the features of the CMC register in the Philippine data. Perhaps writers in this corpus prefer to drop the apostrophe in this contracted form while the writers in the other corpora do not. Normalised per 100,000 words, *lets* and *let's* occur 12.96 and 5.55 times in the Philippine data. In the other three corpora together, they occur 8.06 and 7.76 times, respectively. So while there seems to be a more marked preference for not using the apostrophe in this case in Philippine English, there is also an overall higher number of uses of the word in the Philippine corpus when the versions with and without the apostrophe are combined. However, there is one point of caution to make about such results that researchers should bear in mind when using keyword comparisons such as this one. We are comparing results from one corpus with the aggregated results from three other corpora. The aggregation of the three other corpora masks the fact that some of the other corpora are more similar to the Philippine data, others less so. For *lets* and *let's*, they occur per 100,000 words, 10.99 and 4.58 times in the Indian data, 8.3 and 6.45 times in the UK data, and 5.11 and 11.92 in the US data. So the US data is very different from the Philippine data in this respect, while the Indian data is somewhat similar to it. If we look at the non-contracted *let us*, a similar pattern emerges with the phrase used, per 100,000 words, 9.16 times in the Indian corpus, 7.4 times in the Philippine corpus, 0.92 times in the UK corpus, and 0.85 times in the US corpus. However, the mean of the use of *let us* per 100,000 words in the three non-Philippine corpora is 3.58 times—wholly unlike any of the corpora making up that collection of data. The use of a standard deviation measure can help to spot issues such as this, of course, and is certainly recommended, especially when different types of material are combined together, as is the case with the reference corpus in this study. For the purposes of this brief study, however, I merely note the issue here and would caution users of any aggregated data to be mindful that it may not characterise their data perfectly.

The word *right* in the Philippine data is interesting; it occurs 152 times and splits largely between two meanings: entitlement (50 examples) and judgement (63 examples). As an entitlement, it relates to the discussion of rights in examples such as

> 'that doesn't give anyone the right to disrespect u'. [PH_FR_09]

As a judgement, it is realised in expressions such as

> 'Leading someone on is not right'. [PH_FR_14]

This word allows us to look at an example where a semantic field is shared between two of the subcorpora. In the first example, the Judgement semantic field in the Philippine corpus is complemented by a field indicating an evaluation of something or someone as wrong, as evidenced by the word *sin*. This field is shared with the Indian subcorpus. In the case of *right*, while the word in its sense of judgement is key only in the Philippine data, the entitlement sense is shared between the Philippine data and the US data. Let us consider the moral overtones of right and wrong first and then return to look at entitlement.

The keyword *sin* in the Philippine corpus falls into the *wrong* semantic field. In the Indian subcorpus, the keyword *evil* falls into this field. Both entail a strong moral judgement that something is wrong. In the case of *sin*, there is an overt religious dimension to the word, as evidenced by the fact that the word *god* is the strongest collocate of *sin* in the subcorpus.[3] In the Indian data, there is also a strong religious overtone to the word *evil*, with *god* (which is a keyword in the subcorpus) being the second strongest collocate of the word. Two preoccupations become notable here, one which links the Philippine and the Indian data and one which separates them. The preoccupation that separates them is shown by the top collocate of *evil* in the Indian material: *society*. The discussion of *sin* in the Philippine material is personal (as evidenced by collocates such as *we*, *you*, and *he*). In the Indian material, the *evil* is not personal, it relates to the abstract notion of *society*. No pronouns collocate with *evil* in the Indian data; indeed, other than *god* and *society*, no other content words collocate with *evil* in that subcorpus. This meshes with a theme that is unique to the Indian corpus: keywords talking about a way of life, one of which is *society*, the other of which is *culture*. Both indicate an abstract notion of a system by which human life is organized. Yet only in the Indian subcorpus does this focus become associated with keywords. So the judgement of what is wrong, while common to both corpora, also highlights a fundamental difference between them in terms of how this concept is used. The second preoccupation has already been suggested by the collocates: the Indian and Philippine subcorpora have keywords that fall into the semantic fields of Religion and Religious Identity, the other two subcorpora do not. In the Indian data, the keywords *faith*, *god*, *islam*, *religion*, *religions*, and *religious* relate to Religion, while *muslim* describes a Religious Identity. In the Philippine data, *jesus* and *sacrifice* relate to Religion, while *christian* and *christians* are Religious Identities. This simultaneously shows a difference and a similarity between the Indian and Philippine material: both are more focussed on religion and religious identities than the UK or US material, but both have quite distinctive focuses with regard to religion.

Let us return to the concept of entitlement. This links the Philippine and US subcorpora. There is a discussion of entitlement through the word *right* which is key for both varieties. Yet while the meaning of the word splits in the Philippine material, there is a single dominant meaning of entitlement linked to *right* in the US subcorpus as indicated by the collocates of the word in that subcorpus—*privilege*, *abortion*, *woman*, and *women* being in the top ten collocates of the word. Some of these collocates are shared in the Philippine material with *abortion* and *woman* also being in the top ten collocates for the word, neatly demonstrating the importance of *right* as entitlement in both subcorpora. So this is an example of a similarity shown by keywords made apparent by the semantic field analysis of the keywords and underscored by the use of concordance and collocation analysis.

Taking the analysis of the Indian, Philippine, and US material so far, it may be possible to jump to a conclusion that the Indian and Philippine material are closely linked by religious preoccupations, while the Philippine and US material also evidence a link on a discussion of rights. But the picture is much more complex than that. There are themes that link all three—for example, all three subcorpora have keywords that fall into the semantic field of Political Systems, while the UK data does not. Keywords such as *govt* (India),[4] *constitution* (Philippines), and *running* (US) indicate a preoccupation with a discussion of, admittedly different, features of political systems. Another shared semantic field between the three is People populated with keywords indicating people in general as in *human* (India) and *ones* (Philippines and US). The two strongest collocates of *human* in the Indian subcorpus are *beings* and *being*, while in the case of *ones*, the reference is to a number of people, of unspecified size and identity, in examples such as

> 'And the ones who oppose same sex marriage seem to always hide behind the bible'. [PH_SC_04]

No clear pattern of collocation emerges from the use of *ones* to help us to distinguish it from *beings*—more data may allow for this, but this is an important point in itself. Keywords may provide sufficient data to allow a difference or similarity to be outlined, but an expressly qualitative analysis may be required to explain that difference where sufficient data is not available to allow the deployment of other corpus analysis techniques, such as collocation, in support of that keyword analysis. In this case, I would argue that the use of *human* in the Indian data is abstract, while in the Philippine and US data, *ones* is used differently. In both cases, the usage is largely as a demonstrative pronoun, but in the Philippine data, the demonstrative pronoun seems to be used as a rhetorical device that allows, at times, an under-specification of the scale and identity of a group. This blurs the scale of a problem, as in examples such as

> 'the ones that need to be educated for responsible parenthood'. [PH_FR_21]
>
> 'the ones who don't have enough income to sustain their families'. [PH_FR_21]

In the US data, *ones* seems to be vague in terms of number, but it more often seems to be linked to groups with whom the writer is intimate and/or friendly in examples such as

> 'I'm in a group of my friends, they're the ones I call when something has happened'. [US_FR_02]
>
> 'a person should speak with the family members that are organizing the funeral because these are usually the ones closest to the deceased'. [US_SC_18]

In the US data, *ones* occurs 42 times, 12 of which match this usage. By contrast, the Philippine data contains only 19 examples of *ones*, none of which match this usage.

Conspicuous by its absence so far has been a discussion of the UK data. There are many examples of the UK data overlapping with the other datasets, but to conclude this brief exploration of the keywords in the three subcorpora, I will look at one feature which is unique to the British data and a second feature that it shares with one other subcorpus. I will then look at a third feature that is shared across all four subcorpora to complete this illustrative study of different aspects of the keywords revealed by this analysis.

Perhaps the most eye-catching of the fields that are unique to the UK data is the category of Politeness in which occurs the keyword *sorry*. The word is important in conversational English (as is apparent in its extensive treatment in Aijmer 2014 and its frequency in spoken British English, as reported by Rayson, Leech, and Hodges, 1997), so seeing it in the UK subcorpus, given that CMC often carries features of the spoken language, is not such a great surprise. As in Aijmer's analysis of the word, in CMC communication, its use as a politeness marker is varied; for example, it can be used as a bald apology 'If I was wrong, I do say sorry'. However, 18 of the 58 examples of the word in the UK corpus are used as a politeness maker to introduce disagreement, accompanied by an explicit *but* in 11 cases in examples such as

> 'Sorry but that's just an opinion'. [UK_PG_02]
> 'm sorry but i totally disagree with having the royal family'. [UK_SC_04]
> 'Sorry, but despite his pleas and apologies later it will happen again'. [UK_SC_12]

While interesting, this is somewhat predictable based on research such as Aijmer's (*ibid*). What is less predictable is the advice semantic field. Here the UK and Philippine data come together in having keywords such as *try* (Philippines) and *advice* (UK). In the Philippine data, the advice offered is to try to do something—over half (58) of the 98 examples of *try* in the data are followed immediately by *to*, introducing an infinitival clause in which the advised course of action is outlined. In the UK data, of the 30 examples of *advice*, 11 are preceded by *my*. Advice is requested as well as given, however, through the word *advice*. The use of the forums to give advice seems quite marked in the Philippine and UK data. An interesting advice word in the UK data links back to *sorry*—it is the word *just*. The word is used to give advice on a course of action as in examples such as

> 'Smile at them and just stare back' and 'Just try to surround yourself with positive people'. [UK_SC_01]

Yet the word is also a politeness marker, minimizing the imposition caused by an action undertaken or suggested. The last example shows clearly how a course of action is introduced by *just*, but the imposition on the reader is also softened by the word. So while the Philippine and UK data share common ground in the salience of keywords indicating the giving of advice in both, the link between the Politeness category, which is unique to the UK data, and the Advice category is salient.

Finally, let us explore a category shared by all four of the corpora. In this case, I will focus on a grammatical rather than a semantic category. All of the subcorpora have modal verbs which are key. The Indian data has four, the

Philippine two, and the US and UK data one each. It is tempting to conclude that perhaps the overall frequency of modals is greater in the Indian data and that explains the number of modals in the Indian keywords. However, this is not true. If we use a part-of-speech tagger on the four datasets, we see there is little notable variation in the number of modal verbs per 10,000 words in the Indian (216.27 per 10,000 words), Philippine (221.55 per 10,000 words), UK (206.13 per 10,000 words), and US (217.66 per 10,000 words) data. There is certainly no indication that modals are unusually frequent in the Indian subcorpus. The answer to the difference lies in which modals are key in the Indian subcorpus: *can*, *must*, *should*, and *will*. Compare this to the modals which are key for the UK and US data: *would* and *might*, respectively. An exploration of the Indian data reveals its key modals to be strong modals of obligation. By contrast, the key modal in the US data is the weak epistemic modal *might*, while the UK has only one strong modal, *would*. This finding is quite in line with findings of changes in modal use in British and American English over time (e.g. Leech, Hundt, Mair, & Smith, 2009; Baker 2010), where it has been suggested that British and American English are moving away from modals of obligation, with the effect being more pronounced for American English. This shared category shows both some evidence in support of that and an indication that modals of obligation are not as in such marked decline in Indian English. With regard to the Philippine data, it too retains strong modals, with *will* being key.[5]

Conclusion

This review of the keywords in the dataset is incomplete; there is much more of interest to be mined from the keywords extracted. However, the study in this chapter shows that, using this technique, we may extract interesting similarities and differences between corpora. In doing so, we may confirm what is in the literature or make a fresh insight into some feature as yet unexplored. However, the keyword technique requires analysis and contextualization. If there is insufficient data for that contextualization, the analysis may need to switch to more expressly qualitative modes of investigation. In this chapter, the analysis comes from grouping similar keywords together and undertaking part-of-speech analysis. The contextualization comes from close reading of concordances and the exploration of collocations around the keywords. Yet data is key and without it our analysis becomes less distinct, less incisive. Similarly, tools which are able to deal with the data are necessary. As noted in this chapter, both a semantic and part-of-speech tagger used to look at the data experienced elevated rates of error because they were not trained to run on CMC material. Also, the results of keyword analyses need to be securitized carefully, as was shown with the analysis of *lets* in the Philippine and non-Philippine material. Keywords also need further interpretation.

In conclusion, while undoubtedly helpful, keywords are best used in concert with other methods—a conclusion I would draw for any method.

Postscript

It was with trepidation that I approached writing this reflection on my chapter. I have always firmly believed that corpus linguistics is best described as a set of methods and that those methods are largely complementary to one another. One of the pleasures of being involved in this book is that a large-scale triangulation study has tested these beliefs. While that was the cause of some nervous anticipation, the end result of the process is one not simply of relief but of a very real sense of fascination. The fascination arises from how the disparate methods used in the book have resulted, overwhelmingly, in results that are complementary to one another.

One area where this is apparent is in the comparison between the findings in this chapter and those in the chapters by Brezina and Potts. For example, Brezina picked up lexis that was indicative of some of the varieties of English in the data just as keywords did in my analysis. Potts's study, using semantic tagging, is striking in terms of its similarity to this study. For example, both studies picked up i) the strong theme of religion and the supernatural in the Indian data, ii) that government was key in the Philippine data, iii) issues related to politeness in the UK data, and iv) that there was a frequent use of CMC acronyms in the Indian data. So there was agreement between the analyses.

However, there were also areas where findings in one chapter were not shared by others. What should we make of these? My advice on approaching those would be to treat the apparent mismatches with caution. The chapters we were asked to write were short. Many observations that we could have made were not made due to limitations of space. A close inspection of the keywords listed at the beginning of my study helps to show this. For example, Potts notes the salience of a military discourse in the US data. The word *military* is a keyword in the US data—this was a point that could have been discussed. Similarly, Potts's point about the US orientation of the UK data is ably supported by the keywords *america* and *americans* in the UK data. So some of the apparent differences of emphasis in the analyses presented are actually researcher choices—the authors chose to highlight certain features, in the limited space given, that they found to be of interest. With more space available, these apparent differences should evaporate.

Additionally, there are also almost certainly differences caused by differences in researcher choice when setting the parameters for their techniques. For example, in my study, I made decisions about what counted as a keyword. I used fairly stringent criteria, which reduced the number of keywords produced. This was done, of course, with a view to the limited amount of space available to write the results of the study up. While I was aware that inevitably I would not be able to discuss all of the keywords I found, I limited the keywords that were available for potential discussion by using the parameters used to define keyness in such a way as to limit the number of keywords produced. So as well as there being keywords shown at the beginning of the chapter which are not discussed, there are other potential keywords which are not listed at all because the parameters used meant they did not qualify as keywords. With a more permissive set of parameters, it may be that some features absent from my study, but observed through other methods, may have been apparent in the keywords also.

Such observations may be a cause for concern. However, the first type of difference can be easily dismissed—it is an artefact of the limited space given to the study. While such omissions probably often occur, as long as the full set of keywords retrieved is reported, the reader is at least shown what is not studied as well as what is studied—there is no effort to 'hide away' keywords. The second type of difference is potentially more troubling. These are keywords which neither the analyst nor the reader are aware of. Yet the response to this is a standard feature of the reporting of scientific findings—one must be clear about one's method to permit replication and to allow researchers to experiment with different conditions to test what effect they have on a study. So reporting on the conditions used to determine keyness is important both in terms of empowering readers to critically explore the results presented but also to make it clear that there is a process whereby data is analysed and reduced prior to interpretation. That process may be varied, but without an accurate report of how the process was undertaken, replication and critical exploration, if not thwarted, become very difficult.

Nonetheless, my overall impression is that while there is a degree of convergence in the findings, which is reassuring, there is also a degree of divergence. Some techniques are more likely to spot some things than others. So the approach of Friginal and Biber, for example, which is very much oriented towards register and grammatical features, shows some of these issues in a much more clear fashion than other methods, such as keywords, which are more lexically focussed. On the other hand, techniques such as keywords and collocation seem to show discourses and issues related to word meaning in sharper contrast. So the idea that corpus linguistics is a set of compatible methods, all with slightly different strengths, seems well supported by the findings in this book. I could not finish, however, without noting the results from the qualitative study. These also agreed, to a high degree, with the corpus-based findings. This is not a great surprise to me—qualitative analysis is often a point of departure for my own work, with close reading of a few texts being my entry point for an analysis of a large body of data. It is also often my guide as I interpret the findings of a corpus-based study. What the corpus studies clearly offer to qualitative analyses is a confirmation or refutation at scale of some observations coupled with some findings which the qualitative analysis did not pick up on.

If I had one wish, it would be that the book was written again two or three times, as I am sure that further studies could iterate these analyses again, digging into the data afresh with new insights based on these studies, refining, and providing further depth to the results.

Notes

1 WordSmith has a default p value of 0.000001. However, using this p value with the other settings for dispersion and minimum frequency resulted in a very small number of keywords, many of which were only key due to appearing in a small number of files, so a decision was made to increase the p value to 0.001 in order to produce a larger, yet manageable, set of keywords.
2 In this chapter, semantic fields will be spelt with initial capitals.
3 Collocates were calculated using the Mutual Information statistic, with a window of +/- 5 words and a minimum collocate frequency of five. The MI of *sin* and *god* in the Philippines data is 6.25.
4 Both *government* and *govt* combine in the Indian data to make this a word that is focussed on much more in that subcorpus than the other subcorpora. The combined frequency of the word per 100,000 words in the four corpora are 70.53 (India), 67.56 (Philippines), 39.64 (UK), and 45.12 (US). The contracted form *govt* is much more frequent in the Indian data, hence its keyness.
5 I am setting aside the keyword *cant* here as it is systematically mistagged in all four of the subcorpora. The part-of-speech tagger used to analyse the data was not designed for use on CMC material and, in this case, this led to the tagging of the word being so inaccurate as to be unusable. I note, however, that the modal in question is a strong modal, albeit negated.

References

Aijmer, K. (2014). *Conversational Routines in English: Convention and Creativity*. New York: Routledge.
Aston, G. & Burnard, L. (1997). *The BNC Handbook*. Edinburgh: Edinburgh University Press.
Baker, P. (2006). *Using Corpora in Discourse Analysis*. London: Continuum.
Baker, P. (2010). *Sociolinguistics and Corpus Linguistics*. Edinburgh: Edinburgh University Press.
Culpeper, J. (2009). Words, parts-of-speech and semantic categories in the character-talk of Shakespeare's Romeo and Juliet. *International Journal of Corpus Linguistics*, 14(1), 29–59.
Leech, G., Hundt, M., Mair, C. & Smith, N. (2009). *Change in Contemporary English: A Grammatical Study*. Cambridge: Cambridge University Press.
Ooi, V. (2002). Aspects of computer-mediated communication for research in corpus linguistics. In P. Peters, P. Collins & A. Smith (Eds.), *New Frontiers of Corpus Research* (pp. 91–104). Amsterdam: Rodopi.
Rayson, P., Leech, G. & Hodges, M. (1997). Social differentiation in the use of English vocabulary: Some analyses of the conversational component of the British National Corpus. *International Journal of Corpus Linguistics*, 2(1), 133–152.
Scott, M. (1997). PC analysis of key words—and key words. *System*, 25(1), 1–13.

3 Lexical Bundles

Bethany Gray

Introduction

Phraseological research has increasingly been relying upon fully inductive analyses of corpora to investigate extended multi-word units. Different types of phraseological phenomena have been investigated under a variety of terms and definitions, such as collocations, lexical phrases, formulas, prefabricated expressions, idioms, n-grams, lexical bundles, frames, and collocational frameworks. One such phraseological unit that has received considerable attention has been the 'lexical bundle'. Biber and colleagues coined the term 'lexical bundle' in the *Longman Grammar of Spoken and Written English* (1999) to refer to continuous sequences of three or more words that recur frequently across a range of speakers/writers in natural discourse, such as *may be due to*, *on the basis of*, *it may be that*, or *the end of the* (Biber, Johansson, Leech, Conrad, & Finegan, 1999; also see Cortes 2015 on the origins of the term).

The lexical bundles approach is a fully corpus-driven methodology in that it '[begins] with simple word forms and [gives] priority to frequency to identify recurrent word sequences' (Biber 2009: 282). The bundles approach processes each word in a corpus and identifies and tallies every possible multi-word sequence of a specified length (commonly three-, four-, or five-word sequences) attested in a corpus. Sequences which meet a pre-established frequency threshold and are distributed across a range of texts in the corpus (ensuring that the sequence is not recurring due to its use by an individual or small number of speakers/writers) are considered lexical bundles (Biber et al. 1999: 992–993).

Lexical bundle researchers have proposed that these units, which are identified purely based on frequent recurrence in corpora, function as 'important building blocks of discourse, associated with basic communicative functions' (Biber, Conrad, & Cortes, 2004: 400), signal cohesion and coherence in a text (Nesi & Basturkmen 2006; Hyland 2008), and indicate 'competent language use within a register' (Cortes 2004: 398). Thus lexical bundles are seen as basic components of discourse construction which can help language users carry out particular discourse functions.

Defining Characteristics of Lexical Bundles and Their Use in Natural Discourse

The lexical bundles that have been identified through this corpus-driven methodology typically have characteristics which distinguish them from other types of formulaic language (Biber 2009: 283–284; also see Cortes 2015):

- extremely common, based on distributional criteria representing both frequency of occurrence and distribution across speakers/writers;
- typically incomplete structural units, often bridging two units (but with strong grammatical correlates as they are usually constructed from clausal or phrasal components);
- non-idiomatic meaning and not particularly perceptually salient.

After their identification in a corpus, lexical bundles are typically described according to their structural makeup and typical discourse functions. The framework for classifying bundles along these two parameters presented in Biber, Conrad, & Cortes (2004) is the most widely adopted framework and has been shown to provide good coverage of lexical bundles identified in a range of registers and across languages (Cortes 2015). Table 3.1 summarizes these structural and functional categories, which are illustrated with examples from the Q+A corpus.[1]

After being categorized functionally and structurally, corpora can be described in terms of their use of lexical bundles, considering the number of bundle types, the frequency of bundle use, and the structural types and discourse functions of bundles that are prevalent.

Research on lexical bundles has revealed register patterns in the relative distributions, structural types, and typical discourse functions of bundles in spoken and written registers (see Biber et al. 1999; Biber 2009):

- Conversation typically uses more bundles than academic writing, both in terms of number of bundle types and overall frequency of occurrence.
- Lexical bundles in conversation are most commonly verb phrase or dependent clause bundles, and these bundles can thus be considered 'oral' bundles. Most bundles in academic writing are noun phrase–based bundles, which can be considered 'literate' bundles.
- Conversation relies heavily on lexical bundles which serve stance functions, followed by discourse organizing bundles. In contrast, academic prose primarily employs referential bundles.

Biber and Barbieri (2007: 265) point out that 'each register employs a distinct set of lexical bundles, associated with the typical communicative purposes of that register', and bundles have thus been investigated in a range of specialized registers. Spoken and written academic registers have received

Table 3.1 Structural and functional framework for categorizing lexical bundles (adapted from Biber, Conrad, & Cortes 2004)

Structural types of bundles	*Description*	*Example bundles from the Q+A corpus*
Verb phrase fragments	Incorporate fragments of *verb phrases*, including subject pronouns followed by a verb phrase, the beginning of a verb phrase, and question fragments	*what do you think* *you are not a* *you don't have to* *it all depends on*
Dependent clause fragments	Include both *verb phrase fragments* and components of dependent clauses (e.g., complement clauses)	*if you don't want* *not be able to* *I think you should* *you need to get*
Noun phrase and prepositional phrase fragments	Consist of noun phrases, often with a *head noun* and the start of a post-modifier (commonly a prepositional phrase, but also relative or complement clauses)	*nothing to do with* *in the middle of* *the end of the* *the best way to*
Discourse Functions of Bundles	*Description*	*Example Bundles from the Q+A Corpus*
Stance expressions	Indicate epistemic, attitudinal, modal, or evaluative assessments, including assessments of certainty or likelihood, desire, obligation/directive, intention/prediction, and ability	*there is nothing wrong* *I think it is* *if you want to* *it depends on the* *you need to get*
Discourse organizers	Signal relationships between previous and forthcoming discourse, by introducing topics, stating focus, or elaborating/clarifying a topic	*I would like to* *on the other hand* *nothing to do with*
Referential expressions	Reference physical, abstract, or textual entities, often to identify/focus on that entity, indicate imprecision, or detail attributes such as quantity, framing, time, place	*for the sake of* *the two of you* *end of the day* *is one of the* *the rest of the*

a great deal of attention (Biber Conrad & Cortes, 2004; Nesi & Basturkmen 2006; Biber & Barbieri 2007; Cortes 2008, 2013; Hyland 2008; Liu 2012; Csomay 2013), along with discourse produced by language learners and/or novice first language (L1) writers (Cortes 2004, 2006; Chen & Baker 2010; Ädel & Erman 2012; Biber & Gray 2013; Paquot 2013; Staples,

Egbert, Biber, & McClair, 2013). Bundles have also been investigated in non-academic registers, including political debates (Partington & Morley 2004), written EU documents (Jablonkai 2010), legal genres (Breeze 2013), and hotel websites (Fuster-Márquez 2014). These investigations have shown that each specialized register utilizes lexical bundles in distinctive ways. Thus it seems likely that a specialized register like Internet-based question-and-answer forums will likewise rely on a distinctive set of lexical bundles matched to the register's purpose, topics, and mode.

The Present Study

The goal of the present study is to investigate the phraseological patterning of language in the Q+A corpus, specifically the use of lexical bundles. Based on the identification of frequent four-word lexical bundles in the Q+A corpus, the following research questions will be addressed in this study:

1 In what ways does the use of lexical bundles in online Q+A forum responses differ across four world English varieties (India, Philippines, UK, and US) in terms of the frequency, structure, and discourse function of the bundles?
2 In what ways does the use of lexical bundles in online Q+A forum responses differ across three topic areas (Family & Relationships, Politics & Government, and Society & Culture) in terms of the frequency, structure, and discourse function of the bundles?

Methodology

This study focuses on four-word lexical bundles identified using the fully corpus-driven lexical bundles methodology (Biber 2009), which inductively identifies all possible word combinations of a specified length in a corpus and tracks their recurrence. Frequency thresholds are set to identify explicit criteria as to how frequently a sequence must occur in a given corpus in order to be considered a bundle. A typical frequency threshold in lexical bundles studies is ten times per million words (Biber et al. 1999; Cortes 2015).[2]

A complicating factor to the lexical bundle methodology, however, is corpus size. The Q+A corpus is well under one million words (c. 400,000 words for the complete corpus, and c. 100,000 words for each country subcorpus). It is mathematically possible to normalize the raw counts for bundles extracted from the Q+A corpus to one million words, thus extrapolating frequencies beyond what is actually observed in the corpus. For example, any sequence occurring four times (raw) in the Q+A corpus, such as *who are you to*, would reach the ten times per million words threshold if normalized to one million. However, four instances is quite a low level of recurrence in the lexical bundle tradition. It is possible that a sequence such as *who are you to* would occur more times in a larger sample of Q+A texts and thus reach the frequency threshold, but the extrapolation required to make this assumption introduces the risk of the over-identification of bundles. That is, there is no guarantee that bundles occurring fewer than ten times (raw) in a small corpus would reach the threshold even if the corpus were one million words (see Cortes 2002; Chen & Baker 2010: 32; Cortes 2015: 204–205).

Thus a conservative approach is needed for small corpus sizes; the approach used here is to identify four-word bundles that occur at least ten times (raw) in the Q+A corpus,[3] with a range of five texts to ensure that the use of the bundle is distributed across a range of writers and posts. Using these criteria, a specialized computer program was written in Perl to identify all four-word sequences not crossing punctuation boundaries (or question/answer entries within a text), tally its total occurrences in the full Q+A corpus, and track the number of different texts it appears in. At the same time, this program compiled the frequency of the sequences in the four by-country subcorpora (India, Philippines, UK, US) and the three by-topic subcorpora (Family & Relationships, Politics & Government, Society & Culture). These frequency and range criteria resulted in the identification of 82 four-word lexical bundles.[4]

Each of the 82 lexical bundles was categorized structurally and functionally according to the framework set out by Biber, Conrad, and Cortes (2004) illustrated in Table 3.1. For bundles not explicitly labeled in this previous study, comparisons were made to similar bundles, along with an examination of KWIC (keyword in context) lines using MonoConc Pro 2.2 (Barlow 2004) to verify the most appropriate category based on the typical use of the bundle in the Q+A corpus. The bundles were classified by the same rater twice at a two-month interval: the intra-rater reliability for the structural categorization was 98%, and 96% for the functional categorization. Differences between the two coding points typically occurred for bundles that are highly multi-functional, and a final decision was arrived at by examining all of the KWIC lines for that bundle.

In order to compare the use of the lexical bundles across the country and topic subcorpora within the Q+A corpus, normalized rates of occurrence per 100,000 (the approximate size of the smallest subcorpus) were calculated for each bundle in each subcorpus.[5]

Results & Discussion

The resulting 82 lexical bundles, which are listed in frequency order in the Appendix, occur a total of 1,265 times (raw) in the Q+A corpus overall, with the most frequent four-word bundle (*if you want to*) occurring 48 times in the corpus. Table 3.2 displays the distribution of these 82 bundle types by structure and discourse function and shows that most (71%) of the bundle types in Q+A forums are either verb phrase (e.g., *I do not think, it depends on the*) or dependent clause fragments (e.g., *if you want to, I don't know what, should be able to*); thus the Q+A register appears to rely on

Table 3.2 Distribution of 82 Q+A lexical bundle types by structure and discourse function

	Structural characteristics				*Discourse functions*				
	Verb Phrase Fragments	*Dependent Clause Fragments*	*Noun Phrase Fragments*	*Total*	*Stance*	*Discourse Organizing*	*Referential*	*Special Functions*	*Total*
Number of bundle types	22	36	24	82	45	7	28	2	82
Percentage of bundle types	27%	44%	29%	100%	55%	9%	34%	2%	100%

more 'oral' bundles than 'literate' bundles (Biber, Conrad, & Cortes, 2004), despite the written mode of the register. This interpretation is further supported by the fact that more than half of the bundle types (55%) carry a primary stance function (e.g., *you really want to, I think you should, you need to be*), while bundles with referential functions account for 34% of the bundle types (e.g., *is one of the, the rest of the, a lot of people*), with very few discourse organizing bundle types.[6] A preliminary interpretation of this finding is that the interactional nature of Q+A forums reflects similar characteristics to conversation, a spoken register, as participants share a context (they are all responding to a posed question, often near to the time that the question has been posted), discuss concerns of everyday life, and carry out communicative purposes such as giving advice, sharing opinions, and expressing concerns.

The discussion to this point has considered the nature of the 82 bundle types identified in the Q+A corpus. Using these 82 bundles, I now turn to their frequency of use represented by rates of occurrence per 100,000 words in the four varieties of English (Research Question 1) and the three topic areas (Research Question 2).

Lexical Bundles Across Varieties of English

The overall frequency of lexical bundle use across the four varieties of English is displayed in Table 3.3, showing that Q+A forums in the Philippines use lexical bundles to a slightly greater extent than forums in India, the UK, or the US, with relatively little variation between forums from India, the UK, and the US. The overall use of bundles is not significantly different across the four varieties: χ^2 (3) = 4.49, $p = 0.21$.

However, it is possible that the approach of identifying bundles based on the whole Q+A corpus masks potential differences between the four varieties due to unidentified bundles that are variety specific (i.e., occurring frequently in one of the smaller subcorpora but not reaching the conservative frequency cutoff of ten). To account for this possibility, an experiment was conducted to also calculate overall bundle use based on bundles identified at two frequency thresholds: ten times raw in the whole corpus *or* five times raw in *one* subcorpus (range = 5 in the whole corpus), resulting in a list of 115 bundles. Table 3.3 shows that with this approach, India and the US remain fairly similar to one another in terms of overall bundle use, while texts from the UK appear more similar to the higher bundle use in the Philippines. However, there is still not a significant difference between the four varieties: χ^2 (3) = 2.42, $p = 0.49$.[7]

Despite fairly minimal differences between overall bundle use across the four varieties, Figures 3.1 and 3.2 show more variation in the structural types and discourse functions of the bundles. These figures reflect the overall higher frequency of lexical bundles in forums from the Philippines, and Figure 3.1 demonstrates that this difference is in part due to the much higher

Table 3.3 Distribution of lexical bundles (frequency) across four varieties

	Frequency per 100,000 words	
	82 bundles occurring 10 times in whole corpus	*115 bundles occurring 10 times in the whole corpus* or *5 times in one subcorpus*
India	298.96	350.57
Philippines	335.94	381.13
UK	289.81	377.45
US	293.00	348.89

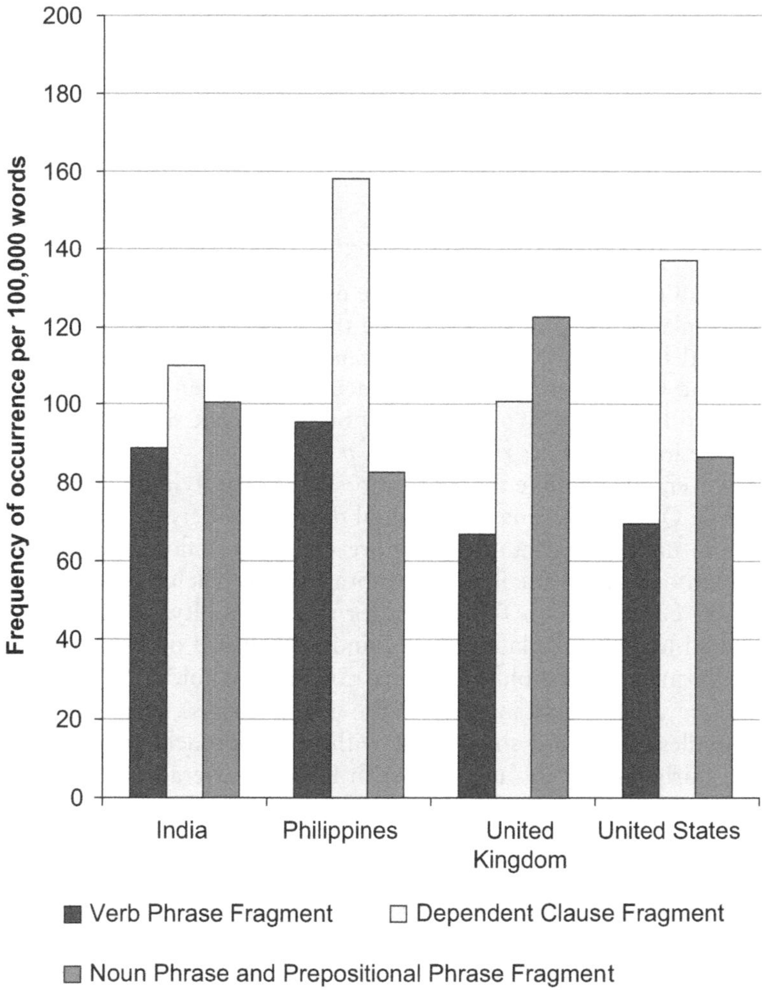

Figure 3.1 Distribution of bundles across four varieties: Structural type

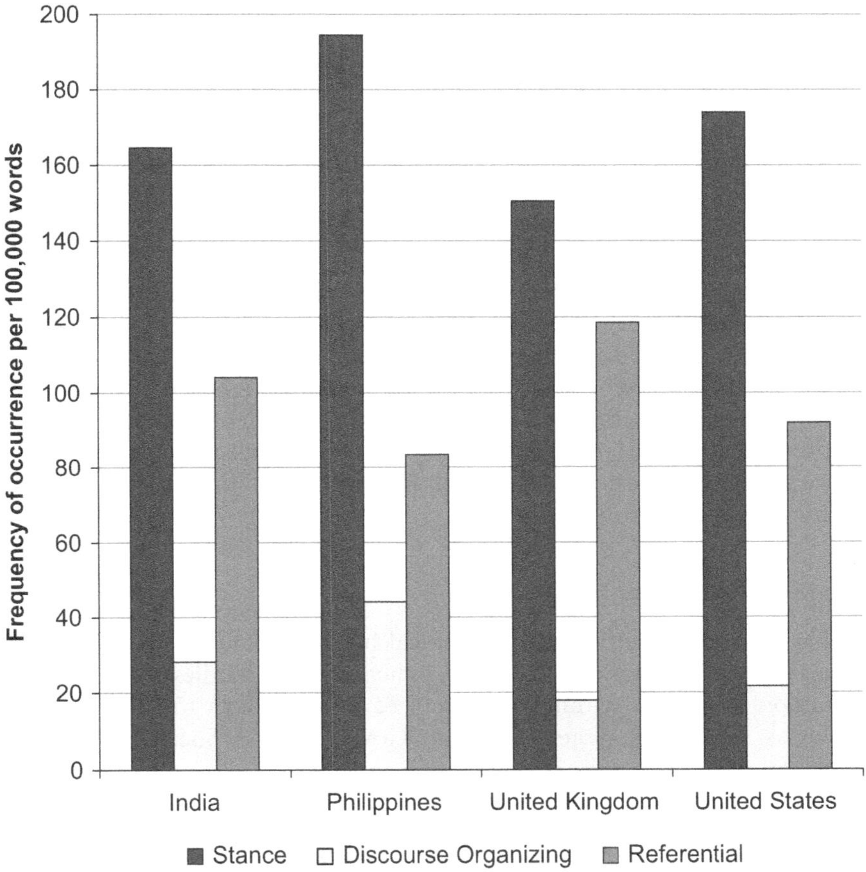

Figure 3.2 Distribution of bundles across four varieties: Discourse function

frequency of dependent clause–based bundles in the Philippines (and slightly higher use of verb phrase–based bundles). The use of verb phrase–based bundles is notably lower in forums from the US and UK, and the UK texts are the only variety in which noun phrase–based bundles are the most frequent type of bundle, in part due to a few phrases that seem to be particularly characteristic of UK language, such as *end of the day* and *in the first place*.

These structural trends are reflected in the patterns in the most frequent discourse functions for these lexical bundles. Figure 3.2 shows a consistent trend for conveying stance as by far the most frequent function of lexical bundles in all varieties, particularly through the use verb phrase– and dependent clause–based bundles focused on the wants, needs, and thoughts of forum participants (e.g., *if you want to, you don't have to, I think you should, I would like to*). In fact, the higher use of stance bundles in forums from the Philippine accounts for a good portion of the overall higher use of verb phrase– and dependent clause–based bundles in the variety observed earlier. Referential bundles are the next most frequent, while discourse organizing bundles are rare comparatively (although notably higher in forums from the Philippines).

These patterns are reflected in the bundles that are particularly distinctive of each variety.[8] Bundles distinctive of the Philippine forums include primarily verb phrase and dependent clause bundles, many of which additionally have a stance function (e.g., *have the right to, to be able to, what do you think, you don't need to*). However, it is important to note that even if a bundle was attested as particularly distinctive of one variety, it was often the case that a similar or related bundle was distinctive in another variety (e.g., *if you really want* is distinctive in India, *I think it would* and *I would have to* in the UK, and *if you want to* and *I think that you* in the US). Thus despite minor variations in the exact phrasing of some bundles across country subcorpora, there are relatively few bundles which truly distinguish one variety from another. It turns out that much more variation in lexical bundle use occurs when comparing topic areas.

Lexical Bundles Across Q+A Topic Areas

Table 3.4 shows the frequency of lexical bundle use across the three topic areas represented in the Q+A corpus, indicating that bundles are much more common in forums within the Family & Relationships topic—about 1.5 times as frequent as either Politics & Government or Society & Culture, which use lexical bundles to similar extents.

Figures 3.3 and 3.4 show the distributions of these bundles in the three topic areas across structural type and discourse function, respectively. In terms of the structural types of bundles, the Politics & Government and the Society & Culture subcorpora are nearly identical in their equal reliance on dependent clause– and noun phrase–based bundles, and lower use of verb-phrase-fragment bundles. While the use of noun phrase–based bundles is similar across all three topic areas, the Family & Relationships subcorpus exhibits a markedly higher use of dependent clause-fragment bundles: these are nearly twice as frequent in that topic area and any other structural type, and any other topic area (see Figure 3.3).

Table 3.4 Distribution of lexical bundles (frequency) across three topic areas

	Frequency per 100,000 words
Family & Relationships	400.32
Politics & Government	260.27
Society & Culture	255.50

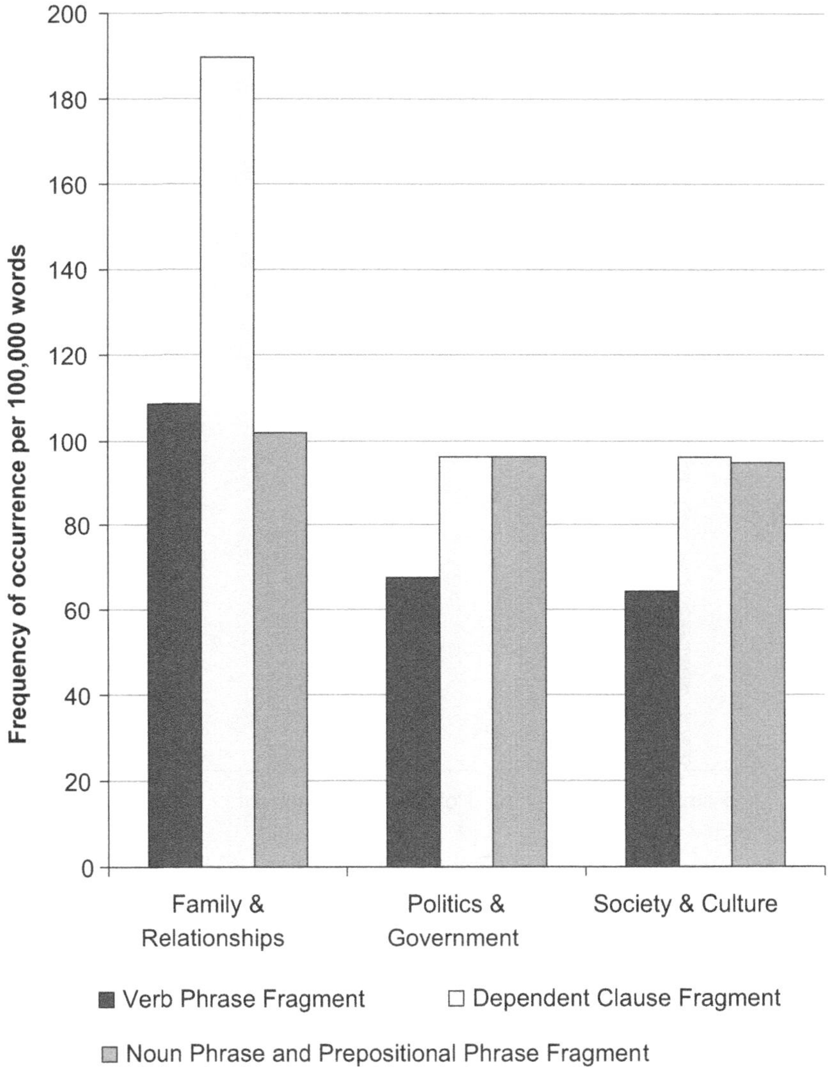

Figure 3.3 Distribution of bundles across three topics: Structural type

Figure 3.4, focused on the discourse functions of bundles, also reflects this trend, with stance-conveying bundles almost twice as common in Family & Relationship than in Politics & Government or Society & Culture. This is highly related to the structural patterns discussed earlier, as many of the stance-conveying bundles are also dependent clause–based bundles. Figure 3.4 shows a remarkable consistency, however, in the general trend for the discourse function of bundles: in all three topic areas, stance bundles are

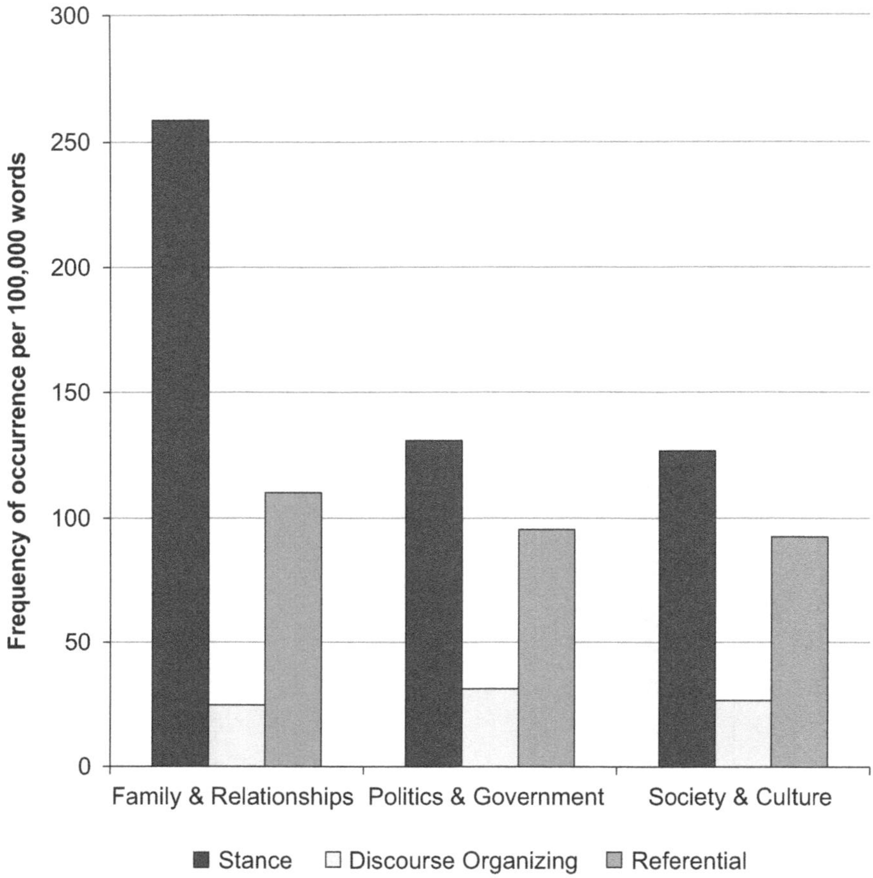

Figure 3.4 Distribution of bundles across three topics: Discourse functions

most common, followed by referential bundles, with discourse organizing bundles comparatively rare (as they are in the corpus overall).

The higher frequency of stance bundles in Q+A forums warrants a bit of additional attention on these bundles, and the reliance on stance bundles can be connected to the purpose of this register: to answer questions, give advice, and share opinions. This purpose is reflected in the more specific, specialized functions that are common within those stance-conveying bundles. As Hyland (2008) and Cortes (2015) point out, as the register being studied becomes more specific, bundles common to that register follow, also becoming more specialized in function.

For example, approximately 30% of the stance bundles in the Q+A corpus indicate personal obligation or give advice to 'you', the person who posted the initial question on the forum (*you don't have to, I think you should, you have to do, I would have to, tell her that you, you need to do, you have to be, that you have to, you need to be, you need to get, then you need to, I think that you*). Although this function occurs across the three topic areas, it is much more common in the Family & Relationships topic area, with each attested bundle with this function occurring 3.69–16.26 per 100,000 words in that topic (compared to frequencies of 0.00–4.85 in Politics & Government and Society & Culture). Many of the bundles that are distinctive of the Family & Relationships subcorpus (e.g., *I think you should, you have to do, tell her that you, you have to be, the only way to, you need to get, I think that you, I think it would*) are focused on making recommendations and giving advice:

(1) Well it all depends on what the fight was about if you were both at fault though **I think you should** probably be the bigger person and apologize first instead of letting the fight linger on that will get you nowhere. [UK_FR_10]
(2) This is delicate. Since she will be your MIL, it's tricky terrain. I would suggest that you **tell her that you** appreciate her input, but like you said; your Mom knows you and your taste better. [PH_FR_20]
(3) The key to any relationship is honesty. **You have to be** honest, if your spouse can't get any reply out of u apart from 'im fine' then it will drive him/her mad and things could go wrong. [IN_FR_12]
(4) **I think you should** talk with an adult family member who you trust and tell them about the problem. [US_FR_12]
(5) Well, here's my two cents: **You don't HAVE to** do anything. BUT proper etiquette says that *even though* you brought a shower gift, it is customary and expected that you also buy a wedding present/cash if you are attending the wedding and reception. [US_SC_14]

These bundles are most often used to give a directive to the initial posters, but they are also sometimes used to criticize them:

(6) why? if their only offense is being homeless and poor than **you need to get a** heart. [US_SC_13]
(7) she is going to be your family and frankly, **i think that you** are sounding very rude. [PH_FR_20]
(8) **You need to get** a grip on reality guy! Do bad things happen? Yes. [IN_PG_13]

A second common specialized function occurs with bundles containing first-person pronouns and epistemic verbs (e.g., *I think it is, I don't know if, I don't know what, I think it would, I do not think, I don't know how*) to provide the writer's personal opinions or knowledge. These bundles are more evenly distributed across the three topic areas, but they are still slightly more common in the Family & Relationships topic (see Appendix). These bundles provide frames for writers to give their opinion or state what they do or don't know and to position their statements as their opinions or thoughts (rather than facts):

(9) **I think it is** high time the Filipino people realize that it is not the church that raise their families. [PH_FR_21]

(10) **I think it is** because some women are so jaded about men, they only see what is bad in them. [US_SC_09]

(11) Good god, thats a tough one, **i think it would** take a lot of guts to do this but i would have to stop the wedding and investigate further for real . . . [UK_FR_03]

(12) **I don't know what** the fuss is about. The Cornish did this by applying for protected status for the word 'Cornish' in front of pasties. [UH_PG_17]

While the categories of epistemic stance and personal obligation/directive were recognized subcategories of stance bundles in the Biber, Conrad, and Cortes (2004) framework, an additional stance function arose out of the analysis of the Q+A corpus: that of hedging or putting conditions on the opinions or advice offered. Bundles like *it depends on the, it all depends on, as long as you,*[9] and *as long as it* typically frame the writer's advice or opinion as being conditional, only applying if certain situations are met:

(13) **It depends on the** situation, because sometimes silence is good and then sometimes communication is good. . . . [IN_FR_12]

(14) **As long as you** both know where you stand and you're at the same level with what you want from the relationship, go for it! [UK_FR_07]

(15) I think it's up to the person to do whatever that person wants to; **as long as it** does not compromise his or her faith. [PH_SC_01]

Other more specific stance functions can indicate the writer's evaluation or point of view: *the best way to, the only way to, right thing to do, is nothing wrong with, there is nothing wrong*:

(16) There **is nothing wrong with** having a girl as a friend especially over the internet. [IN_FR_17]

(17) **The best way to** grasp the differences is to carefully compare whatever translation you are using with a Tanach. [PH_SC_13]

(18) **The only way to** know is to compare the important ingredients between different brands and that involves reading labels carefully. [UK_SC_19]

Although this range of stance functions are the most common function of lexical bundles in the Q+A forums, the even higher frequency of these bundles in the Family & Relationships area seems to indicate that the giving of personal advice dealing with interpersonal concerns is particularly constructed through the use of stance bundles that indicate obligation, provide directives, comment on the epistemic status of the writer's idea, and provide conditions to that advice. This provision of conditions is particularly interesting, as it reflects one of the non-linguistic characteristics of this register: that the individuals posing questions and those responding to those questions do not know each other and that the original questions are typically short and sometimes decontextualized; that is, those responding to questions do not have all of the background information about the situation or the people involved to offer firm advice but rather feel the need to hedge this advice as applicable only in certain situations. The frequent use of this stance function in the Family & Relationships subcorpus also helps to explain the structural patterns that were observed, as dependent clause–based bundles (which are frequency stance bundles in this study) were much higher in that subcorpus than the other two topics.

Conclusion

This study has considered the overall distribution of lexical bundles in the Q+A forum registers and has investigated possible variation among Q+A forums based on the variety of English and on the specific topics being addressed. Findings from this analysis reveal that the Q+A forum, although written in mode, relies extensively on lexical bundles that are often associated with 'oral' discourse modes:

- Q+A forums have a higher reliance on lexical bundles that contain verbs, with verb phrase and dependent clause–fragment bundles making up approximately 68% of all bundles in these corpora (compared to only 32% of the bundles representing noun phrase/prepositional phrase fragments).
- Q+A forums have a higher reliance on bundles that convey epistemic, attitudinal, modal, and evaluative stance.

These findings correspond well to the non-linguistic characteristics of Q+A forums. Although written in mode, the communicative purpose of the register is to convey advice and opinions—it thus has a stance-oriented communicative purpose (see Biber & Conrad 2009, Chapter 2), which is more common of oral registers. Likewise, the interactive nature of Q+A forums, where there is direct contact between the participants in the discourse, is similar to many face-to-face spoken registers.

These trends for the reliance on 'oral' bundles were particularly marked in the subcorpus representing the Philippines and in the Family & Relationships topic area. Although this finding relative to English variety requires further exploration and explanation, the trends observed in the Family & Relationships topic can be related to the nature of this topic area, which is concerned with personal relationships and what individuals should (or should not) do within those relationships. Finally, this study has found that the specialized nature of Q+A forums, particularly within this Family & Relationships topic area, leads to specialized stance functions related to giving advice and stating opinions.

The study is, of course, not without limitations. As many researchers have noted before, lexical bundles are often multi-functional, and not all instances of one bundle type may carry exactly the same discourse function in all contexts of use. This study has focused on the most common, or primary, discourse function based on visual inspection of concordance lines; however, a more detailed analysis might consider every occurrence of these bundles, allowing for different instances of the same bundle type to be included in counts for separate functional categories, thus yielding more precise estimations of the discourse functions of bundles in Q+A forums. This might also lead to the development of a more register-specific framework for classifying the discourse function of bundles in this register.

Postscript

There has been wide interest in lexical bundles in corpus-based research, in part because they represent frequent formulaic, phraseological patterns that can only be discovered through corpora. Beyond their formulaic status, however, lexical bundles have received continued attention in part because of the functional and structural insights about discourse that they can offer. Thus it is not surprising that I immediately saw connections between the bundles I observed in the Q+A corpus and the findings presented by researchers taking different analytical approaches.

In some instances, these connections represented observations that I noted but which I did not report on in the chapter itself because the specialized functions represented a relatively small set of the data. For example, the chapters on keywords (McEnery), semantic annotation (Potts) and stance-taking (Levon) uncovered trends related to politeness (and impoliteness) markers in Q+A forums. As I analyzed the discourse functions of the bundles I identified from the corpus, I noted the use of bundles like *you need to get* to frame criticisms, often in an impolite manner:

(1) **You need to get** a grip on reality guy! [IN_PG_13]
(2) A war historian, nah, your more like someone who doesnt know his facts and is clinging onto dreams. **you need to get** your facts straight, the russians who were supposedly liberating those behind enemy line. [US_PG_05]
(3) I think **you need to get** your facts straight. Just because your last gf was bad don't generalize. [US_SC_09]
(4) why? if their only offense is being homeless and poor than **you need to get** a heart. [US_SC_13]

While this impoliteness function was immediately apparent from my analysis of the KWIC lines for the bundle *you need to get*, I did not report on this observation because (a) it represented a relatively small proportion of uses for this particular bundle (4 out of 12 instances in two different subcorpora) and (b) to truly characterize the use of bundles to convey impoliteness would have required a manual analysis of every concordance line for every bundle, a task which was beyond the scope of the present study. Yet the fact that politeness/impoliteness has come up in multiple analyses may indicate that politeness/impoliteness functions for bundles is worthy of further investigation. Indeed, impoliteness functions were also noted on occasion for other bundles:

(5) If you are going there just to mess with her **then you need to** grow up. [FR]
(6) **I don't want to** make you feel bad but that sounds quite shallow. [IN-FR]

Similarly, I also noticed bundles that signaled religiously oriented discourse, an observation made by four other studies. And indeed, these references were most prevalent in the Indian and Philippine subcorpora, although I also noted that these occurrences came from a relatively small set of texts (indicating a possible influence of corpus composition on the nature of the findings):

(7) I wouldn't teach my kids **that there is no** God. I'd explain that some people believe and some don't, and hope they make an educated decision when they're older. [PH_SC_20]
(8) That's why you continually see terrorists killing innocent non-Muslim civilians **in the name of** 'Allah', as such things are deemed to be the duty of all good Muslims. [IN_PG_12]
(9) and unfortunately the terrorists who whip up hatred **in the name of** Islam are those that get the airtime. [IN_SC_17]

At the same time, however, an analysis on the extent to which bundles are used to frame religious discourse would require extensive manual analysis to produce quantitative findings for such uses, as illustrated by the fact that other instances of these same bundles were not religiously oriented:

(11) So the answer is, **that there is no** answer. [IN_FR_13]
(10) Stop. . . . **in the name of** love . . . before you break my heart. . . .! [UK_FR_03]

Thus, in addition to their primary or general discourse functions, the bundles observed in the Q+A corpus also revealed more specialized uses—but these specialized uses represented only a portion of the instances of particular bundles and requires a more extensive manual analysis.

In other cases, the findings from the analyses carried out under different analytical approaches pushed me to think about the lexical bundles data in new ways. In particular, the initial lexical bundles analysis revealed very few differences in bundle use across the varieties of English. Yet others' findings about variation across these four subcorpora provided potential paths for better making sense of bundle variation by country. For example, the keywords analysis (McEnery) indicated higher levels of advice giving and obligation modals in the Philippine subcorpus, while the audience perception analysis (Egbert) revealed that answers from the Philippine subcorpus were judged as more biased than those from other countries.

Although I found few systematic differences in the overall use of bundles across countries, I *did* find that the use of stance bundles was markedly more frequent in the Philippine subcorpus than in other countries. On one hand, this finding seems to support the findings from the chapters by McEnery and Egbert. On the other hand, this connection also pushed me to consider additional ways that bundles could be grouped to potentially reveal different patterns of variation across the country varieties. For instance, to see if I could find further evidence that obligation meanings are most prevalent in the Indian and Philippine subcorpora, I grouped all bundles with the second-person pronoun *'you'*, which seemed to be directing the reader to do something or think in a particular way (e.g., *I think you should, you have to do, tell her that you, you need to do, you have to be*), and created by-country counts. Similarly, I used the same approach to consider the issue of bias raised by Egbert's chapter by looking at all bundles with first-person pronouns (e.g., *I think you should, I would like to, I think it is, I would have to, when I was a, I don't know if, I don't want to, I think it would, I think that you*) with the hypothesis that the use of the first person may be associated with perceptions of bias. A final grouping was created for bundles which might downplay author bias by hedging or demonstrating that the author is considering multiple perspectives (e.g., *at the same time, on the other hand, it depends on the, as long as you*). Table 3.5 presents the results of these preliminary analyses.

Table 3.5 Frequency of obligation and first-person bundles by country (normalized to 100,000 words)

	India	*Philippines*	*US*	*UK*
Bundles containing '*you*' and obligation meanings	42.86	50.10	45.08	30.87
Bundles containing first-person pronoun *I*	27.28	44.19	49.58	56.78
Bundles hedging or acknowledging other perspectives	37.99	29.46	37.88	32.88

This preliminary analysis does seem to support the finding that the Philippines in particular focuses on obligation and advice giving, although a full analysis would need to consider other bundles which also convey personal obligation and offer advice. In the current lexical bundles framework employed in my chapter, these bundles are all grouped under the larger 'stance' category. However, more specific 'obligation' functions could be partitioned out to add further evidence about the extent to which varieties rely on obligation meanings in Q+A texts.

In contrast, the first-person pronouns test analysis is less clear, with the US (perceived as the least biased) actually using first-person pronouns with the second highest frequency! This seeming contradiction opens many avenues for follow-up research, for example, by considering whether the use of first-person pronouns contributes to readers' evaluation of bias, and if so, in what way? (i.e., does it make the discourse seem more biased or does it make it seem less biased because the presence of the first-person pronouns acknowledges or attributes the claims/ideas as belonging to the writer rather than presenting them as bald assertions?). Finally, the bundles which seem to acknowledge multiple perspectives are used most frequently in the US and India, which generally reflects Egbert's findings.

In sum, it is possible that a bundles analysis can be used to offer additional support or triangulation to other methods of analysis or to challenge those findings. It is also possible, however, for findings from other approaches to inform a lexical bundles analysis by providing the impetus for alternative, more register-specific functional categories for bundles (e.g., impoliteness markers, advice giving).

Notes

1 The framework in Biber, Conrad, and Cortes (2004) contains multiple subcategories within each structural and functional type of bundle. Only the main category is used in this study, although it should be noted that most of the subcategories within this taxonomy are represented by the bundles identified from the Q+A corpus.

2 However, note that different frequency cutoffs are often employed for bundles of different lengths due to the decreasing frequency of multi-word sequences as those sequences increase in length, for practicality reasons, or for answering particular research questions (see Biber, Johansson, Leech, Conrad, & Finegan, 1999; Biber, Conrad, & Cortes, 2004; Chen & Baker 2010).

3 This is considered conservative, as even if additional texts were added to the Q+A corpus to increase its size to one million words, all of the bundles identified in this study would maintain their bundle status. On the other hand, it is also possible that this approach under-identifies other sequences which might be identified as bundles if more texts were included in the corpus. A similar approach is used in Chen & Baker 2010.

4 Two additional four-word bundles (*want to get married, there is no God*) were excluded from the analysis because they were highly topic-specific bundles that occurred due to the specific topics of a few forums. Both were relatively low frequency, low range, and typically occurred primarily in one of the subcorpora. For

example, *there is no God* occurred 13 times in 6 texts but nearly exclusively (9/13) in the Philippines/Society & Culture subcorpus. *Want to get married* occurred 10 times in 5 texts, with eight-tenths coming from the UK/Family & Relationships subcorpus.

5 Because of the relatively low frequency of any individual bundle in a single text, no per-text rates of occurrence were calculated. Rather, frequencies for bundles are reported per corpus or subcorpus. Although necessary from a quantitative perspective, this methodology is also theoretically motivated since the interest in bundles is on their frequent recurrence across texts produced by different writers/speakers.

6 Two bundles, *to take care of* and *to get to know*, were categorized as 'special function', as they represent infinitive clauses with multi-word verbs and do not fall under the three primary functional categories. They are excluded from subsequent analysis.

7 To extend the test, Figures 3.1–3.4 were replicated with the expanded list of bundles. The same patterns of variation were attested with this combined approach, adding support that the whole-corpus approach is appropriate when making comparisons between several smaller subcorpora.

8 Bundles which occurred in a subcorpus at a rate of at least 1 SD above the mean were considered 'distinctive' for that subcorpus. However, this does not mean that the bundles were never used in the other subcorpora.

9 Note that the bundles, *as long as you* and *as long as it* can carry referential rather than stance, functions, as in the following example: 'Deep breathing exercises—inhale for 5 seconds, completely filling the lungs, hold for 20 seconds (if you can't hold it that long, hold for **as long as you** can) and then completely exhale for 10 seconds' [IN_SC_16]. However, an examination of the KWIC lines for these bundles reveals that most of the examples carried the stance rather than the referential function and were thus categorized as stance bundles.

References

Ädel, A. & Erman, B. (2012). Recurrent word combinations in academic writing by native and non-native speakers of English: A lexical bundles approach. *English for Specific Purposes*, 31, 81–92.

Barlow, M. (2004). *MonoConc Pro 2.2*. Houston, TX: Athelstan.

Biber, D. (2009). A corpus-driven approach to formulaic language in English. *International Journal of Corpus Linguistics*, 14(3), 275–311.

Biber, D. & Barbieri, F. (2007). Lexical bundles in university spoken and written registers. *English for Specific Purposes*, 26, 263–286.

Biber, D. & Conrad, S. (2009). *Register, Genre, and Style*. Cambridge: Cambridge University Press.

Biber, D., Conrad, S. & Cortes, V. (2004). *If you look at. . .*: Lexical bundles in university teaching and textbooks. *Applied Linguistics*, 25(3), 371–405.

Biber, D. & Gray, B. (2013). *Discourse Characteristics of Writing and Speaking Task Types on the TOEFL iBT Test: A Lexico-Grammatical Analysis. TOEFL iBT Research Report (TOEFL iBT-19)*. Princeton, NJ: Educational Testing Service.

Biber, D., Johansson, S., Leech, G., Conrad, S. & Finegan, E. (1999). *Longman Grammar of Spoken and Written English*. London: Longman.

Breeze, R. (2013). Lexical bundles across four legal genres. *International Journal of Corpus Linguistics*, 18(2), 229–253.

Chen, Y-H. & Baker, P. (2010). Lexical bundles in L1 and L2 academic writing. *Language Learning & Technology*, 14(2), 30–49.

Cortes, V. (2002). Lexical bundles in published and student disciplinary writing in history and biology. Unpublished PhD dissertation. Northern Arizona University.

Cortes, V. (2004). Lexical bundles in published and student disciplinary writing: Examples from history and biology. *English for Specific Purposes*, 23(4), 397–423.

Cortes, V. (2008). A comparative analysis of lexical bundles in academic history writing in English and Spanish. *Corpora*, 3, 43–57.

Cortes, V. (2013). 'The purpose of this study is to': Connecting lexical bundles and moves in research article introductions. *Journal of English for Academic Purposes*, 12(1), 33–43.

Cortes, V. (2015). Situating lexical bundles in the formulaic language spectrum: Origins and functional analysis developments. In V. Cortes & E. Csomay (Eds.), *Corpus-Based Research in Applied Linguistics: Studies in Honor or Doug Biber* (pp. 197–216). Amsterdam: John Benjamins.

Csomay, E. (2013). Lexical bundles in discourse structure: A corpus-based study of classroom discourse. *Applied Linguistics*, 34(3), 369–388.

Fuster-Márquez, M. (2014). Lexical bundles and phrase frames in the language of hotel websites. *English Text Construction*, 7(1), 84–121.

Hyland, K. (2008). As can be seen: Lexical bundles and disciplinary variation. *English for Specific Purposes*, 27, 4–21.

Jablonkai, R. (2010). English in the context of European integration: A corpus-driven analysis of lexical bundles in English EU documents. *English for Specific Purposes*, 29(4), 253–267.

Liu, D. (2012). The most frequently-used multi-word constructions in academic written English: A multi-corpus study. *English for Specific Purposes*, 31(1), 25–35.

Nesi, H. & Basturkmen, H. (2006). Lexical bundles and discourse signalling in academic lectures. *International Journal of Corpus Linguistics*, 11(3), 283–304.

Paquot, M. (2013). Lexical bundles and L1 transfer effects. *International Journal of Corpus Linguistics*, 18(3), 391–417.

Partington, A. & Morley, J. (2004). From frequency to ideology: Investigating word and cluster/bundle frequency in political debate. In B. Lewandowska-Tomaszczyk (Ed.), *Practical Applications in Language and Computers—PALC 2003* (pp. 179–192). Frankfurt: Peter Lang.

Staples, S., Egbert, J., Biber, D. & McClair, A. (2013). Formulaic sequences and EAP writing development: Lexical bundles in the TOEFL iBT writing section. *Journal of English for Academic Purposes*, 12(3), 214–225.

Appendix

Table 3.6 All lexical bundles occurring at least ten times in five different texts in the Q+A corpus (normalized per 100,000 words)

Bundle	*Overall Q+A corpus data*			*Data per variety of English (normed)*				*Data per topic area (normed)*			*Bundle information*	
	Raw Count	*Number of Texts*	*Per 100,000 Words*	*India*	*Philippines*	*United Kingdom*	*United States*	*Family & Relationships*	*Politics & Government*	*Society & Culture*	*Structural Type*	*Discourse Function*
if you want to	48	42	11.54	10.71	10.81	8.96	15.33	16.25	11.03	7.62	DC	stance
you don't have to	34	26	8.18	2.92	8.84	9.96	10.82	14.77	0.74	9.00	VP	stance
as long as you	32	23	7.70	6.82	6.88	10.96	6.31	11.82	2.94	8.31	NP/PP	stance
i think you should	29	24	6.97	3.90	2.95	10.96	9.92	16.25	1.47	3.46	DC	stance
nothing to do with	28	26	6.73	9.74	6.88	5.98	4.51	7.39	5.88	6.92	NP/PP	DO
you are going to	26	22	6.25	3.90	11.79	5.98	3.61	11.82	2.94	4.15	VP	stance
the end of the	25	22	6.01	1.95	2.95	12.95	6.31	9.60	5.88	2.77	NP/PP	referential
the rest of the	25	22	6.01	5.84	3.93	9.96	4.51	2.22	8.82	6.92	NP/PP	referential
in the first place	25	21	6.01	4.87	1.96	9.96	7.21	7.39	4.41	6.23	NP/PP	referential
to be able to	24	22	5.77	4.87	10.81	1.00	6.31	4.43	8.09	4.85	DC	stance
a lot of people	22	20	5.29	3.90	3.93	4.98	8.11	3.69	5.15	6.92	NP/PP	referential
at the same time	22	19	5.29	7.79	2.95	5.98	4.51	5.17	5.88	4.85	NP/PP	referential
the best way to	22	18	5.29	8.76	3.93	2.99	5.41	2.22	3.68	9.69	NP/PP	stance
you have to do	22	18	5.29	5.84	7.86	3.98	3.61	10.34	1.47	4.15	VP	stance
you don't want to	21	17	5.05	4.87	9.82	1.99	3.61	12.56	1.47	1.38	DC	stance
on the other hand	20	18	4.81	3.90	9.82	1.00	4.51	3.69	5.15	5.54	NP/PP	DO
i would like to	19	14	4.57	1.95	8.84	3.98	3.61	2.95	7.35	3.46	DC	DO
at the end of	19	19	4.57	1.95	2.95	10.96	2.70	7.39	2.94	3.46	NP/PP	referential
have the right to	19	11	4.57	3.90	8.84	1.00	4.51	1.48	12.50	0.00	VP	stance
i think it is	18	15	4.33	3.90	3.93	6.97	2.70	5.17	2.94	4.85	DC	stance
i would have to	18	13	4.33	0.97	0.00	10.96	5.41	5.91	2.21	4.85	VP	stance
it depends on the	17	12	4.09	7.79	0.98	3.98	3.61	8.12	1.47	2.77	VP	stance
has nothing to do	16	15	3.85	6.82	4.91	2.99	0.90	4.43	3.68	3.46	VP	DO
is one of the	16	15	3.85	9.74	2.95	1.99	0.90	3.69	1.47	6.23	VP	referential
should be able to	16	11	3.85	2.92	4.91	5.98	1.80	4.43	4.41	2.77	DC	stance
tell her that you	16	6	3.85	0.97	6.88	0.00	7.21	11.82	0.00	0.00	DC	stance
when it comes to	15	13	3.61	4.87	5.89	1.99	1.80	3.69	3.68	3.46	DC	referential
for the rest of	15	14	3.61	1.95	2.95	5.98	3.61	5.17	5.15	0.69	NP/PP	referential
have a lot of	15	13	3.61	3.90	3.93	1.99	4.51	5.91	2.94	2.08	VP	referential

to take care of	15	7	3.61	1.95	8.84	1.99	1.80	1.48	2.21	6.92	VP	special function
if you are not	15	15	3.61	3.90	3.93	1.99	4.51	2.95	3.68	4.15	DC	referential
not be able to	15	13	3.61	1.95	5.89	1.99	4.51	2.95	5.88	2.08	DC	stance
you need to do	15	14	3.61	4.87	3.93	1.99	3.61	8.12	0.74	2.08	DC	stance
you want to do	15	7	3.61	1.95	4.91	0.00	7.21	5.17	5.15	0.69	DC	stance
you have to be	15	14	3.61	4.87	4.91	1.00	3.61	5.91	2.94	2.08	VP	stance
when i was a	14	8	3.37	0.00	4.91	4.98	3.61	6.65	1.47	2.08	DC	referential
rest of the world	14	11	3.37	3.90	1.96	5.98	1.80	0.74	6.62	2.77	NP/PP	referential
you want to be	14	13	3.37	6.82	0.98	1.99	3.61	4.43	2.94	2.77	DC	stance
in the middle east	13	11	3.13	5.84	1.96	2.99	1.80	0.74	5.88	2.77	NP/PP	referential
it is not the	13	12	3.13	5.84	3.93	1.00	1.80	4.43	2.94	2.08	VP	referential
i don't know if	13	12	3.13	1.95	4.91	0.00	5.41	2.95	2.94	3.46	DC	stance
i don't know what	13	13	3.13	1.95	3.93	2.99	3.61	4.43	2.21	2.77	DC	stance
that you have to	13	12	3.13	3.90	3.93	2.99	1.80	5.17	1.47	2.77	DC	stance
what do you think	12	11	2.89	1.95	4.91	1.00	3.61	2.95	4.41	1.38	VP	DO
that there is no	12	9	2.89	2.92	4.91	1.00	2.70	3.69	0.00	4.85	DC	referential
end of the day	12	11	2.89	0.00	0.00	10.96	0.90	5.17	1.47	2.08	NP/PP	referential
in the name of	12	7	2.89	7.79	0.98	2.99	0.00	1.48	3.68	3.46	NP/PP	referential
the rest of your	12	10	2.89	1.95	1.96	3.98	3.61	7.39	1.47	0.00	NP/PP	referential
the way it is	12	12	2.89	3.90	3.93	2.99	0.90	2.22	3.68	2.77	NP/PP	referential
don't know how to	12	10	2.89	0.97	3.93	1.99	4.51	3.69	1.47	3.46	DC	stance
if you really want	12	10	2.89	3.90	2.95	1.99	2.70	4.43	1.47	2.77	DC	stance
you need to be	12	8	2.89	4.87	1.96	1.99	2.70	7.39	0.74	0.69	DC	stance
you need to get	12	10	2.89	1.95	2.95	3.98	2.70	3.69	2.21	2.77	DC	stance
the only way to	12	10	2.89	5.84	2.95	1.00	1.80	4.43	2.21	2.08	NP/PP	stance
a	12	7	2.89	9.74	0.00	1.00	0.90	0.00	6.62	2.08	VP	stance
if you have a	11	10	2.65	1.95	2.95	1.99	3.61	2.95	0.74	4.15	DC	DO
and a lot of	11	11	2.65	0.97	2.95	2.99	3.61	1.48	4.41	2.08	NP/PP	referential
in the middle of	11	10	2.65	0.97	2.95	1.99	4.51	0.00	2.94	4.85	NP/PP	referential
the two of you	11	10	2.65	2.92	3.93	1.99	1.80	6.65	0.74	0.69	NP/PP	referential
it is not a	11	10	2.65	3.90	0.98	1.00	4.51	1.48	2.94	3.46	VP	referential
you are not a	11	11	2.65	3.90	1.96	1.00	3.61	5.17	0.74	2.08	VP	referential
i don't want to	11	10	2.65	4.87	1.96	1.00	2.70	4.43	2.94	0.69	DC	stance
then you need to	11	11	2.65	3.90	3.93	0.00	2.70	5.91	0.00	2.08	DC	stance
you really want to	11	10	2.65	4.87	1.96	2.99	0.90	4.43	1.47	2.08	DC	stance
as long as it	11	11	2.65	3.90	1.96	1.00	3.61	2.22	2.94	2.77	NP/PP	stance
to do with the	10	10	2.40	1.95	5.89	1.00	0.90	0.74	4.41	2.08	VP	DO

(Continued)

Table 3.6 (Continued)

Bundle	*Overall Q+A corpus data*			*Data per variety of English (normed)*				*Data per topic area (normed)*			*Bundle information*	
	Raw Count	*Number of Texts*	*Per 100,000 Words*	*India*	*Philippines*	*United Kingdom*	*United States*	*Family & Relationships*	*Politics & Government*	*Society & Culture*	*Structural Type*	*Discourse Function*
that there is a	10	9	2.40	2.92	1.96	1.00	3.61	0.00	2.21	4.85	DC	referential
for the sake of	10	9	2.40	3.90	2.95	1.00	1.80	2.95	0.74	3.46	NP/PP	referential
to get to know	10	9	2.40	0.00	4.91	1.00	3.61	5.17	0.00	2.08	VP	special function
even if it is	10	10	2.40	2.92	2.95	1.99	1.80	1.48	2.94	2.77	DC	stance
i don't know how	10	10	2.40	0.00	5.89	1.00	2.70	2.22	2.21	2.77	DC	stance
i don't think i	10	8	2.40	0.00	0.98	5.98	2.70	2.95	0.74	3.46	DC	stance
i think it would	10	10	2.40	0.97	2.95	3.98	1.80	4.43	0.74	2.08	DC	stance
i think that you	10	10	2.40	2.92	0.98	1.99	3.61	4.43	2.21	0.69	DC	stance
if you are a	10	9	2.40	1.95	2.95	1.99	2.70	2.95	3.68	0.69	DC	referential
if you don't want	10	8	2.40	0.97	6.88	1.00	0.90	3.69	2.94	0.69	DC	stance
know what to do	10	9	2.40	0.97	2.95	3.98	1.80	6.65	0.74	0.00	DC	stance
right thing to do	10	10	2.40	0.97	4.91	1.00	2.70	0.74	3.68	2.77	NP/PP	stance
i do not think	10	9	2.40	3.90	1.96	1.99	1.80	2.22	4.41	0.69	VP	stance
is nothing wrong with	10	9	2.40	1.95	2.95	3.98	0.90	5.17	1.47	0.69	VP	stance
it all depends on	10	8	2.40	0.97	0.98	3.98	3.61	2.95	3.68	0.69	VP	stance
there is nothing wrong	10	9	2.40	1.95	2.95	3.98	0.90	4.43	1.47	1.38	VP	stance

4 Semantic Annotation

Amanda Potts

Introduction

This chapter utilises the method of semantic field analysis to describe and compare various subcorpora of online question-and-answer forum texts. This is achieved through automated semantic tagging and calculation of statistical significance using USAS and Wmatrix.

The use of semantic categories is particularly helpful when comparing subcorpora of relatively small sizes, as with this dataset. This is because restricting one's view to the word level disadvantages infrequent words; this is a particular problem in small corpora, where many lexical items—particularly open class words which may be of special interest—are certain to occur infrequently. Using this method, it is possible to group many types with similar meanings together, increasing the frequency of the category to a threshold that allows for analysis of a greater variety of statistically significant features. In other words, I demonstrate a systematic approach to the comparison of corpora by using 'corpus-based comparative frequency evidence to drive the selection of words for further study' (Rayson 2008: 523).

Tools

Analysis in this chapter has been carried out in Wmatrix,[1] a web-based corpus analysis and comparison tool developed by Paul Rayson at Lancaster University. Wmatrix is unique in its total integration with the CLAWS part-of-speech tagger (Garside 1987) and the UCREL Semantic Annotation System (Archer, Wilson, & Rayson, 2002). While part-of-speech tagging is crucial, it is further automated *semantic* tagging that forms the basis of exploration in this chapter and therefore bears further discussion.

The UCREL Semantic Annotation System (USAS) is a framework for automatic semantic tagging of input text. USAS draws upon an extensive lexicon to assign one or more semantic tags (semtags) to each word or multi-word-unit (MWU) in a given text. The tagset is hierarchical, with 21 major discourse fields (Table 4.1) further expanded into over 230 category labels (Archer, Wilson, & Rayson, 2002: 2). This type of annotation is

Table 4.1 Structure of USAS major discourse field distinctions (from Archer, Wilson, & Rayson, 2002: 2)

USAS broad category	*Description*
A	General and abstract terms
B	The body and the individual
C	Arts and crafts
E	Emotion
F	Food and farming
G	Government and public
H	Architecture, housing, and the home
I	Money and commerce in industry
K	Entertainment, sports, and games
L	Life and living things
M	Movement, location, travel, and transport
N	Numbers and measurement
O	Substances, materials, objects, and equipment
P	Education
Q	Language and communication
S	Social actions, states, and processes
T	Time
W	World and environment
X	Psychological actions, states, and processes
Y	Science and technology
Z	Names and grammar

useful for analysis seeking to highlight broad themes and discourse relationships within texts, as '[t]he semantic tags show semantic fields which group together word senses that are related by virtue of their being connected at some level of generality with the same mental concept' (Archer, Wilson, & Rayson, 2002: 1).

Using the Wmatrix Tag Wizard, users may upload and automatically tag their corpora before performing standard corpus-linguistic analyses, such as concordance and keyword. However, as all items are additionally assigned semantic tags, it is possible in Wmatrix to extend the keyness method, producing and comparing frequency lists of semantic tags rather than words. This reduces the number of items to be analysed and allows for more objective identification of categories of meaning for analysis. However, identification of key semtags is not intended to be comprehensive; it is merely from this starting point that the researcher intervenes and carries out qualitative examination, including concordance analysis and sense disambiguation.

Methods

Addressing the main research question entails undertaking a comparative approach, which in itself requires a point of meaningful comparison. To generate reference corpora that would adequately highlight the unique features of a given target corpus, a reference corpus containing every country's data, excluding that of the target country, was compiled. For instance, the US English corpus was compared to a reference corpus containing each English sample *except* the US (i.e., IN, PH, and UK). This method was replicated for topic clusters regardless of country, e.g., a target corpus containing all Politics & Government threads was compared to a reference corpus of all threads from the Family & Relationships and Society & Culture forums. Standardisation/ regularisation of spelling has not been attempted; the corpora were used as provided and examples from the data appear *sic erat scriptum*.

Key semantic tags were then calculated. Wmatrix makes use of the log-likelihood (LL) test as a confidence indicator of keyness, providing a measure of the certainty that one can have that resulting keywords or semantic domains are not occurring due to chance (Rayson, Berridge, & Francis, 2004). This is not uncontroversial; the use of LL for identifying and ranking keywords has recently been problematized (see for instance, Gabrielatos & Marchi 2012), but it remains the most widely used keyness statistic. Therefore, it has been adopted here not as a personal endorsement but rather due to the lack of a new accepted standard keyness measurement and also in the hope of highlighting common findings between this and other chapters also using LL.

Some cut-off frequency thresholds have also been applied after tagging, for ease and clarity of analysis. Only key semantic tags and constituent lemmata appearing across more than three threads in a given country subcorpus are considered. Lexical items with frequencies of ten or higher are considered in close discussion. These cut-offs guarantee that space is maximised in discussing reasonably well-distributed, frequent items that might be generalisable beyond single threads or isolated discussions.

Analysis

The nature of key semantic tag analysis—i.e., highlighting overuse of certain semantic meanings in one corpus versus another—makes it more useful for certain types of contrastive analyses and dramatically less valuable for others. For instance, when texts have already been segregated by topic, key semtags echo this classification. Consequently, key semantic domains in the Family & Relationships subcorpus include: KIN (S4), PERSONAL RELATIONSHIP: GENERAL (S3.1), PEOPLE: FEMALE (S2.1), RELATIONSHIP: INTIMACY AND SEX (S3.2), and PEOPLE: MALE (S2.2). Texts from Politics & Government contain key semtags such as POLITICS (G1.2), GOVERNMENT (G1.1), WARFARE, DEFENCE, AND THE ARMY; WEAPONS (G3), and LAW AND ORDER (G2.1). Finally, Society & Culture texts show overrepresentation in the semantic fields of RELIGION AND THE SUPERNATURAL (S9), THE MEDIA: BOOKS (Q4.1), and MUSIC AND RELATED ACTIVITIES (K2).

These findings, while not particularly helpful for forming hypotheses, do indicate that the topic categories imposed externally (e.g., Family & Relationships) are reflected discourse internally (e.g., in overrepresentation of lexical items such as *parents, daughter, marriage*, and *divorce*, all contributing to overall keyness of tag S4, KIN). In this way, we see how key semtags indicate the 'aboutness' or themes of a given collection of texts. Therefore, when texts are not externally categorised by theme but by country, generating key semtags will indicate frequent threads of meaning suggestive of common nationwide interests. In this aim, Sections 4.1 through 4.4 that follow detail key semantic tags for subcorpora defined by country alone. These are ordered alphabetically by corpus name.

Key Semantic Tags: India (IN)

Key semantic tags in the IN dataset appear in Table 4.2 (those discussed in more detail are highlighted in bold). It is striking that two semtags from the broad category X (PSYCHOLOGICAL ACTIONS, STATES, AND PROCESSES) appear in this list and nowhere else in the key semtag tables in this small study. It seems that the Indian corpus is more preoccupied with indicators of psychological states; indeed, the semtag with the highest LL value by some margin is X5.1+ ATTENTIVE.

The most frequent components of X5.1+ in the IN corpus include *concentration* (frequency: 59), *concentrate* (22), *focus* (24), and *attention* (17). Lexical items *concentration, concentrate*, and *concentrating* are largely restricted to one thread, IN_SC_11, where the original poster asks, 'WHAT IS THE DIFFERENCE BETWEEN MEDITATION AND CONSENTRATION'. Both *focus* and *attention* appear in this same thread but also in 11 additional (nonexclusive) others. Concordance lines containing *attention* explain methods of drawing and commanding attention, for instance, of a potential romantic partner or of an audience to a performance. Discussions of *focus* are more self-centred, with posters recommending that others retain, for example, *focus* on their own happiness or on surrounding themselves with positive people. Even without an object, *focus* is positively evaluated as a (nominal) goal of its own, as in one recommendation to 'be passionate for that language, solve your mistakes, increase your memory

Table 4.2 Key semantic tags in the IN corpus

Item	*Description*	*IN freq.*	*IN freq./ 100k*	*PH+US+ UK freq.*	*PH+US+UK freq. /100k*	*LL*
X5.1+	**Attentive**	**169**	**171.36**	**89**	**29.53**	**191.19**
S9	**Religion and the supernatural**	**1157**	**1173.15**	**2305**	**764.86**	**133.67**
Z99	Unmatched	2433	2466.97	5608	1860.88	129.67
F4	Farming & horticulture	95	96.33	57	18.91	97.18
X2	Mental actions and processes	118	119.65	99	32.85	87.33

and *focus* . . .' (IN_SC_20). Items semtagged X5.1+ relate to self-betterment and in many threads work in tandem with the next key semtag discussed in the next section.

Keyness of the S9 semtag (RELIGION AND THE SUPERNATURAL) can largely be related to two extremely frequent lexical items in the IN corpus: *god* appears 269 times and *religion* appears 128 times. Compare this to 512 occurrences of *god* and 71 occurrences of *religion* in the three other corpora combined. *God* appears in 36 of the 69 files comprising the IN corpus, spread across the Politics & Government, Society & Culture, and Family & Relationships threads. Other lexical items that might be classed as relating to 'religion in general' include *religious* (34), *sacred* (30), *religions* (28), *Satan* (24), *heaven* (23), *hell* (22), *spirit* (20), *soul* (2), *spiritual* (18), *bless* (15), *pray* (15), *divine* (13), *worship* (12), and *sacrifice* (10). Religion is invoked in such a variety of threads that it might take up the entirety of this chapter to attempt to describe the nuances of this semtag. Suffice to say that in this subcorpus, religion (particularly *god*) is offered as an answer to many of life's difficulties; when one poster asks how to be happy despite pain, the answer voted best gives a list that begins, '1—Be closer to *God*—prayer gives strength—& support' (IN_FR_07). Aside from being a personal support system, *god* is also acknowledged as empowering others and therefore providing the explanation for interpersonal struggles: 'You don't force no one to love you because *god* gave us freewill that's something that no magic can change not even god himself'. (IN_FR_06).

Occurring in 15 threads, *religion* is not as well dispersed as *god* and tends to cluster around questions explicitly linked to faith (opposed to being introduced independently by commenters to an otherwise secular discussion). In these threads, *religion* as an abstract concept is questioned in its role in modern society; commenters debate whether *religion* is good for humanity (IN_SC_18) or whether it hampers integration in India (IN_PG_21). These debates relate to (and lead to) more specific discussion of particular religious groups occurring with less variety and in smaller frequency than general religious words, including *muslims* (41), *muslim* (40), *islam* (37); *bible* (30), *rosary* (16), *church* (12), *Christians* (12); and *jews* (18). Though spirituality and *religion* on the whole are positively appraised as methods of improving one's personal life, specific religions (or religious practitioners) are negatively evaluated across a dozen threads. In IN_PG_15, the original poster (OP) asks, 'Who do you think is responsible for the current situation in the Middle East?' and the best answer responds, '*religious* extremists. . . . *muslim*, *christian* and *jewish*. extremism in any form is dangerous'. It is notable that the majority *religion* in India—Hindu—is not present in this semtag. We might conclude, then, that negative appraisal of practitioners is in fact negative appraisal of religious 'others', whereas positive appraisal of *religion* is presumed to be the common (popular) *religion* and *worship* thereof.

In addition to semtags in categories highlighted for analysis, it might be noted that the IN corpus is the only one to feature Z99 (UNMATCHED) in the top-five semtags ranked by LL value. This indicates that this corpus contains a disproportionate number of items not recognised by the USAS tagger, in this case, many features of Internet language (such as *im* instead of 'I'm', *wat* instead of 'what' and *pls* instead of 'please'). The (American/British) English-centric nature of the tagger also appears to lack recognition for items which mark the text's social context, e.g., the festival *diwali* and common given name *Jeeyen*. Attempts to represent gender-neutral pronouns, e.g., with a slash, *he/she, him/her*, and *his/her*, are also not recognised by the tagger but appear in relatively higher number in the IN corpus. This highlights a shortcoming of the application of any method relying on automated tagging to corpora comprised of non-standard (e.g. Internet) language.

Key Semantic Tags: Philippines (PH)

The USAS semtag with the highest LL value in the Philippine corpus is G1.1 GOVERNMENT (see Table 4.3). A large number of items semtagged G1.1 appear more than ten times; these may be loosely (manually) categorised as follows:

- **People:** *president* (169), *officials* (18)
- **Localities:** *country* (104), *nation* (37), state (29)
- **Descriptors:** *official* (60), presidential (18)
- **Political process:** *constitution* (45), *constitutional* (11)
- **Abstract concepts:** *imperialism* (13)

President is both highly frequent (occurring 169 times in the PH corpus) and well distributed (across 20 threads). However, a number of threads are explicitly themed on this topic. Five such threads deal with the President of the Philippines asking for opinions on the President's state of the nation address (PH_PG_02), the possibility of former President Joseph Estrada running once more for the presidency (PH_PG_20), creation of an official residence for the vice-president (PH_PG_18), appropriate personal spending on the President's behalf (PH_PG_21), and even which Philippine presidential

Table 4.3 Key semantic tags in the PH corpus

Item	*Description*	*PH freq.*	*PH freq./ 100k*	*IN+US+ UK freq.*	*IN+US+UK freq. /100k*	*LL*
G1.1	**Government**	**676**	**689.86**	**1307**	**432.79**	**91.55**
P1	**Education in general**	**360**	**367.38**	**619**	**204.97**	**72.78**
Q4.1	The Media: Books	141	143.89	159	52.65	71.21
S9	Religion and the supernatural	1067	1088.88	2395	793.05	71.02
G1.2	Politics	540	551.07	1119	370.53	54.53

candidate commenters one would most like to date (PH_PG_19). Within these threads, presidents past, present, and prospective are assessed, frequently on personal attributes. Former President Joseph Estrada is appraised as 'bogus' due to past criminal convictions (PH_PG_20). The best answer (as rated by readers) to the question of whether the vice-president should have an official residence (PH_PG_18) is a damning indictment of greed, calling the request lavish and stating that '[The vice-president] claims to have lived a life of a poor man then do so even when many of his wealth is hidden and he does live very well contrary to image'. The majority of responses in PH_PG_21 dealing with the purchase of a second-hand Porsche by President Benigno Aquino III negatively appraise this action as morally wrong, with the leader's lack of personal austerity considered a negative model for citizens who expect public officials to 'lead modest lives'. Contrary to my initial reading of thread PH_PG_19, commenters do not qualify their 'date' choices with judgements on presidential candidates' personal appearance or public persona; rather, they weigh up which candidates they would most like to discuss politics with. This underscores the level of personal engagement in politics exhibited by PH corpus contributors.

Beyond those threads based on Philippine politics, multiple threads also deal with another nation, both explicitly and implicitly. Explicitly, OPs ask, 'Will this elections for US *president* make History?' (PH_PG_03) and 'Why are Republicans such Hypocrites?' (PH_PG_04). The main question in PH_PG_08 asks, 'What's so bad about *imperialism*', with the extended query, 'The left is particularly boisterous about claiming that America is in a war for *imperialism* because of our role in Iraq, and then never giving solid evidence to back up this claim'. In PH_PG_18, the OP is asking whether elections can be simplified, but in the extended query, it is clear that this is also in the US context: 'I don't think all American voters really understand the electoral process/2-party system anyway—I don't'. Thread PH_PG_12 discusses the possibility of enforcing a test or academic standard for American presidential candidates. In this and other threads, it's clear that not only people from the Philippines contribute to the PH corpus. Indeed, American discourses (identifiable through inclusive pronouns and other forms of identity positioning) are overrepresented in this subcorpus and also in others (see Section 4.3). This is likely due to the site of corpus collection: Yahoo! appears to be more popular with certain nations than others. However, this shows that researchers must have a good understanding of the characteristics of the texts contained within a corpus to guard against over-interpretation that may result without further analysing these threads and concordance lines.

Moving to the next key item, the PH corpus is the only dataset containing a key semtag in the P (EDUCATION) broad category (see Table 4). This unique preference may be indicative on its own, but through the scope of semantic annotation, we can also discuss the lexical components contributing to this keyness. Key semtag P1 is varied, including: *school* (50), *taught* (28), *teach* (25), *college* (20), *education* (19), *lesson* (12), *test* (10), and *high school* (10). These items are discussed at more length in the following section.

The highest frequency item in this semtag—*school(s)*—appears in a wide variety of contexts: describing driving or helping to prepare for school as the sweetest thing that a father has done, used as an attribute to portray a time of life or bracket of age, a setting for various life vignettes, etc. As such, the only pattern that can be meaningfully ascribed to its keyness is that *school* is talked about often and regarded as important, both as a feature of identity and a milestone or a staging area for formative events. This also goes for *high school* and for *college*, save for the instances where *college* is incorrectly categorised outside of its bigram, *Electoral College*. The value of strong academic performance comes across strongly across the threads.

The concordance lines for a more broad linguistic term—*education*—gives further insight into the attitudes commenters hold towards the institution. In the PH corpus, commenters make clear that they believe the government should focus on *education* and the further promotion of social equality; lack of access to proper *education* (and nutrition) for all citizens is one reason offered in support of population control. Academic merit is also considered to be one major aspect of gaining a meaningful relationship; one original post (PH_FR_09) details the reasons that her relationship is failing, largely attributing this to her boyfriend's family deriding her inferior qualifications. Commenters urge the original poster to 'try to make them understand that education is something but love is something else', but do not denounce the possibility of this type of discrimination.

It is in more abstract nouns that the conceptualisation of EDUCATION IN GENERAL comes into better focus. Concordance lines of *lessons* range from institutional (e.g., school, golf, and music *lessons*) to abstract (life *lessons*). Strikingly, the singular *lesson* is, in all 12 instances, used in the abstract sense. These appearances are sometimes related to the negative concepts of 'learning (one's) lesson' or 'teaching (one) a lesson', but more often in a thread relating stories of a (positive) life *lesson* learned from young people, such as the value of honesty, forgiveness, and gratitude.

Key Semantic Tags: United Kingdom (UK)

Key semtags for UK English can be found in Table 4.4. Readers may find the appearance of S1.2.4-IMPOLITE interesting, as this may key into certain cultural stereotypes about the UK. However, the most highly key semtags (by LL) are Z2 GEOGRAPHICAL NAMES and F1 FOOD. As I will demonstrate, these concepts are not as dissimilar as they might first appear.

UK semtag Z2 makes up approximately 1.07% of the corpus overall and contains a wide variety of lexical items which might be grouped into categories themselves. The most numerous in terms of variety and frequency are self-reflexive, indicating *British* (74) interests, broadly in the *UK* (56)

Table 4.4 Key semantic tags in the UK corpus

Item	*Description*	*UK freq.*	*UK freq./ 100k*	*IN+PH+ US freq.*	*IN+PH+ US freq./ 100k*	*LL*
Z2	**Geographical names**	**1035**	**1072.15**	**1766**	**581.94**	**228.15**
F1	**Food**	**477**	**493.09**	**608**	**200.35**	**203.75**
Z8	Pronouns	15638	16194.13	44831	14772.99	97.02
S1.2.4-	Impolite	92	95.3	60	19.77	90.78
O4.2-	Judgement of appearance: ugly	159	162.64	196	64.59	72.05

and *Britain* (23), for *Brits* (10) but also more specifically in reference to *Scotland* (41) and the *Scottish* (38), *England* (34), and the *English* (14) and locally to the *Cornish* (11). In the UK subcorpus, self-reflexive discourse defines Britain as being a nation with strong military history, defined by royalty, and full of humour that is misunderstood by people from other countries, namely Americans. Strain between *English* and *Scottish* (and in one case, Irish) identity appears in multiple threads, with some commenters displaying unease with describing the makeup of *Britain* itself.

The second most frequent pattern in terms of frequently semtagged lexical items shows a preoccupation with the culture of another country: *american* occurs 81 times; *americans*, 70; *america*, 31; and *USA*, 14. This may be in part due to a number of Politics & Government threads explicitly dealing with the topic. These range from ideologically neutral attempts at intercultural communication, such as UK_PG_05's opening query, 'As an American, I'm curious about what you think of Obama?', to more confrontational remarks, such as 'Why do Americans try to take all the credit for WW2?' (UK_PG_02), to the openly hostile, 'Are all americans idiots?' (UK_PG_08). The position of *America* as a world superpower seems to be keenly felt, particularly in the UK where emotions about the President run high. The best answer to the UK_PG_05 query about the US President says:

> He seems like a breath of fresh air, enthusiastic and a 'do-er' rather than just a complainer. A bit early to tell how it';s gonna turn out, but I wish him, you, us all the best. Edit: can anyone do any worse than that imbecile you had last?

Here we see that President Obama is positively appraised, particularly in contrast to his negatively evaluated predecessor, George W. Bush. However, other commenters are less kind, calling him 'a Socialist joke' and an 'Overhyped talentless ethnic'. However, the influence of non-UK (indeed, US) contributors affects the results, as in Section 4.1.

Certain European superpowers also feature, namely *Germany* (17), *german* (15), and *french* (14), with *Europe* generally appearing 11 times. *Germany* and *german* appear usually to do with discussions around WWII and Hitler's leadership, though some other patterns occur, such as commenters calling the British Royal Family a 'bunch of free loading *germans*' (UK_SC_04) or forming long comparisons such as the one in UK_SC_15:

> It seems that humour that's droll like ours is understood by some nations and not others, ie. the Dutch, *German* and continental countries share and understand this. *American* people tend to have a different style of humour that isn't as droll, so they often take us too literally.

Z2 items from further afield include *Israel* (31), *arab* (13), *Iraq* (12), and *asylum seekers* (12), though these are limited to one or two threads and cannot be generalised in any meaningful way to UK discourse as a whole.

Food, the next most key semtag, is also defined according to its region or recipe for creation. For instance, some foods (e.g., cheddar *cheese*, Cornish *pasties*) appear in conversations about the distinctions that are made in some foods' qualification for a certain nomination, with others (types of *fast food, fried onion* rings) showing up in explanations of items that might not be familiar to some readers, as they are described as being more popular in places like the US. Awareness of UK minority group food preferences also appears, though these are negatively appraised. A number of commenters acknowledge that Muslims don't want to handle *pork* but that measures taken by chain store Marks & Spencer allowing them to avoid this activity are overly sensitive.

The UK semtag F1 contains a great variety of lexical items above the minimum frequency of ten, including *chocolate* (42), *eat* (38), *food* (31), *eating* (19), *sugar* (15), *onion* (15), *foods* (11). When describing a broad category of food denoting the *nutritional* content, commenters use the plural: *foods*. These are grouped together as bad foods to be avoided ('processed', 'packaged', 'prepared', 'genetically modified', 'low fat', 'fat free') versus good foods to be consumed ('healthy'). Dieters are advised not to eat *bread*, monitor *salt* intake, eliminate sugar, and keep an eye on the calorie content of *nuts*.

Concordance lines of *chocolate* (appearing in five threads) also show an ethical awareness of consumption. One original poster asks, 'Is eating chocolate morally wrong?' (text UK_SC_10), problematizing western profit leveraged from African child labour. In 37 responses containing *chocolate*, only two state explicitly that eating *chocolate* is morally wrong, with 11 asserting that it is not wrong. It is the act of child labour and not the specific product that is considered 'wrong' by three commenters. These patterns indicate that the source of products is important to many people in the UK, and though they may not avoid problematic foods, they are inclined to be conscientious consumers where possible.

Key Semantic Tags: United States (US)

Key semantic tags in the US dataset with the five highest LL values compared to a reference corpus consisting of the data from the IN, PH, and UK appear in Table 4.5. Notable here are the overrepresentation of the concepts of WARFARE, DEFENCE, AND THE ARMY; WEAPONS and medicalisation of discourse indicated by the presence of MEDICINES AND MEDICAL TREATMENT in the key list. The semtags with the two highest LL values are H4- (NON-RESIDENT) and O4.3 (COLOUR AND COLOUR PATTERNS), discussed in turn in the following section.

The semantic tag H4- NON-RESIDENT does not refer, as might be assumed, to those lacking legal residency in the US. Rather, NON-RESIDENT denotes a lack of residence, e.g., *homeless* (39) and *homelessness* (16). These words are dispersed at the minimum threshold across the corpus, with the highest concentration in a single thread beginning with the question, 'Should *Homeless* people be sent to jail?' (US_SC_13). In 59 responses, 53 provided a firmly negative response, with several respondents negatively appraising the OP (e.g., calling the question/asker heartless or ridiculous). Nearly all negative responses state that *homeless* people should only be sent to jail if they commit a crime, with many obliquely stating that *homelessness* in itself is not (and should not be) criminalised. Of the six responses giving affirmative or alternative responses, one seems hyperbolic ('send them to iraq'), with the other more sarcastic: 'YES. free food, sex, cable, gym, library, protection. thanks for the advice. i'm going *homeless* right now. ciao'. Three responses indicate that jail would allow for meals and shelter, with one of these stating that 'They should be allowed to come and go'. The final coded as ambiguous states 'if they have over 400$', the exact meaning of which is unknown, but might relate to cost of imprisonment or definitions of 'real' versus 'fake' *homelessness*.

Table 4.5 Key semantic tags in the US corpus

Item	*Description*	*US freq.*	*US freq./100k*	*IN+PH+UK freq.*	*IN+PH+UK freq./100k*	*LL*
H4-	**Non-resident**	**59**	**55.2**	**1**	**0.34**	**146.18**
O4.3	**Colour and colour patterns**	**244**	**228.28**	**240**	**81.87**	**122.34**
S3.1	Personal relationship: General	520	486.51	815	278.03	94.32
B3	Medicines and medical treatment	255	238.58	329	112.23	77.45
G3	Warfare, defence, and the army; weapons	421	393.88	698	238.12	63.26

The two other threads containing items tagged H4- both belong to the Politics & Government category, and neither begin with questions specifically related to *homelessness*. In US_PG_04, the original poster asks, 'Why do the Americans not care about any one but themselves?' While the question deals with issues of (specifically Mexican) immigration and difficulty in obtaining citizenship status, the responses derail into arguments about problems considered to be more pressing. One respondent says:

> 'Doing the right thing and giving you welfare, medicare, etc' Are you crazy? Whos says we owe you anything? If you are a citizen of this country that is one thing but illegals have no rights ezcept in the country where they are a citizen. We have people who are still *homeless* and displaced from hurricanes katrina and rita and you want us to give you welfare? when pigs fly!

This underscores the general sentiment of *homelessness* as a prevailing social problem in the US, but one which is more important than the needs of non-citizens and immigrants, perhaps due to this concordance line's linkage with environmentally displaced people rather than chronically homeless people. Another take on this appears in US_PG_16 where the OP asks, 'So why do libs think health insurance is more important than putting food on the table?' One response states, 'Because liberals don't care about starving people. sick people. homeless people, honest people. . . And they don't care about minorities or abused women either'. This clearly constructs a group of deviants (containing *homeless* people) to whom liberals are construed as being unsympathetic.

Naming strategies and segregation of 'norms' and 'deviants' are further evident in items tagged O4.3 COLOUR AND COLOUR PATTERNS. The highest frequency items in this semantic tag are *black* (65), *white* (47), and *color* (34). Of these, 61 instances of *black*, 36 instances of *white*, and 42 of *color* come from file US_FR_07, where the original poster asks, 'Is a *black* wedding dress Ok for a wedding? Because *white* has bored me to no end, and I would prefer any other *color*?' However, this leaves 13 additional files containing *white*, nine containing *black*, and three featuring *color*—more than meeting the minimum dispersion frequency.

However, we must resist over-interpretation, even on the basis of this frequency and dispersion; explicit ethnic/racial marking through use of *black*, *white*, and *colour* is a minority pattern—albeit a strong minority—forming the basis of four of those threads mentioning *black*, four mentioning *white*, and one containing *color*. (Other n-grams contributing to keyness of this semtag in the US corpus include '*White* House' and '*black* magic'.) Threads in which *white*, *black*, and *color* refer to ethnicity often indicate social tension in the US. In one thread (US_FR_12), the original poster shares that 'My parents hate white girls? (I'm 14)?' Notably, this thread contains only four responses, two of which support the OP starting an interracial relationship, while the other two state that the OP is too young to date, with one of these adding,

'I have to agree with your parents cause whats wrong with dating your own race were you come from? black'. In another thread asking whether posters trust President Barak Obama (US_PG_02), one comment states:

> Hey I have nothing wrong with a *black* president! But Obama? His wife HATES *whites*, he grew up in a muslim house [. . .] he has YET to provide a birth certificate to show he was born in the USA [. . .] If obama doesn't get us all killed by inviting his terrorist buddies over, he has plenty of secondary options.

Here issues of political 'trust' become muddled with emotions about ethnicity and perceived tensions between people of different backgrounds. The ethnic 'other' is linked to religious and national 'others', and likened to a terrorist. From small-scale interactions (e.g., parents resisting their child's wish to begin an interracial relationship) to larger-picture implications (e.g., citizens proclaiming heads of state to be untrustworthy on the basis of a set of attributes loosely and mostly erroneously related to being *black*), these patterns do indicate that prominence of O4.3 COLOUR AND COLOUR PATTERNS highlights an underlying feature of language in this society.

Discussion

This brief analysis has highlighted one way in which key semantic tag analysis might be used to highlight differences between two or more corpora.

Broadly speaking, it was found that the IN corpus contained a number of themes pertaining to spirituality and religion, though these were sometimes highlighted as potential areas of tension in society, and did indicate 'othering' discourses. Key topics in the PH corpus were government and education, with posters showing interest in public spending, election processes, and the future development of the nation's youth and the nation as a whole. In the UK corpus, key semtags relating to geography indicated interest in societal differences and positioned the country as one rich in culture and humour, particularly in comparison to other regions. Food was also salient in the UK, though posters encouraged moral awareness of its production. Finally, in the US corpus, major social problems such as homelessness and ethnic/racial divisions came to the fore as posters discussed welfare and distribution of social services.

This was one example of teasing out meanings by using key semantic tag analysis, ranked by LL, and taking into account both dispersion and frequency cut-offs. Three alternative ways of approaching the data through semantic tagging would be to 1) analyse the contents of each semantic tag belonging to a certain broad semantic category for each corpus, 2) compare and contrast all items from a specific semtag of special relevance for a given research question, 3) avoid using LL as an effect size approximate by downsampling through use of a different measure, such as coefficient of variation. For instance, one researcher might find differences in keyness of the S (SOCIAL ACTIONS, STATES, AND PROCESSES) category to be illuminating for social-contrastive analysis, whereas another might be more concerned with frequency of PRONOUNS (Z8) alone.

By way of a caveat, I would also add that this method is best conceived as a matter of first enquiry rather than a comprehensive approach to analysis. It is best employed to indicate broad patterns in meaning that might not be accessible to the researcher through intuition alone. Normally, I would employ semantic annotation and analysis of key semantic domains alongside a battery of other analyses. Particularly with such small corpora, the inclusion of one thread on a specific (semantic) topic skews all results. As a result, key semantic tag analysis is most effectively employed when bolstered by the same measures that many types of corpus-based methods benefit from, namely, performance on a somewhat large and well-designed corpus in pursuit of response to well-defined research questions and informed by efforts at triangulation.

Postscript

Writing this analysis was a challenging exercise in brevity. In reading other authors' submissions, it does seem that more space might have allowed me to reiterate a small number of findings uncovered using other methods.

In this chapter, I was able to show the five key semtags with the highest LL value in each country, but due to space constraints, I opted to only drill down on the 'top-two' semtags and to discuss the most frequent headwords contained within. These cut-offs—more arbitrary (in the case of the 'top-two' semtags) and more principled (where a minimum frequency of ten indicates that a headword comprises 0.01% of any given country's overall corpus)—allowed me to identify some interesting differences between the countries, but they have also obviously truncated the possible range of analysis.

In two cases appearing in this chapter, semantic annotation did echo findings of other authors, but this was not expanded upon due to the semtags ranking third, fourth, or fifth in descending LL value (rather than first or second). For instance, in the PH corpus, S9 RELIGION AND THE SUPERNATURAL appears in the fourth position in Table 4.3, with a LL value of 71.02. So looking beyond the first two key positions would have enabled me to corroborate McEnery, Brezin, and Levon's findings regarding the importance of religion in the Philippines. Further, in Chapters 2 and 10, McEnery and Levon note an '(im)politeness' category in UK English. The semtag S1.2.4- IMPOLITE appears in the fourth key position for the UK in Table 4.4 (LL: +90.78). The most frequent headword by a far margin in the S1.2.4- semtag in the UK is *rude*; concordance lines show that staring, making comments about someone's appearance, and speaking a language other than English in front of English-only speakers are considered to be *rude* by posters (though in the last instance, eavesdropping on these conversations is also called *rude!*). In this case, then, the appearance of S1.2.4- indicates a cultural policing of impoliteness rather than an overabundance of impolite speech acts in the corpus.

On other occasions, considering the full set of key semtags appearing earlier, a certain LL cut-off would have exposed patterns identified in other chapters. For instance, in Chapter 9, Baker notes that the US has a higher number of female terms than male. Indeed, with a LL score of +24.90, S2.1 FEMALE is key semtag #13 for the US corpus. Deeper concordance analysis might also have exposed more nuanced meanings; for instance, two head-words from PH key semtag G1.1 GOVERNMENT (*constitution* and *constitutional*) were included under a category I have called 'political process'. In associated concordance lines, these often key constitutional *rights*, a pattern indicated by McEnery in Chapter 2.

Writing a chapter for this book has been an unusual experience in many ways. First, the dataset provided is drawn from sources outside of my usual remit and is not necessarily one which I would choose to semantically annotate. The choices that I made regarding cut-offs were in the aim of showing the strength of semantic annotation to its best effect, this being a method that I highly value and use (in combination with other corpus-linguistic tools) in a large proportion of my work. As a side effect, these choices have disallowed me from triangulating a small number of additional findings. Overall, however, I believe that findings from the great majority of this volume would have been impossible to come by using semantic annotation; Chapters 5, 7, and 11 are particularly striking in their different approaches and nearly entirely novel findings. Other chapters touch on similar themes but were able to dedicate more time to discussing them. In hindsight, I see more fully that it was not only method but also—very critically—methodological choices that have made the difference between what was included and what was left unanalysed in the final work. While more space might have presented the opportunity to be more inclusive in qualitative analysis, the necessity of establishing some cut-offs would have meant that no amount of words would have allowed me to explore every interesting feature of the data thrown up by semantic keyness. Luckily, a range of other interesting contributions has filled some of these gaps and—if I may—made a very strong argument for triangulation in our everyday work!

Note

1 http://ucrel.lancs.ac.uk/wmatrix/

References

Archer, D., Wilson, A. & Rayson, P. (2002). Introduction to the USAS Category System. Accessed online at: http://ucrel.lancs.ac.uk/usas/usasguide.pdf

Gabrielatos, C. & Marchi, A. (2012). *Keyness: Appropriate Metrics and Practical Issues*. Paper presented at the CADS International Conference 2012, 13–14 September, University of Bologna, Italy.

Garside, R. (1987). The CLAWS word-tagging System. In R. Garside, G. Leech & G. Sampson (Eds.), *The Computational Analysis of English: A Corpus-Based Approach*. London: Longman. (pp. 30–41).

Rayson, P. (2008). From key words to key semantic domains. *International Journal of Corpus Linguistics*, 13(4), 519–549.

Rayson, P., Berridge, D. & Francis, B. (2004). Extending the cochran rule or the comparison of word frequencies between corpora. In G. Purnelle, C. Fairon & A. Dister (Eds.), *Le Poids des Mots: Proceedings of the 7th International Conference on Statistical Analysis of Textual Data (JADT 2004)* (pp. 926–936). Louvain-la-Neuve, Belgium: Presses universitaires de Louvain.

5 Multi-Dimensional Analysis

Eric Friginal and Doug Biber

Introduction

Despite the growing amount of online language produced by digitally literate users and the ubiquity of the Internet worldwide, there is still a paucity of linguistic research on these digital domains (Grieve, Biber, Friginal, & Nekrasova, 2010; Friginal, Waugh, & Titak, 2015). As it is, new web-based registers continue to emerge and evolve quickly, illustrating the dynamic nature of language development online and the need to examine such emerging texts. Given the size of the global Internet and increasing reader participation in social media (including Q+A forum pages), there is no doubt that web-based domains are a valuable resource for extensive linguistic research studies (Gries 2011; Herdağdelen 2013).

The chapters in this book attempt to answer the primary question, 'In what ways does language use in online Q+A forum responses differ across four world English varieties: India, Philippines, UK, and US?' In this chapter, we seek to answer this question by examining the linguistic features of Q+A forum responses through a multi-dimensional (MD) analysis methodology developed by Biber (1988). Many corpus-based studies of cross-linguistic variation focus largely on isolated linguistic and functional features of texts. There have also been multiple studies making use of corpora in comparing and contrasting English registers and varieties of English (or 'Englishes'). Some examples of such research include the work of Balasubramanian (2009) profiling register variation in Indian English from lexical and grammatical distributions in spoken and written registers of English in India, Bautista (2011) and Friginal's (2011) analyses of Philippine English texts, several studies of global varieties of English from ICE (or the International Corpus of English), and comparisons of grammatical features of second-language writing from the International Corpus of Learner English (ICLE) and similar learner corpora.

A complementary approach to this type of distributional research is to examine the overall linguistic profile of corpora using statistical tools without an a priori set of target features. Biber (1988, 1995, 2003) pioneered the MD analysis methodology, which classifies texts according to clusters of co-occurring linguistic features in a cross-register comparison (Friginal 2013a).

For MD analysis, over 100 grammatical, syntactic, and semantic features are tagged and tallied for each text. These feature counts are then subjected to a multivariate statistical analysis to identify clusters of co-occurring features, and the results are interpreted through qualitative analyses using text samples with reference to the identified functions of the register or sub-register in the corpus.

Multi-dimensional Analytical Framework

Biber's (1988) multi-feature, multi-dimensional analytical framework has been used in the study of a variety of spoken and written registers, including web-based texts. MD analysis data come from factor analysis (FA), which considers the sequential, partial, and observed correlations of a wide range of variables producing groups of occurring factors or dimensions. According to Tabachnick and Fidell (2001), the purposes of FA are to summarize patterns of correlations among variables, to reduce a large number of observed variables to a smaller number of factors or dimensions, and to provide an operational definition (i.e., a regression equation) for an underlying process by using these observed variables. These purposes of FA support the overall objective of corpus-based MD analysis, which aims to describe statistically correlating linguistic features and group them into interpretable sets of linguistic dimensions. The patterning of linguistic features in a corpus creates linguistic dimensions which correspond to salient functional distinctions within a register and allows cross-register comparison (Friginal 2013a). Some MD analysis studies have focused on the application of Biber's (1988) dimensions (the approach pursued in this chapter), while others have generated new dimensions within specialized corpora by running a new FA. The findings in various MD analysis studies indicate that this approach can be effectively conducted using most corpora, including those from more controlled sub-registers in a specialized corpus (Forchini 2012). The MD analysis approach has also been remarkably useful in predicting the extent to which the occurrence of specific linguistic features varies across texts.

Involved Versus Informational Production Features of Q+A Forum Responses

Biber's (1988) Dimension 1, which we focus on in this chapter, was functionally interpreted as Involved versus Informational Production (see Table 5.1 for Dimension 1 features). The positive features of Dimension 1 suggest 'Involved Production' characteristics of texts. The combination of private verbs (e.g., *think, feel*), demonstrative pronouns, first- and second-person pronouns, and adverbial qualifiers suggests that the speaker or writer is talking about his/her personal ideas, sharing opinions, and involving an audience (the use of *you* or *your*). The discourse is also informal and hedged (*that* deletions, contractions, *almost*, *maybe*). At the other

Table 5.1 Biber's (1988) co-occurring features of LOB (Lancaster-Oslo-Bergen Corpus) and London-Lund for Dimension 1

Factor	*Co-occurring features—Positive*	*Co-occurring features—Negative*
Factor 1	Private verb (e.g., *believe, feel, think*)	Noun
	'*That*' deletion	Word length
	Contraction	Preposition
	Verb (uninflected present, imperative, and third person)	Type/token ratio
	Second-person pronoun/possessive	Attributive adjective
	Verb '*do*'	(Place adverbial)
	Demonstrative pronoun	(Agentless passive)
	Adverb/Qualifier—Emphatic (e.g., *just, really, so*)	(Past participial WHIZ deletion)
	First-person pronoun/possessive	(Present participial WHIZ deletion)
	Pronoun '*it*'	
	Verb '*be*' (uninflected present tense, verb, and auxiliary)	
	Subordinating conjunction—Causative (e.g., *because*)	
	Discourse particle (e.g., *now*)	
	Nominal pronoun (e.g., *someone, everything*)	
	Adverbial—Hedge (e.g., *almost, maybe*)	*Features in parentheses are not statistically 'strong' features in this factor
	Adverb/Qualifier—Amplifier (e.g., *absolutely, entirely*)	
	Wh- question	
	Modals of possibility (*can, may, might, could*)	
	Coordinating conjunction—Clausal connector	
	Wh- clause	
	Stranded preposition	

end of the continuum, negative features combine to focus on the giving of information ('Informational Production') as a priority in the discourse. There are many nouns and nominalizations (e.g., *education, development, communication*), prepositions and attributive adjectives (e.g., *smart, effective, pretty*) appearing together with very limited personal pronouns. This co-occurrence of features suggests that informational data and descriptions of topics are provided without particular focus on the speaker or writer. More unique and longer words are used (higher type/token ratio and average word length), and the texts appear to be formal in structure and focus.

The Focus of This Chapter

This chapter focuses on the linguistic differences and similarities between Q+A forum responses from the UK, US, India, and the Philippines, compared across Biber's (1988) dimensions. The subcategories of these Q+A texts are grouped according to country of origin and topics (Family & Relationship, Politics & Government, and Society & Culture). Specifically, we examine comparative data from Dimension 1 'Involved versus Informational Production' across these groups of texts. Dimension 1, more distinctly than the others, provided us with more defined and easily interpretable variation that potentially shows the influence of first-language background and/or cultural orientations in how these groups of texts have been written by Q+A participants from the three different forum topic areas.

Methodology

The Q+A forum corpus was POS-tagged (part of speech tagged) using the Biber Tagger (Biber 1988, 2006) and an additional program (TagCount) was used to produce normalized counts for various semantic and grammatical features. The Biber Tagger was designed to incorporate a large number of linguistic features and return an output that can easily be processed for automatic tag counting and norming. This tagger was designed to incorporate a large number of linguistic features, extending the tagset from the Lancaster's Constituent Likelihood Automatic Word-Tagging System (CLAWS). Grieve et al. (2010) reported that the Biber Tagger has a 94% accuracy rate for formal written registers (e.g., research articles, newspaper articles), with only slightly lower accuracy for spoken texts. (Note that the Biber Tagger is not freely available online but may be accessed by contacting Douglas Biber's Corpus Linguistics Research Program at Northern Arizona University).

Computing Dimension Scores

The normed frequencies of co-occurring linguistic features in the Q+A forum corpus, comprising Dimensions 1 to 5 from Biber's (1988) dimensions, were standardized using z-scores. This process allowed highly different distributions in the dataset to be more comparable with one another, summing up and averaging scores that reflected a feature's range of variation. Each dimension comprised linguistic features that significantly co-occurred with one another and contained both positive and negative loadings. Standardization of frequencies provided for these complementary patterns of polarity. In other words, when a text contains frequent instances of one group of co-occurring linguistic features (positive or negative), the features from the opposite group are likely to be absent (Biber 1988; Friginal & Hardy 2014b).

Using the composition of Biber's (1988) dimensions, the standardized frequencies of the linguistic features in the Q+A forum corpus were then added to obtain dimension scores per individual text. Once scores in all five dimensions had been calculated for each text, mean scores per sub-groups (i.e., texts from UK, US, India, and Philippines; texts across country and topic groups) were obtained by averaging the texts' dimension scores. Detailed instructions on how to conduct an MD analysis, compute dimension scores, and functionally interpret factors/dimensions can be found in Biber (1988) and Conrad and Biber (2001). Instructions to run MD analysis using the statistical package SPSS can be found in Friginal and Hardy (2014b).

Results

Our comparison data of the linguistic similarities and differences between sub-groups of texts from the Q+A forum corpus across the five dimensions from Biber (1988) are summarized in Table 5.2. We also discuss our findings using a dimensional scale for Dimension 1 (Figure 5.1), supported by brief qualitative interpretations and text samples. As a whole, Table 5.2 suggests that Q+A forum responses are primarily involved and personal rather than informational. The negative scores on Dimension 2 show that they are also non-narrative (very few past tense verbs co-occurring with third-person pronouns and public and perfect aspect verbs), while the positive scores on Dimension 4 indicate a persuasive writing style (high frequencies of infinitives, prediction modals, suasive verb, and conditional subordination).

Table 5.2 illustrates that Dimension 1 (highlighted in bold) produced the most interesting and most diverse patterns of variation across country groups and topic categories in the Q+A forum corpus compared to the other four dimensions. Although results from the other dimensions also provided patterns that could be further investigated in depth and more qualitatively in future studies, Dimension 1 clearly showed a more extensive and definitive range of variation (as indicated in the group averages or mean scores for Dimension 1 by country and topic groups). Overall, Q+A forum responses, as a sub-register of written discourse, resemble the linguistic composition of spoken texts, such as telephone and face-to-face conversations, spontaneous speeches, and oral interviews (based on Biber's 1988 comparison). These online texts are also similar in structure to more involved and informally written texts, such as personal letters and emails. This comparison to emails was based on data from an MD analysis of emails from the Enron corpus conducted by Titak and Roberson (2013).

Country and Topic Comparisons in Dimension 1

Figure 5.1 shows the country average scores for the UK, US, Philippines, and India for Dimension 1. These four groups of texts averaged on the positive side of the scale. As previously noted, this suggests a more involved (and also informal and interactive) production focus of writing in their linguistic composition.

The UK forum responses have the highest average Dimension 1 scores, with Indian texts having the lowest scores (16.849 and 10.939, respectively). The US and Philippine mean scores are quite similar (US = 15.195, Philippines = 14.517) and fall between averages from the UK and Indian

Table 5.2 Comparison of dimension scores

Registers	*Dimension 1 Involved vs. informational production*	*Dimension 2 Narrative vs. non-narrative discourse*	*Dimension 3 Elaborated vs. situation-dependent reference*	*Dimension 4 Overt expression of argumentation*	*Dimension 5 Impersonal vs. non-impersonal style*
India–Family & Relationships	**20.836**	–2.044	–0.875	5.301	–0.477
India–Politics & Government	**3.124**	–1.820	1.481	3.547	1.695
India–Society & Culture	**8.857**	–2.878	3.164	0.584	1.100
Phil–Family & Relationships	**20.676**	–1.811	–2.622	5.922	0.351
Phil–Politics & Government	**7.555**	–1.847	2.008	2.629	1.727
Phil–Society & Culture	**15.320**	–1.687	0.808	4.372	0.934
UK–Family & Relationships	**25.351**	–0.927	–1.259	4.878	–0.218
UK–Politics & Government	**9.235**	–0.727	1.098	1.646	1.745
UK–Society & Culture	**15.961**	–1.947	–0.679	3.150	0.528
US–Family & Relationships	**23.212**	–0.980	–2.552	5.438	–0.326
US–Politics & Government	**10.633**	–1.827	1.010	2.312	1.274
US–Society & Culture	**11.734**	–1.844	0.193	2.159	1.452

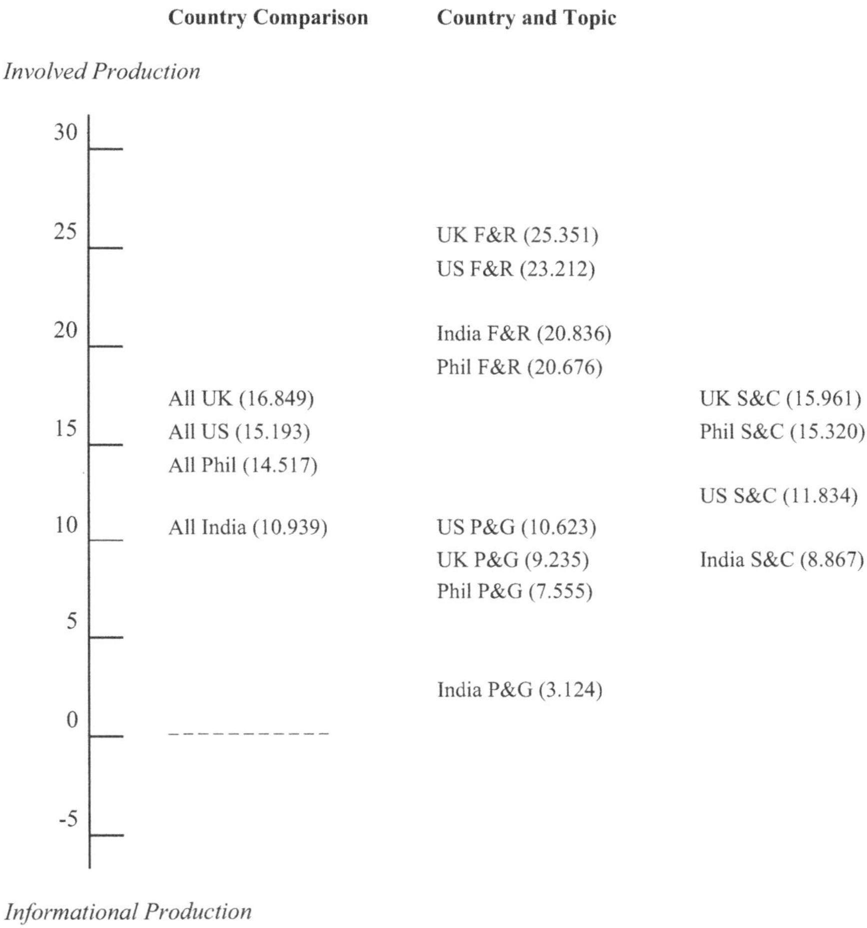

Figure 5.1 Comparison of average factor scores in Q+A forum responses for Dimension 1

subcorpora. UK texts appeared to be more interactive compared to the three other groups, and authors made use of many personal references, especially first-and second-person pronouns and private verbs. The Indian subcorpus had the highest number of texts with negative average scores in Dimension 1, indicating informational production focus in responding to questions by many Indian contributors.

Interestingly, some Indian texts made use of verbatim excerpts from websites such as Wikipedia in responding to a user question. In the text excerpt that follows, for example, a response to a 'definition of God' question from a forum participant in India was directly cut and pasted from Wikipedia by the author, instead of hyperlinking the information from the actual wiki page. As expected in this scholarly and highly *informational* Wikipedia entry, there are more nouns (highlighted in bold font), prepositions, and attributive adjectives in this excerpt. The text (S&C 05) overall has a Dimension 1 score of –17.85.

Text Sample 1. Response from India, S&C 05 (Dim1 Score = –17. 85)

> **God** denotes a **deity** who is believed by **monotheists** to be the sole **creator** and **ruler** of the **universe**. **Conceptions** of **God** can vary widely, despite the use of the same **term** for them all.
>
> The **God** of **monotheism**, **pantheism** or **panentheism**, or the supreme **deity** of **henotheistic religions**, may be conceived of in various **degrees** of **abstraction**: as a powerful, human-like, supernatural **being**, or as the **deification** of an **esoteric**, **mystical** or **philosophical category**, the **Ultimate**, the summum bonum, the **Absolute Infinite**, the **Transcendent**, or **Existence** or **Being** itself, the **ground** of **being**, the **monistic substrate**, etc. The more **abstract** of these **positions** regard any **anthropomorphic mythology** and **iconography** associated with **God** either sympathetically as mere **symbolism**, or unfavourably as blasphemous.
>
> Source(s): http://en.wikipedia.org/wiki/God

The average scores for country by topic for Dimension 1 are also shown in Figure 5.2. Family & Relationships forum responses have the highest positive averages (22.519) while Politics & Government responses have the lowest (7.637). Society & Culture responses have an average Dimension 1 score of 12.968. For the most part, UK and US responses are more involved, interactive, and informal across the three topic areas compared to Philippine and Indian texts. Indian responses have the lowest average scores in Politics & Government and in Society & Culture.

These distributions may indicate how writers from four varieties of English represent themselves as they respond to Q+A forums online. Writers with 'educated Englishes' (Gonzalez 1992) from India and the Philippines may have responded to online posts more formally, structurally more 'organized' (i.e., written in a more academic manner and possibly edited more extensively), and less personally than native speakers of English from the UK and the US. This observation is consistent with studies based on data from the International Corpus of English (ICE), especially those that argue for the presence of systematic patterns of variation in 'world Englishes' and between native and non-native varieties (e.g., Xiao 2009; Bautista 2011; Friginal & Hardy 2014a).

The classification of new or emerging Englishes and colonization models in countries such as India (colonized by the British) and the Philippines (colonized by the Americans) are common topics of comparative studies that could be further explored using online registers, such as these Q+A forum responses. It appears, based on the current data on involved versus informational production features of these texts, that MD analysis may have also captured some of these potentially systematic variations. Gonzalez (1998) noted that, 'Philippine-American English' is a legitimate variety of the English language which is in the process of developing its set of standards for itself in pronunciation (the segmental and suprasegmental elements), lexis (including words and collocations as well as new meanings and uses for words from the source language and idioms which consist of loan translations from the Philippine languages), and in specific syntactic structures (Hardy & Friginal 2012). Filipino questions and responses in these online forums, when presented completely in English (as contrasted with code-switched norms in English and Tagalog or other local languages) reflect the characteristic features of this English variety that has emerged in more professional and educated settings. In India and the Philippines, access to the Internet and participation in predominantly English discourses online are still utilized primarily by those who have achieved higher levels of education and professional affiliations.

Both India and the Philippines have been very receptive to a range of British and American influences, not only in language but also in popular culture, such as music, television and movies. English publications written by Indians and Filipinos, which have typically been based on these British and American English influences, have increasingly changed over the years, resulting in a variety characterized as emerging 'educated' norms (Hardy & Friginal 2012; Friginal 2013b). These norms are typically acquired from university contexts, often based on written discourse. In the Philippines, for example, a survey conducted by the Social Weather Station in the late-1990s reported that 75% of the Philippine population claimed to understand and follow commands in English. The actual level of English proficiency among the general population, however, varies from *beginner* to *near native* (Salazar 2008).

In a study exploring the linguistic differences between Filipino and American blogs, Hardy and Friginal (2012) found that Filipino bloggers (with blogs written exclusively in English, with very limited code-switching) had a more 'academic' or 'formal' tone than most American bloggers in these Filipinos' treatment of personal issues and observations about current business, economic, and political events. This distinction was attributed to the individual characteristics of bloggers from the US and Filipinos who are blogging in English. While US-based bloggers represented a wide range of demographics (e.g., age, profession, and educational attainment) and topical concerns, Filipino bloggers typically came from a more homogeneous group of educated, young professionals in major cities such as Metro Manila and Cebu, pursuing very similar sets of contexts as they wrote and published their blogs in English.

Involvement and Personalization in Q+A Forum Responses

Texts with high scores in Dimension 1 typically have a high level of interaction, involvement, and personal affect (Biber 1988). Many references to *I* and *you* are repeated, and these co-occur with other features such as wh-questions, emphatics (e.g., *really, very, so*), causative subordination (e.g., *because*), and informal writing features, such as contractions, discourse markers, and hedging. The typical format of Q+A forums in online sites directly influences how responses are structured to be interactive and involved. Responses are 'other-directed', as evidenced by the frequent use of *you* and *your*. Posted questions across various topic areas are often personal and user responses are addressed to the particular poster or participant, often focusing on expressions of opinion and subjective interpretation of issues. Private verbs (e.g., *think, feel, believe*) with first-person *I* form egocentric sequences and personal/private affect in user responses. Interpersonal content appears to be the primary production focus rather than the immediate delivery of information. Text Sample 2 illustrates personal affect (highlighted in bold are personal references, private verbs, and second-person pronouns) in a Society & Culture response from a participant based in the US.

Text Sample 2. Interaction and Personal Affect, US S&C 18 (Dim 1 Score = 22.93)

I think that it is ok as long as it is done right and for the right reasons.

> **My** husband is a photographer and he was once asked to provide out of town family members with pictures of the deceased and the flower arrangements. **We** did make arrangements to do the work prior to family and friends arrival.
>
> There is no right answer to **your** question. **You may feel** that it is perfectly ok to take a picture at **someones** funeral and **someone else** believes that it is totally taboo. **I** say, **you** do whatever comforts **you** during a time of great loss. **I,** however, **would** do it very discreetly and when **no one else** was around.

Figure 5.2 shows the distribution of first-person pronouns (including possessives) and private verbs in the four country groups of the Q+A forum corpus (normalized per 1,000 words). Indian responses used the fewest personal references (first person = 30.43; private verbs = 18.30) compared to the three other groups. Both native speaker varieties had more first-person pronouns and private verbs than their non-native counterparts. US responses had slightly more private verbs than UK responses (20.21 and 19.55, respectively).

There are related corpus-based studies comparing and contrasting British and Indian Englishes that also mirror the distributions shown in Figure 5.2. For example, Xiao (2009) found variations in ICE texts in 'future projection' (e.g., use of future time expressions from modals *will, would, shall*; conditionals and expressions of definiteness). British English had the highest frequencies of these features in written registers and private conversations, while Indian English had the lowest. Patterns of English usage with future projection in other ICE subcorpora such as Hong Kong and Singapore appeared to be similar to British English, further differentiating Indian texts especially in the use of future time expressions from other ICE corpora collected in Asia. Xiao attempted to interpret this particular result, while referencing the need for additional research, as well as the need to examine such data from a sociocultural perspective. He cited Shastri (1988), who suggested that the Indian mind and its communicative expressions in English

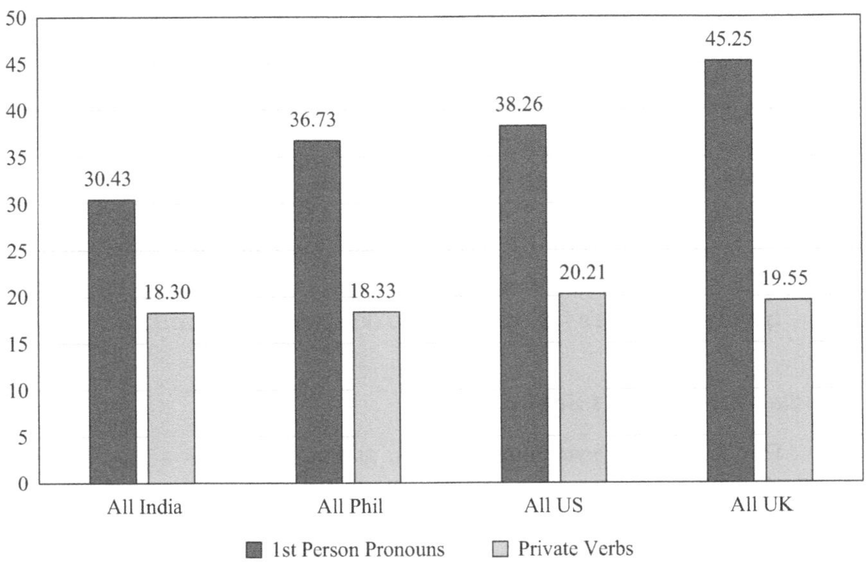

Figure 5.2 Distribution of first-person pronouns and private verbs in Q+A forum responses (normalized per 1,000 words)

may not be inclined to thinking much in terms of the future. Related to this observation are distributions from ICE spoken texts that significantly show that Indian speakers made use of the fewest first-person pronouns compared to other spoken Asian Englishes from the Philippines and Singapore. A comparable ICE MD analysis conducted by Friginal (2010) reported that spoken registers of the Indian subcorpus reflected the structure and linguistic composition of some formal written texts.

Text Samples 3 compare two responses from the UK and India on the topic of Family & Relationships. The two excerpts were based on very similar questions focusing on women and relationships. The response from the UK (Dimension 1 Score = 34.15) explicitly shows the writer's personal affect and opinion more than the response from India (Dimension 1 Score = 4.82). Both of these responses made use of the second-person *you*, but there are clear differences in how this feature is used. *You* from the UK response is primarily personal and addressed to the person who posted the question in the forum board. In the Indian excerpt, *you* was impersonal and was not directly addressed to the person who posted the question (e.g., 'If **you** look like a magazine model, **you** can have a personality of standing tap water, and the smarts of a garden slug . . .'). There was no first-person pronoun in the Indian excerpt despite the very subjective nature of the post.

Text Samples 3. Personal Affect in UK and Indian Responses

UK F&R 15 (Dim 1 Score = 34.15)

You have to do what ***your*** heart wants to do, even if that means taking him back. **I** unfortunately '**thought**' **I** loved my ex, and **I** took him back. That was the worst year of **my** life, even when it should have been the best because **our** daughter was born. **I** regretted it, sooo much! Had **I** not done that, **I think I** would miss him and eventually 'work things out' with him. Now that **I've** rid of him, **I feel** much better.

To **me** this made sense. It hurt to do it, but **I** found out what type of guy he is and he's not worth it. ***You*** don't know until ***you*** try.

India F&R 04 (Dim 1 Score = 4.82)

Read through these answers, ***you*** are bound to get a lot of spin. Women by a large do not want to seem as shallow as men. they want to believe that they see relationships and love as more of an emotional thing. That women fall in love with their ears and mind . . . yeah right.

In spite what they (women) say, they basically go for the 3 Cs: [C] assanovas, [C]adds (bad boys), and [C]ashmen. If ***you*** look like a magazine model, ***you*** can have a personality of standing tap water, and the smarts of a garden slug, and the women will be knocking themselves out of the way to be on ***your*** arm.

Informational and Scholarly Responses

Texts with more informational production foci in Dimension 1 are often not concerned with interpersonal and affective content. These texts have high frequencies of nouns, prepositions, attributive adjectives, and longer words. In Biber's (1988) study, these texts also have a higher type/token ratio, owing in part to a careful selection of words similar to writing in academic or scholarly registers. English varieties in India and the Philippines made use of more nouns and prepositions than their native English counterparts in the Q+A forum corpus as shown in Figure 5.3.

The following text samples show Politics & Government responses from India and the Philippines. Both responses have negative Dimension 1 scores (India = -4.17; Philippines = -8.25), suggesting that these responses have higher information density and that the writers spent more time editing their entries than in more interactive or personal responses. Nouns,

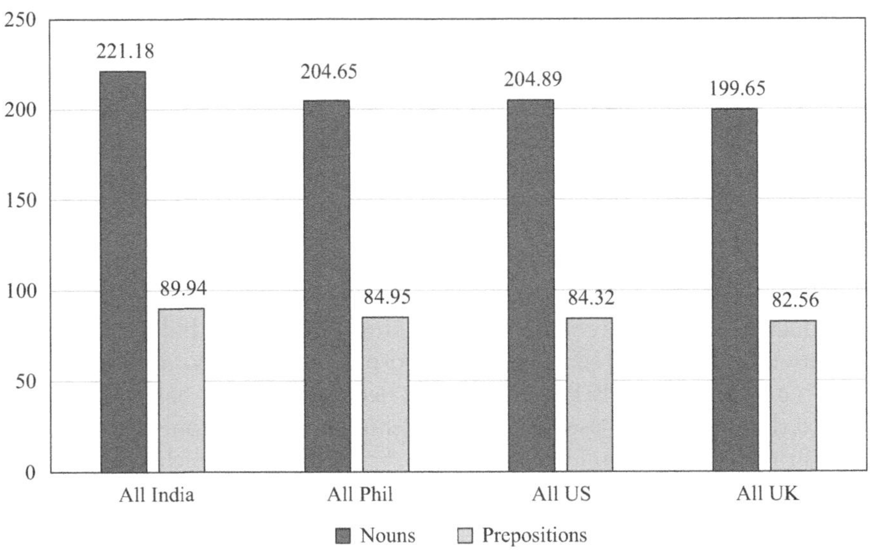

Figure 5.3 Distribution of nouns and prepositions in Q+A forum responses (normalized per 1,000 words)

nominalizations, and longer words were frequently used, and the responses based on two similar political questions show a high level of awareness of contexts and related issues.

Text Samples 4. Informational Production Focus in Indian and Philippine Responses

India P&G 01 (Dim 1 Score = -4.17)

> That a broad **political spectrum** of this **country** never was taken into full **confidence** during **negotiations** of the **deal** in **question** has led to this **state** of **affairs**. Left **Support** to the **Govt** was never unconditional and **CMP** has been only the **link** between the ruling **coalition** and the **left**. The **govt** as well as the **party** are possibly paying the **price** for their **complacency** or their over **confidence** in convincing their **left supports** This can never be called bucking under **pressure**.

Phil P&G 18 (Dim 1 Score = -8.25)

> The **vice-president** should have an **official residence** because in **case** the **president** would be **abroad** and he is designated as the acting **president**, there is no need for him to relocate his **confidential aides** and **secretaries**. A permanent **setup** in an **office** would be handy. Second, the **vice-president** should be given a **cabinet post** so that he may justify an **official residence**.
>
> The rationale here is that even the First Lady has a social office. In the case of Binay, he should be given responsibility, like as foreign affairs secretary to justify his request for an official residence.

In her book *Register Variation in Indian English*, Balasubramanian (2009) conducted a large-scale empirical investigation of English in India using a combination of the corpus she compiled ("Corpus of Contemporary Indian English") and sections of ICE-India. Among her many results, Balasubramanian noted that the English used in India is 'definitely distinct from other varieties like British or American English' (p. 233). Spoken registers included more easily recognizable *Indianisms* and various situational variables (e.g., contexts, production, and medium foci and addressees) influence the distribution of linguistic features such as circumstance adverbials, subject-auxiliary inversion in wh-questions, and stative verbs in the progressive. Indian Q+A responses, structurally and functionally resembling informational and scholarly texts, are perhaps influenced by these situational variables of written production. These results appear to be very similar to those Filipino researchers have also reported as characteristic features of written Philippine English, again, as Gonzalez (1998) called it, 'Philippine-American' English, namely, formal and scholarly in contexts where very limited code-switching is expected.

The register of online feedback and user responses may be considered, in general, as comprising more or less informal written texts similar to blogs (Argamon, Koppel, Fine, & Shimoni, 2003). However, 'native' and 'non-native' English writers may be addressing the production features of these texts differently. Hardy and Friginal (2012), as noted earlier, suggested that American bloggers may come from many different backgrounds or demographics, representing more diverse groups including level of education, socioeconomic status, age, and profession with much easier access to computers with Internet connection. In contrast, a Filipino (and also quite possibly an Indian) who blogs in English might be more likely to come from an educated or professional background and typically based/located in major cities. Such a person is skilled and confident enough to publish in English online, and he/she also assumes that readers are proficient enough in English to understand the writing. One might expect that this more specific audience (i.e., Filipinos interested in reading an English blog or response to a forum question) would have influenced Filipino bloggers to focus more on structurally accurate features and more organized, carefully edited and cohesive discourse. In contrast, American or British bloggers and forum participants may not necessarily consider their readers' language backgrounds and are perhaps are more concerned with communicating content and/or affect rather than structural or organizational norms of what they typically see as informal texts.

Conclusion

This chapter applied Biber's MD approach in comparing the linguistic characteristics of Q+A forum responses from the UK, US, India, and Philippines across three topic groups (Family & Relationships, Society & Culture, and Politics & Government). Group dimension scores from established dimensions of spoken and written registers from Biber (1988) were computed to compare the linguistic preferences and characteristics of participants in these online forums. Specifically, we focused our analysis on Involved versus Informational Production (Dimension 1), which provided an interesting range of variation. Our comparisons illustrate variation in forum responses influenced by topics/questions prompts and participants' language background. By using a multi-feature MD analysis, the distribution of linguistic characteristics among these sub-registers was described in this chapter in terms of the functional continuum for Dimension 1. Overall, the online Q+A forum is structurally involved, personal, and interactive, but we noticed interesting patterns that may indicate characteristic contrasts between native and non-native varieties of English and perhaps how non-native forum participants represent themselves in largely informal writing contexts.

Englishes in India and the Philippines, arguably, are still developing their own set of norms and standard markers, especially in expressing informational, personal, narrative, thematic, and interactive foci. The educated variety of English in these two countries typically deviates from personal and involved stylistic features of informal, online writing by those in the US and the UK. This observation seems to reflect the distinctions made in bilingual education or second-language teaching studies, for example, Cummins's (1984) model of teaching interpersonal communication skills and academic language proficiency. As such, in the Philippines, this finding also supports Gonzalez's (1992) claims of the influence that academic English has had on Philippine-American English. Gonzalez (1992: 766) states, for example, that 'Filipinos generally speak the way they write, in a formal style'.

We believe that corpus-based, multi-dimensional analysis could be successfully used as a model to compare varieties of English across macro and micro registers. The same comparative approach developed in this study could be expanded to include other outer circle (Kachru 1996) varieties of English in Asia such as Singaporean or Hong Kong Englishes and also other online texts, especially those from social networking sites. A more detailed focus on other specific linguistic features determined by functional dimensions could disclose the similarities and differences in authors' communicative norms confounded by their cultural and linguistic backgrounds (Hardy & Friginal 2012). Englishes in India and the Philippines have traditionally used American and British *standard* patterns in lexis and syntax, but there are noticeable (or 'emerged') differences in the overall linguistic characteristics of Q+A texts produced in these two countries compared to their norm-providing counterparts.

References

Argamon, S., Koppel, M., Fine, J. & Shimoni, A. R. (2003). Gender, genre, and writing style in formal written texts. *Text*, 23, 321–346.

Balasubramanian, C. (2009). *Register Variation in Indian English*. Amsterdam: John Benjamins Publishing Company.

Bautista, M. L. (Ed.) (2011). *Philippine English: Corpus-Based Studies*. Manila: De LaSalle University Press.

Biber, D. (1988). *Variation Across Speech and Writing*. Cambridge: Cambridge University Press.

Biber, D. (1995). *Dimensions of Register Variation: A Cross-Linguistic Perspective*. Cambridge: Cambridge University Press.

Biber, D. (2003). Variation among university spoken and written registers: A new multi-dimensional analysis. In P. Leistyna & C. F. Meyer (Eds.), *Corpus Analysis: Language Structure and Language Use* (pp. 47–70). Amsterdam: Rodopi.

Biber, D. (2006). *University Language*. Amsterdam: John Benjamins Publishing Company.

Biber, D., & Conrad, S. (2001). *Variation in English: Multi-dimensional studies*. Routledge.

Cummins, J. (1984). *Bilingualism and Special Education: Issues in Assessment and Pedagogy.* Clevedon: Multilingual Matters.
Forchini, P. (2012). *Movie Language Revisited. Evidence from Multi-Dimensional Analysis and Corpora.* Bern: Peter Lang.
Friginal, E. (2010). *Understanding Asian Englishes: A Multidimensional Comparison.* Paper presented at the American Association for Applied Linguistics Conference 2010, Denver, CO.
Friginal, E. (2011). Corpus analysis of the modal verb *would* in spoken and written Philippine English. In M. L. Bautista (Ed.), *Philippine English: Corpus-Based Studies* (pp. 123–145). Manila: De LaSalle University Press.
Friginal, E. (2013a). Twenty-five years of Biber's multi-dimensional analysis: Introduction to the special issue and an interview with Douglas Biber. *Corpora*, 8(2), 137–152.
Friginal, E. (2013b). Linguistic characteristics of intercultural call center interactions: A multi-dimensional analysis. In D. Belcher & G. Nelson (Eds.), *Critical and Corpus-Based Approaches to Intercultural Rhetoric* (pp. 127–153). Ann Arbor: University of Michigan Press.
Friginal, E. & Hardy, J. A. (2014a). *Corpus-Based Sociolinguistics: A Guide for Students.* New York: Routledge.
Friginal, E. & Hardy, J. A. (2014b). Conducting multi-dimensional analysis using SPSS. In T. Berber-Sardinha & M. Veirano Pinto (Eds.), *Multi-Dimensional Analysis, 25 Years on* (pp. 295–314). Amsterdam: John Benjamins Publishing Company.
Friginal, E., Waugh, O. & Titak, A. (2015). *Linguistic Variation in Facebook and Twitter Posts.* Paper presented at the American Association for Applied Linguistics Conference 2015, Toronto, ON, Canada.
Gonzalez, A. (1992). Philippine English. In T. McArthur (Ed.), *The Oxford Companion to the English Language* (pp. 765–767). New York: Oxford University Press.
Gonzalez, A. (1998). The language planning situation in the Philippines. *Journal of Multilingual and Multicultural Development*, 19, 487–525.
Gries, S. (2011). Methodological and interdisciplinary stance in corpus linguistics. In V. Vander, S. Zyngier & G. Barnbrook (Eds.), *Perspectives on Corpus Linguistics* (pp. 81–98). Philadelphia: John Benjamins Publishing Company.
Grieve, J., Biber, D., Friginal, E. & Nekrasova, T. (2010). Variation among blogs: A multi-dimensional analysis. In A. Mehler, S. Sharoff & M. Santini (Eds.), *Genres on the Web: Corpus Studies and Computational Models* (pp. 45–71). New York: Springer-Verlag.
Hardy, J. A. & Friginal, E. (2012). Filipino and American online communication and linguistic variation. *World Englishes*, 31(2), 143–161.
Herdağdelen, A. (2013). Twitter n-gram corpus with demographic metadata. *Language Resources and Evaluation*, 47, 1127–1147.
Kachru, Braj B. (1996). World Englishes: Agony and ecstasy. *The Journal of Aesthetic Education*, 30, 24–41.
Salazar, D. (2008), Modality in student argumentative writing: A corpus-based comparative study of American, Filipino and Spanish novice writers. Unpublished MA Thesis. University of Barcelona.
Shastri, S. V. (1988). The Kolhapur Corpus of Indian English and work done on its basis so far. *ICAME Journal, 12*, 15–26.
Tabachnick, B. G. & Fidell, L. S. (2001). *Using Multivariate Statistics* (4th ed.). Boston: Allyn and Bacon.
Titak, A. & Roberson, A. (2013). Dimensions of web registers: An exploratory multidimensional comparison. *Corpora*, 8(2), 235–260.
Xiao, R. (2009). Multidimensional analysis and the study of world Englishes. *World Englishes*, 28(4), 421–450.

6 Collocation Networks

Exploring Associations in Discourse

Vaclav Brezina

Introduction

Q+A sites as places of information sharing as well as of complex social and linguistic practices have received considerable attention in the literature. These sites have been explored using a number of approaches ranging from content analysis (e.g. Raban 2009; Fichman 2011; Cunningham & Hinze 2014) to various discourse analytical and corpus-based approaches, such as those showcased in this book. From a theoretical perspective, Q+A sites can be seen not only as sources of information but also, and perhaps more appropriately, as online communities of practice (Rosenbaum & Shachaf 2010, cf. Wenger 1998). This theoretical standpoint enables us to view Q+A forums as platforms where people not only seek and receive answers and practical advice in a similar way to looking up information in a reference book but also share their experiences in a more complex and holistic manner that mirrors experience sharing in offline communities (cf. Wilson & Peterson 2002).

The methodology used in this chapter to analyse the complex and multifaceted linguistic processes which underlie the online communities of practice established around the Q+A sites is that of collocation networks. Collocation networks, a concept originally proposed by Phillips (1983, 1985), are based on a very simple observation. Words in texts and discourse systematically co-occur to create a range of cross-associations that can be visualized as networks of nodes and collocates. These associations contribute in various degrees to the meanings created in a text/discourse and can serve to answer the question of 'what is the text/discourse about?' for which the shorthand term 'aboutness' of a text or discourse is sometimes used.

In brief, collocation networks are effective exploratory summaries of different aspects of texts or discourses (Brezina, McEnery, & Wattam, 2015). Brezina, McEnery, and Wattam, (2015) explain how collocation networks are built, starting with an initial node of interest around which first-, second-, third-, etc., order collocates are identified using specialised software (see "Method"). The concept of collocation networks is best demonstrated with the following example (see Figure 6.1), which is based on the Q+A

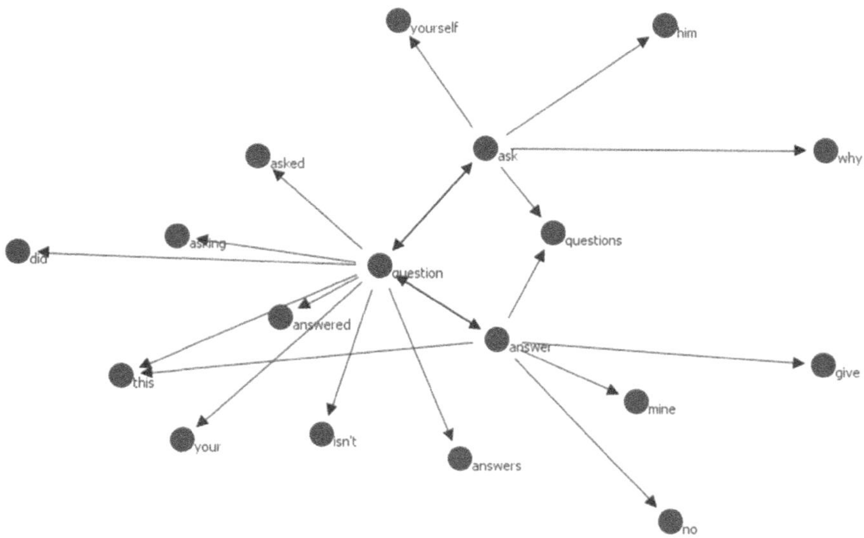

Figure 6.1 Collocation network around *ask* [MI(3), C10, NC10, 5L 5R[1]]

corpus explored in this book. In this example, first- and second-order collocates were identified around the node *ask*. The length of the arrows in the graph indicates the strength of the collocational relationship as measured by the selected association measure, in this case, the Mutual Information (MI) score; the arrow is inversely proportional to the strength of the collocation—the shorter the arrow, the stronger the collocational relationship. A bidirectional arrow signifies a collocational relationship between two nodes that have been expanded for collocates. These nodes are also displayed in a different colour (shade of grey in Figure 6.1).

The resulting collocation network shows not only the strongest immediate associations of *ask* (*question, questions, yourself, him*, and *why*) but also further associations of these associations through which we can explore the discourse in the Yahoo! Answers forums. For instance, although the word *answer* is not directly associated with *ask*, it appears as the second-order collocate, which is linked to *ask* through the first-order collocates *question* and *questions*. This connection, although entirely predictable, is a demonstration of the types of cross-associations that the collocations networks method can reveal.

Method

In this study, the Q+A corpus was analysed using GraphColl, free software for identification of collocation networks in language corpora (for a detailed description see Brezina, McEnery, & Wattam, 2015). GraphColl loads multiple (sub)corpora, which can then be easily compared by running parallel collocation network analyses on different tabs. In this study, the questions and answers in the Q+A discussions were analysed separately with special attention being paid to the four country-based varieties represented in the Q+A corpus: India, Philippines, UK, and US.

Table 6.1 shows the token count for different parts of the Question (Q) and Answer (A) subcorpora of the Q+A corpus. In total, the corpus consists of over 400,000 tokens distributed relatively evenly among the four country-based varieties. For each variety, three topic groups—Family & Relationships, Politics & Government, and Society & Culture—were sampled. The corpus is thus balanced for the country-based variety as well as the topic. An important methodological remark needs to be made at this stage: for the collocation networks analysis to return valid results, comparable and sufficient data needs to be analysed. The Answer (A) subcorpus was considered sufficiently large to be analysed according to the individual country-based subsections, which provide approximately the same amount of evidence; however, the smaller Question (Q) subcorpus could be reliably analysed only as one dataset.

The statistical measure for identification of collocates used in this study is the MI score, which was accompanied by the use of frequency cut-off points to eliminate infrequent combinations. The statistical values used for the creation of the individual graphs are reported in the format proposed in Brezina, McEnery, and Wattam (2015).

Table 6.1 Q+A corpus: Overview

Variety (subsection)	*Q subcorpus*	*A subcorpus*	*Total*
India	2,849	99,131	101,980
Philippines	4,826	96,437	101,263
UK	6,518	93,350	99,868
US	6,282	104,194	110,476
Total	20,475	393,112	413,587

Table 6.2 Collocation parameters notation (CPN)

Notation categories	*Statistic ID*	*Statistic name*	*Statistic cut-off value*	*L and R span*	*Minimum collocate freq. (C)*	*Minimum collocation freq. (NC)*	*Filter*
Example	3a	MI	3	L5-R5	5	1	function words removed
In-text notation (example)	3a-MI2(3), L5-R5, C5-NC1; function words removed						

When corpus examples are provided, the source files are referenced in the following format: Country_Topic_file number, e.g., US_SC_18, which means a US subsection, Society & Culture topic, file number 18.

The research was guided by the following research question:

RQ: What are the typical collocational patterns in the Q+A corpus that characterise the linguistic practices of different communities of practice sampled in the corpus?

Results and Discussion

Identifying Frequent Discourses

As with most corpus techniques, a word frequency list is a useful first step or an entry point into a dataset. Two wordlists were thus built, one for the Q and one for the A subcorpus, to identify frequent lexical items in the discussions. As expected, the top positions in both wordlists are dominated by grammatical words such as *the, and, you*, and *I*. In the Q wordlist, question words also appear in the top positions: *what* (rank 19), *why* (rank 33), *how* (rank 48), *when* (rank 54), and *who* (rank 57). However, it should be noted that wh-words can function both as question words and relativizers in declarative sentences (e.g., *That is why I am so offended by the situation* [US_SC_18]). The analysis of questions therefore requires careful manual checking of the examples. Closer inspection of the data revealed that almost half (131 out of the 265) of the files in the Q subcorpus include at least one instance where a wh-word is used to express either a direct (*How can I just get her to back off and give me room?* [PH_FR_20]) or indirect question (*I don't know what to do about my friend, please help!?* [US_FR_19]).

From the content words, three items in particular stand out. These items occur with high frequencies and a much higher rank than expected when compared with a general English baseline (Brezina & Gablasova 2015). These items are: *god, love*, and *president*. As can be seen from Tables 6.3 and 6.4, these words occur in all country-based sections of the corpus, which points to the cultural universality of the topics. On the other hand, the words are largely domain-specific, as can be seen from their dominant occurrence in specific theme-based sections. This is especially the case with *president*, which occurs mainly in the Politics & Government section (both in the Q (100%) and the A subcorpora (87%)). *God* and *love* occur frequently in Society & Culture as well as in the Family & Relationships section.

The types of questions that include the three words can be seen from the following examples taken from the Indian, Philippine, and UK subcorpora, respectively:

(1) Does *GOD* really exists? If yes then why there are more hungry people than one who eats thrice daily? [IN_SC_15]
(2) I'm in *love* . . . help? [PH_FR_17]
(3) Why is Obama so unpopular as *President*? [UK_PG_18]

As can be noted when comparing Table 6.3 and Table 6.4, *god, love*, and *president* are much more frequent in the A subcorpus than the Q subcorpus, not only in terms of the overall number of occurrences (which is not surprising due to the much larger size of the A corpus) but also in terms of the number of files in which these three words are mentioned. This shows that the three words occur often in the response to questions which do not mention these words explicitly. Let us explore this phenomenon in more detail.

The examples that follow show answers that mention *god, love*, and *president* (italicised in each example). Above each answer is the question that was originally asked. As can be seen, all of the answers are relevant answers to the questions, following the maxims of Grice's (1975) cooperative principle. It should also be noted that the formulation of the questions is sufficiently open to provide space for including references to *god, love*, or *president*.

(4) Q: Do you wish that Hitler won the war?

A: I hate both *God* and Hitler, but somehow *God* is a hero when he does things like Hitler did. [UK_SC_07]

Table 6.3 Typical concepts in questions (Q subcorpus)

Word	*Frequency (no. files out of 265)*	*Predominantly in . . .*	*Countries (files)*
god	47 (19)	Society & Culture (95%)	IN (6), PH (6), UK (2), US (5)
love (both as noun and verb)	36 (29)	Family & Relationships (72%)	IN (8), PH (8), UK (5), US (8)
president	32 (15)	Politics & Government (100%)	IN (2), PH (8), UK (3), US (2)

Table 6.4 Typical concepts in answers (A subcorpus)

Word	*Frequency (no. files out of 265)*	*Predominantly in . . .*	*Countries (files)*
god	738 (117)	Society & Culture (47%) Family & Relationships (29%)	IN (36), PH (33), UK (25), US (23)
love (both as noun and verb)	712 (147)	Family & Relationships (46%), Society & Culture (39%)	IN (44), PH (39), UK (33), US (31)
president	366 (48)	Politics & Government (87%)	IN (11), PH (18), UK (7), US (12)

(5) Q: What really is the difference between democrats and republicans?

A: Work hard, obey *God* and life will be good. In theory, this is a neat way to look at things and in an ideal world, this would be great, but it has a number of flaws. [US_PG_07]

(6) Q: Sex before marriage is wrong or right?

A: Really it's your personal preference. I think that you should wait at least until you're in *love* with someone. [IN_FR_13]

(7) Q: Im sorry! why we need to respect our parent . . . even if they are not resposible and takecare to thier chield . . .

A: It's great if you *love* your family, I *love* mine. I don't believe you are required to. [PH_SC_14]

(8) Q: Does the United Kingdom really need the Royal Family?

A: We just don't want a *president* [UK_SC_04]

(9) Q: Can we remove corruption in this country?

A: *IF THIS IS ACCOMPLISHED / ACHIEVED / DONE by the HON'BLE *PRESIDENT* OF INDIA (by rising above political and personal affiliations/matters), EVERY OTHER THING WILL AUTOMATICALLY START TO COME TO THE DESIRED AND RIGHT PATH. [IN_PG_22]

The examples show how *god, love*, and *president* form a part of what can be described as 'frequent discourses' that construct the Q+A communities of practice as their core building blocks. One of the features of frequent discourses is the fact that they permeate the fabric of the discourse and can potentially appear in a wide range of situations. As can be seen, discussions about religion, emotions, and politics are fairly typical in the corpus and appear in reaction to a number of different, seemingly unrelated, questions. In order to investigate these frequent discourses systematically, collocation networks are used.

Questions

As noted earlier, wh-questions, i.e., questions containing question words such as *what, why, who*, and *how*[2] are frequent in the Q+A corpus. Prototypically, wh-questions are used to seek specific information rather than maintain relationships between participants. This is what Jakobson (1960) calls a 'referential' rather than 'phatic' or 'expressive' function of language. Kearsley (1976), in his classification of interrogative sentences, uses the term 'epistemic referential questions' to indicate that wh-questions prototypically seek knowledge from the addressee, i.e., 'contextual information about situations, events, actions, purposes, relationships, or properties' (pp. 360–361). Similarly, Biber, Johansson, Leech, Conrad, and Finegan (1999: 212) note that wh-questions are typical means of seeking 'information [rather] than to maintain[ing] and reinforc[ing] the common ground among the participants'.

In this study, collocation networks were used to investigate how wh-questions are constructed in the online environment of the Yahoo! Answers communities of practice.

Figure 6.2 shows the collocation network for four question words *what, why, how*, and *who*. We can see that a large number of the collocates are function words supporting the grammatical structure of the questions: *do/does*, *is/are*, and *to* (in *how to . . .* ?) The figure also shows interesting commonalities and connectedness between the questions. For instance, *do* typically follows *what, how*, and *why* but not *who* (the absence of *do* after *who* is the result of a grammatical constraint in situations where *who* is used as a subject). On the other hand, the third-person present singular form *does*, although grammatically possible with *who* as well as the other three question words, is more closely associated with *why*. To see how these patterns translate into the questions that are being asked in the online forums, let us examine the following examples:

(10) What should a wife *do* when she comes to know that her husband chats with a woman every night on internet? [IN_FR_07]
(11) How *do* I convince my parents that I'm not GAY? [UK_FR_21]
(12) How are you going to *do* that WITH ALL The deals made with communist and social countries including OUR FLAG, made in CHINA? [PH_PG_04]

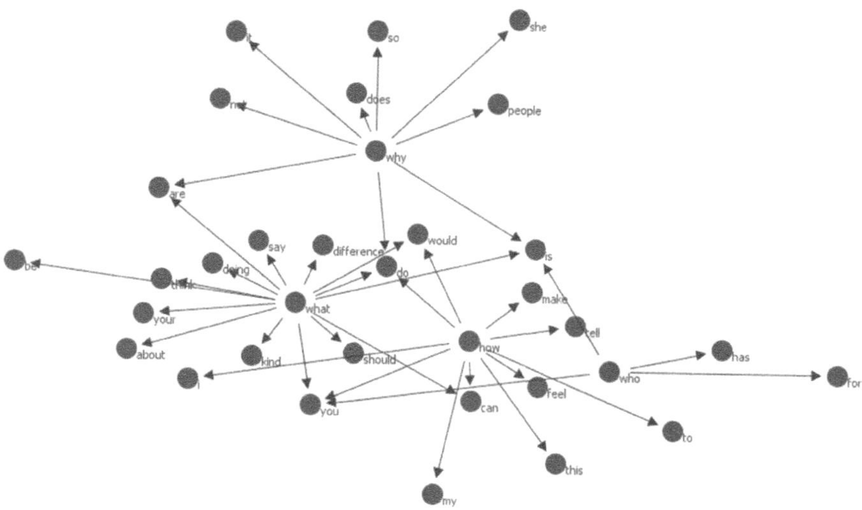

Figure 6.2 Wh-questions in the Q subcorpus [MI(3), C5, NC5, 0L 5R]

(13) Why *does* it happen why *does* not god stop it? [IN_SC_10]
(14) Why *does* republicans always use divisive fear tactics to win? [PH_PG_04]

It is interesting to note the non-standard use of English in example (14), which comes from the Philippine subcorpus. Non-standard uses are fairly common in the data and reflect the position of English as an international means of communication in the Yahoo! Answers communities of practice. Other commonalities include *is* (shared as a collocate by *who*, *what*, and *why*), *are* (shared by *what* and *why*), *would*, and *can* (both shared by *how* and *what*), as well as *you* (shared by *what*, *how*, and *who*). Let us focus on the last three shared collocates. Examples (15)–(18) show the use of the modals *can* and *would* and/or the second-person pronoun *you*, which can be considered as markers of subjectifying strategies. Using these and similar strategies, the online contributors asking the questions usually seek opinions and personal experiences rather than facts.

(15) If God loves me more than I love myself, how *can* there be a hell? [US_SC_06]
(16) *How would you react if this happened to you? [UK_FR_03]*
(17) *What would you buy George Bush for* Christmas? [UK_PG_04]
(18) What do *you* do to overcome stage fear? [IN_SC_16]

Indeed, many of the collocates in the network such as *should*, *think*, *feel*, *your*, *my*, and *I* point to a frequent use of subjectifying strategies. This observation suggests that in the communities of practice created around Q+A sessions, the function of wh-questions has been transformed from the prototypical referential function to a strongly social function, which includes eliciting personal response and building rapport. A similar observation was made by Harper et al. (2009), who discovered a large proportion (36%) of 'conversational questions' in their Yahoo! Answers data. In addition, Harper et al. acknowledge that their estimates about the proportion of conversational questions are fairly conservative because they only take into account clear-cut cases of purely social questions:

> We acknowledge that looking at questions in isolation is not necessarily the best way to classify a Q&A thread. For example, the question 'Why is the sky blue?' might appear to be informational in intent, until you realize that this question has been asked over 2,000 times in Yahoo Answers, and often receives no replies with serious answers to the question.
>
> (pp. 767–8)

The contrast between the social/expressive and referential (informational) function of wh-questions becomes even clearer when we compare wh-questions from the Q+A corpus with wh-questions which people typically ask the Google search engine in the countries for which the Q+A corpus was sampled. Table 6.5 shows wh-questions which Google's auto-complete algorithm outputs when the appropriate wh-word is entered (for more discussion about this function, see Baker & Potts 2013). For individual countries, local versions of the Google search engine were used to capture the regional variation. These questions are based on very frequent queries that the users enter into the search engine in a particular region, as can be seen from questions indexing social and cultural reality in the countries (e.g. the Super Bowl in the US, the festival Holi in India).

We can see that all the Google auto-complete questions are referential questions in response to which the search engine typically returns an encyclopedia article or a similar reference. Interestingly, the question 'why is the sky blue?' discussed by Harper, Moy, and Konstan (2009) as a hidden conversational (social) question in the context of Yahoo! Answers also appears in the auto-complete options (see the Philippines, UK, and US examples). Here, however, Google returns a list of scientific references to address the question.

Table 6.5 Typical questions from Google auto-complete: Compiled 26/3/2015

India	what is my ip?
	how to kiss?
	how to lose weight?
	how to hack wifi?
	when is holi in 2015?
Philippines	what is christmas?
	what is computer?
	why is the sky blue?
	how to make a baby?
	how to download video from youtube?
UK	what time is the eclipse?
	what does bae mean?
	why are oil prices falling?
	why do we yawn?
	why is the sky blue?
	how to make pancakes?
	when is valentine's day?
	who is a in pll?
US	what is isis?
	what is good credit score?
	why is gas so cheap?
	why is the sky blue?
	how to tie a tie?
	how to boil eggs?
	when is the superbowl?
	when was jesus born?
	who is siri?
	who is charles dilaurentis?

Overall, we can say that the collocation network gives us insight into the type of questions asked at the online forums and their preferred phrasing. This is a reflection of the 'local grammar' (Hunston & Sinclair 2001) of asking questions in the online communities of practice. This local grammar shows a strong preference for requests to share personal experience. Personal experience can be elicited via different means, such as opinion-seeking questions, questions seeking personal advice, or even questions that have a surface form typical of questions eliciting facts. The following examples demonstrate the three types of questions.

Opinion-seeking questions (collocates: *people, kind, really)*

(19) Why do *people* join the navy? [PH_PG_10]
(20) What *kind* of god are we dealing with here? [PH_SC_02]

Questions seeking personal advice (collocates: *think, tell, would, you, your*, etc.)

(21) How do I *tell* my boyfriend we should move up a step? [PH_PG_10]
(22) Why or why not? *Tell* us *your* views on this issue. [PH_PG_22]
(23) How would *you* react if this happened to you? [UK_FR_03]

Questions framed as seeking facts with potential subjectifying triggers (collocates: *difference, to*)

(24) What really is the *difference* between democrats and republicans? [US_PG_18]
(25) How *to* eliminate corruption and implement accountability in India? Honest people are afraid. They do not have the resources and financial power to contest the elections. They are threatened, maimed and even killed. The police is hand-in-hands with mafias and dons. We are forced to vote and elect only from the corrupt politicians. [IN_PG_24]

The last type of question is especially interesting. As can be seen from examples (24) and (25), a number of the questions that are framed as asking for specific pieces of information in a neutral factual manner in fact elicit personal response similar to opinion-seeking questions. In example (24), this response is prompted by the epistemic marker *really*, which a number of respondents interpret as a signal to provide their insights and political opinions that go beyond a description in an encyclopedia (e.g., 'Nothing! Same stink, different pile of sh*t!'). In a similar way, the general framing of the question in (25), including the opinion statements about Indian public affairs, prompts reactions of either agreement ('the biggest problem is most of our leaders are illiterate and even don't know how to write there names'.) or disagreement ('the politicians are better. when they could have taken 100 crore they take only 10'.) based on personal assessment of the situation in India.

Answers

While the discussion of the questions in the corpus focused on the characteristics of wh-questions asked and the implications of these questions for the online communities of practice, the discussion in this section concentrates on three specific concepts inherent in the frequent discourses found in the A subcorpus. These discourses include the words *god*, *love*, and *president*. Figure 6.3 is an initial summary of the associations (and their connections) around each of the nodes in the whole A subcorpus.

The figure displays a fairly complex collocation network of the strongest first-order collocates. At this level, the network reveals semantic independence of the political discourse from the other two discourses centred on *god* and *love*, which themselves are interconnected. This finding corroborates the earlier evidence that shows that both *god* and *love* occur frequently in the Society & Culture and Family & Relationships subcorpora, while *president* occurs almost entirely in the Politics & Government subcorpus and has thus more specific collocates that are not shared with the other two words. We can also see that *god* and *love* are connected directly as collocates of one another. The examples that follow show the contexts that give rise to this connection.

(26) Because *God* does not exist, and *God* is *love*, *love* does not exist. [US_SC_08]
(27) lol I still *love God* but I also *love* good literature. [IN_SC_21]

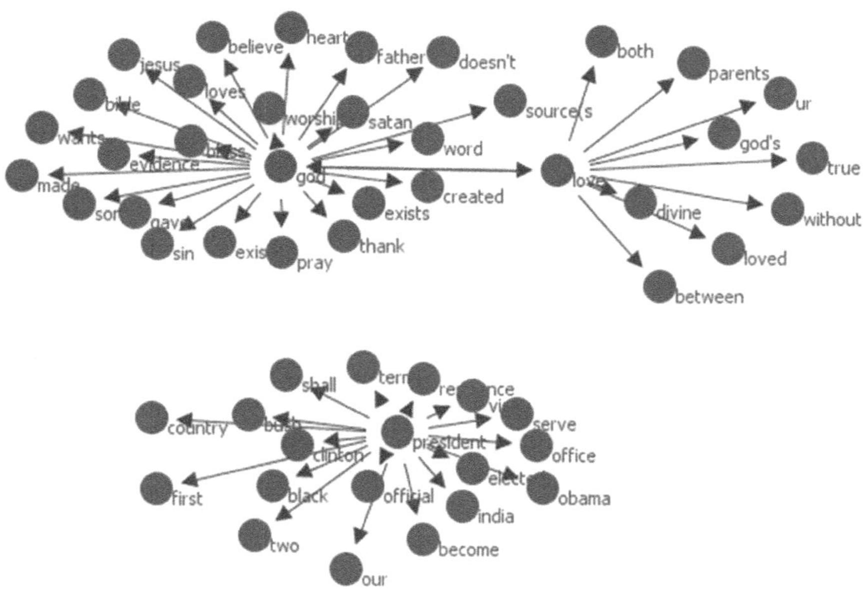

Figure 6.3 *God*, *love*, and *president* in the A subcorpus [MI(5), 10, 10, 5L 5R]

In the remainder of this section, the three frequent discourses will be analysed for the four individual countries (India, Philippines, UK, and US). First, the word *president* will be considered, followed by the discussion of *god* and *love*, which will be treated together due to their interconnectedness.

Figure 6.4 compares the collocates of *president* in the four country-specific subsections of the A subcorpus. Most of the collocates in the

India: 66 occurrences of *president*

Phillipines: 185 occurrences of *president*

Figure 6.4 Continued to the following page

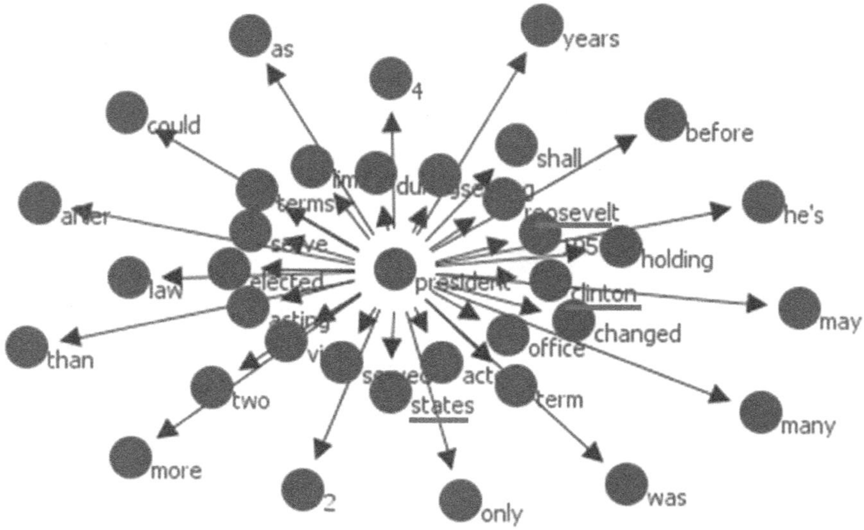

UK: 80 occurrences of *president*

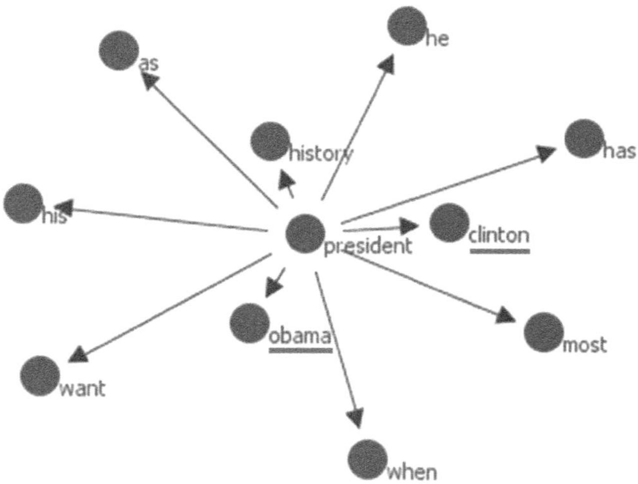

US: 35 occurrences of *president*

Figure 6.4 *President* in the country-based subsections of the A subcorpus [MI(5), 3, 3, 5L 5R] collocates related to American politics underlined.

Figure 6.4a: India: 66 occurrences of *president* *Figure 6.4b:* Philippines: 185 occurrences of *president* *Figure 6.4c:* UK: 80 occurrences of *president* *Figure 6.4d:* US: 35 occurrences of *president*

individual countries (with the exception of the US) refer to the political system, e.g., *serve, elected, term, office, vice-president*, and *prime (minister)*. Surprisingly, the collocation network for the US subsection is relatively sparse with a few grammatical words and two names of American presidents (*obama, clinton*). This sparseness of collocates is related to the fact that the term *president* itself occurs only 35 times in the US subsection and thus yields only a few strong collocates. The lack of direct references using the word *president* in the US context can be explained by the fact that a simple use of a surname is a more common way of referring to a president in the US domestic context. In fact, when we look at the frequency of the forms *obama* (52), *bush* (19), and *clinton* (16[3]) in the US subsection, we can see that they are considerably more prominent (with a combined frequency of 87) than the term *president*, which has a frequency of merely 35.

In the UK section, a large majority of the collocates around *president* (e.g., *states, clinton, roosevelt*) refer to American politics. In the Indian and Philippine sections, the collocation network reveals a split between domestic and international political debates with collocates referring to local (*india/philippines, country, gma*[4]) and American presidents. The collocates associated with American presidents are *bush* and *war* (Indian section), *states, mccain, obama*, and *black* (Philippine section). When we study the data more closely, we also discover an interesting paradox. Although the collocate *our* in the Indian and Philippine data in some cases refers to the local president (*our President Gloria Macapagal-Arroyo*), it is more often used to refer to American presidents by an American contributor (see examples (28), (29) and (30)). As the examples show, the context in which *our* is used to refer to an American president is often negative and distancing. At the same time, *our* as a collocate is entirely absent in the US section, showing an interesting dynamic underlying the references to American presidents in the domestic and international context.

(28) we as americans are proud to hold certain freedoms, but we are led into this by our 'president' and it is US who suffer. i am ashamed of mr.bush and cannot wait for his time to be up. [IN_PG_11]

(29) Well, he's our president. That's why we back him even if we don't agree with him, cringe at his ignorance, and didn't vote for him. [IN_PG_18]

(30) The president was legally elected (I didn't vote for him, but he is our president). If the president commits 'high crimes or misdemeanors', he can be impeached; however, in my opinion, he has not done so. [PH_PG_13]

Since the discourses around the terms *god* and *love* are interconnected both in terms of the overlap in the corpus subsections (Family & Relationships and Society & Culture) as well as in terms of the mutual collocational association as shown in Figure 6.3, they will now be discussed together and the potential cross-association will be explored further using collocation networks. Figure 6.5 displays collocation networks for individual country-based sections.

In three cases—India, Philippines, and US—the connection between the discourses centred around *god* and *love* identified in Figure 6.3 has been

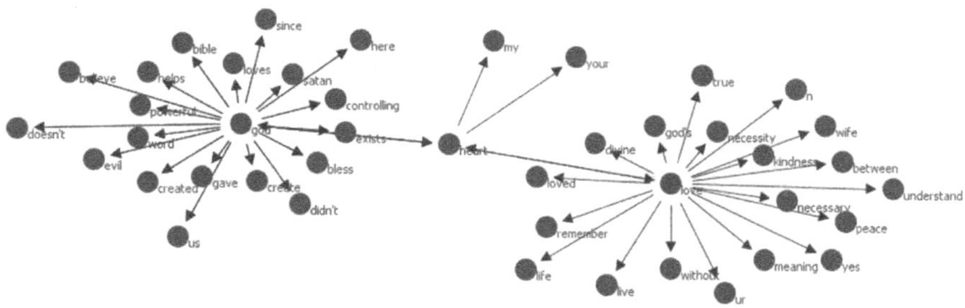

India: 256 occurrences of *god* and 305 occurrences of *love*

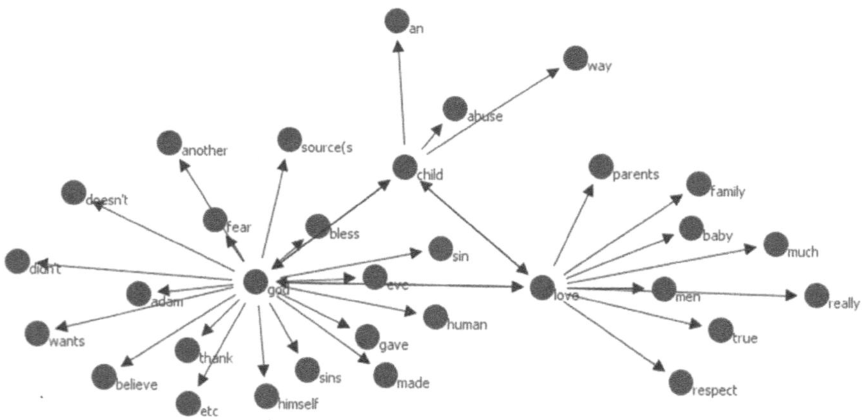

Philippines: 209 occurrences of *god* and 161 occurrences of *love*

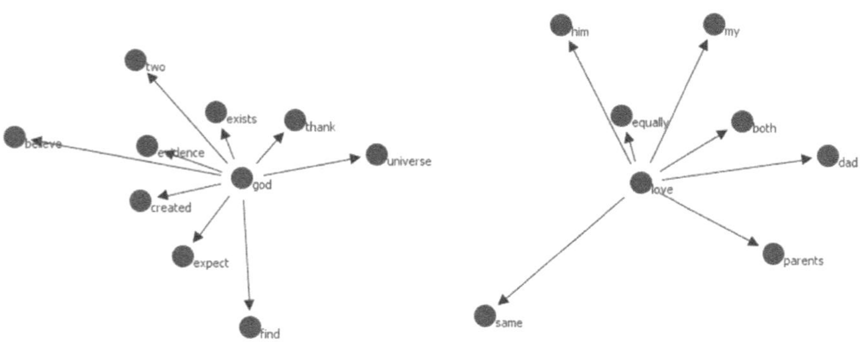

UK: 110 occurrences of *god* and 145 occurrences of *love*

Figure 6.5 Continued to the following page

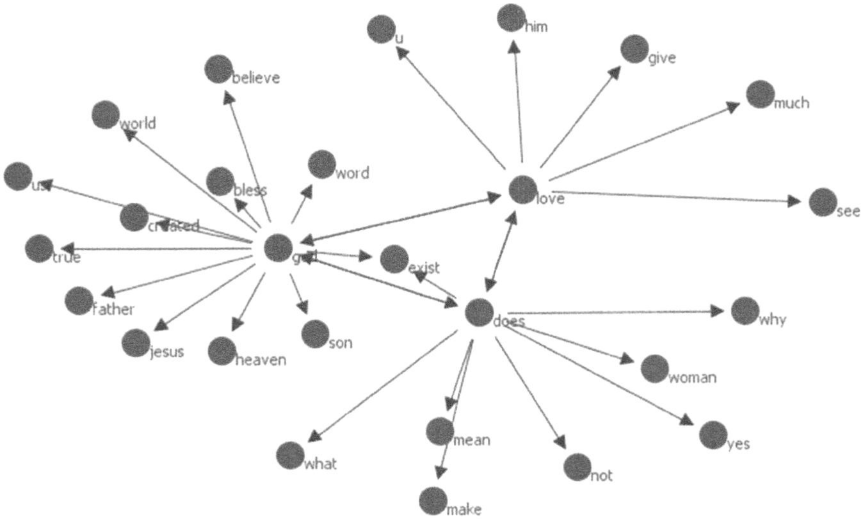

US: 152 occurrences of *god* and 96 occurrences of *love*

Figure 6.5 *God and love* in the country-based subsections of the A subcorpus [MI(5), 5, 5, 5L 5R]

further confirmed. The link appears to be related to Christian rhetoric, as can be seen from examples (31) and (32). By contrast, in the UK subsection, the discourses around *god* and *love* do not show the same type of interdependence.

(31) You win if you seek *God* with all your *heart*, all your soul, and all your strength, and then He will lead you to repentence and acceptance of Jesus as your Lord and saviour. [IN_SC_08]

(32) Remember this *Love* is *God* and *God* has nothing to do with affairs, prostitutes, cheating, etc. [PH_FR_03]

The collocation networks in Figure 6.5 show a competition between religious (e.g., *sins, heaven, divine, god's*) and secular associations (e.g., *thank, life, wife, parents*) of the words *god* and *love*. The largest number of religious associations appears in the Indian section, whereas the UK discourse is largely secular. For instance, in the UK section, *god* appears as a philosophical concept in the discussion about the (lack) of *evidence* for god's existence (example (33)) or in a fixed expression *thank god* that has lost its original religious meaning.

(33) As an atheist, I neither ask for, nor expect to find evidence of God. [UK_SC_03]

This section showed how collocation networks can help examine the context of the use of frequent content words in the A subcorpus—*president*, *god*, and *love*. In all three cases, the examination of collocational networks pointed to the constructs underlying the use of these three words in the four online communities of practice. The analysis revealed both commonalities and differences in belief, social, and political systems of the online users in the four countries analysed.

Conclusion

As demonstrated in this chapter, collocation networks represent an efficient way of analysing complex meaning relationships in discourse. In the case of the Yahoo! online communities of practice, the collocation networks helped shed light on both the local grammar of asking questions as well as on the frequent discourses in the answers centred on *god*, *love*, and *president*. Collocation networks thus enable us to visualize and analyze linguistic practices that give rise to complex meanings of texts and discourses; these linguistic practices can then be easily compared across different subcorpora, such as the country-based sections of the Q+A corpus in this study. At the same time, we need to realise that collocational networks are only one of many exploratory tools in corpus linguistics; this tool has great potential to reveal connections in discourse if we use it appropriately and in combination with other methods, such as concordancing.

Notes

1 For the details of the collocation networks notation see the "Method" section.
2 Other wh-words such as *when*, *where*, and *whose* were excluded from the analysis because of their low frequency in the corpus as question words.
3 This number excludes references to Hillary Clinton.
4 Gloria Macapagal-Arroyo, the president of the Philippines from 2001 to 2010.

References

Baker, P. & Potts, A. (2013). 'Why do white people have thin lips?' Google and the perpetuation of stereotypes via auto-complete search forms. *Critical Discourse Studies*, 10(2), 187–204.

Brezina, V. & Gablasova, D. (2015). Is there a core general vocabulary? Introducing the new general service list. *Applied Linguistics*, 36(1), 1–22.

Brezina, V., McEnery, T. & Wattam, S. (2015). Collocations in context: A new perspective on collocation networks. *International Journal of Corpus Linguistics*, 20(3), 139–173

Cunningham, Sally Jo & Hinze, Annika (2014). Social, religious information behavior: An analysis of Yahoo! Answers queries about belief. *Advances in the Study of Information and Religion*, 4(3).

Fichman, P. (2011). A comparative assessment of answer quality on four question answering sites. *Journal of Information Science*, 37(5), 476–486.

Grice, H. P. (1975). Logic and conversation. In P. Cole & J. Morgan (Eds.), *Syntax and Semantics*. New York: Academic Press. pp. 41–58.

Harper, F. M., Moy, D. & Konstan, J. A. (2009, April). Facts or friends?: Distinguishing informational and conversational questions in social Q+A sites. In *Proceedings of the SIGCHI Conference on Human Factors in Computing Systems* (pp. 759–768). New York, NY: ACM.

Hunston, S. & Sinclair, J. (2001). A local grammar of evaluation. In S. Hunston & G. Thompson (Eds.), *Evaluation in Text: Authorial Stance and the Construction of Discourse* (pp. 74–101). Oxford: Oxford University Press.

Jakobson, R. (1960). Linguistics and poetics. In T.A. Sebeok (Ed.), *Style in Language*. Cambridge, MA: MIT Press

Kearsley, G. P. (1976). Questions and question asking in verbal discourse: A cross-disciplinary review. *Journal of Psycholinguistic Research*, 5(4), 355–375.

Phillips, M. K. (1983). Lexical Macrostructure in Science Text (2 Vol.). Doctoral Dissertation. University of Birmingham.

Phillips, M. (1985). *Aspects of Text Structure: An Investigation of the Lexical Organisation of Text*. Amsterdam: North-Holland.

Raban, D. R. (2009). Self-presentation and the value of information in Q&A websites. *Journal of the American Society for Information Science and Technology*, 60(12), 2465–2473.

Rosenbaum, H. & Shachaf, P. (2010). A structuration approach to online communities of practice: The case of Q&A communities. *Journal of the American Society for Information Science and Technology*, 61(9), 1933–1944.

Wenger, E. (1998). *Communities of Practice: Learning, Meaning, and Identity*. Cambridge: Cambridge University Press.

Wilson, S. M. & Peterson, L. C. (2002). The anthropology of online communities. *Annual Review of Anthropology*, 31: 449–467.

7 Variationist Analysis

Variability Due to Random Effects and Autocorrelation

Stefan Th. Gries

Introduction

The Overall Frequencies of (Co-)occurrence Approach

In contemporary linguistics, corpora are arguably one of the central methodological tools and one of the central sources of data. More and more linguists look into corpora for information on frequencies of occurrence of a particular expression or frequencies of co-occurrence of a particular linguistic expression with other expressions or contextual characteristics. While much earlier work in corpus linguistics involved questions of lexical semantics (often from a lexicographic perspective), for quite some time now, corpus-linguistic applications have become much wider in scope, covering questions from the domains of morphology, (morpho)syntax, and pragmatics from both synchronic and diachronic angles, in both native language and foreign/second languages. One area of research that has seen a particularly strong boost is the study of what I will broadly refer to here as *lexicosyntactic alternations*. With this term, I am referring to instances where speakers (have to) choose one out of a typically small set of several (nearly) equivalent lexical or syntactic options and typically do so without much or any awareness of the factors driving their choices. (1) Shows a few purely lexical choices (of near synonyms), whereas (2) exemplifies cases of either purely syntactic choices (e.g., (2a)) or of choices that involve both lexical and syntactic decisions (e.g., (2b–d)):

(1) a La Forge couldn't make sense of the symmetric/symmetrical pattern(s)
  b Dr. Crusher was annoyed by the shouting/yelling children
  c Picard attempted/tried to kill the Borg
(2) a Picard *picked up the tricorder* versus *Picard picked the tricorder up*
  b *Worf will* kill *the Romulan* versus *Worf is going to kill the Romulan*
  c Picard gave Riker his orders versus Picard gave his order to Riker
  d the admiral's orders versus the orders of the admiral

Given the ease with which frequencies of choices involving lexical material can be extracted from corpora, it comes as no surprise that there are many reference works and studies that report and utilize frequencies of occurrence of the alternants that make up alternations. Maybe the most famous example of the former is Biber et al'.s (1999) comprehensive corpus-based reference grammar of English, which provides normalized frequencies of a large number of grammatical phenomena for different registers (conversation vs. fiction vs. news vs. academic prose) and modes (spoken vs. written). As for the latter, the following are examples from the domain of learner corpus research involving comparisons of native speaker (NS) and (different kinds of) non-native speaker (NNS) data, a very common application in that field:

- Hyland and Milton (1997) compare frequencies of epistemic modality expressions;
- Laufer and Waldman (2011) compare frequencies of V-N collocations across NS and differently proficient levels of NNS;
- Hasselgård and Johansson (2012) compare frequencies of *quite* (in isolation and in colligations).

That is, such studies usually provide (i) normalized frequencies of occurrence of particular expressions (per register, per mode, per L1, . . .) and/or (ii) normalized frequencies of how often particular expressions co-occur with some other (kind of) expression (sometimes explored statistically using many χ^2-tests or the related log-likelihood ratios). Given the regularity with which such frequencies of occurrence are reported, it is probably no exaggeration to assume that this is one of the corpus-based statistics most commonly used in the last three or so decades. However, as I will argue presently, they are also potentially very misleading.

The Variationist Case-by-Variable Approach

While the aforementioned kinds of frequencies of (co-)occurrence are very useful in reference works, their utility in research articles (in particular for learner corpus research but also more generally) is often much more doubtful given how raw/normalized frequencies of occurrence typically divorce the use of an expression from the rich context in which they are used. Consider the use of *may* and *can* by NS and NNS in the data of Gries and Deshors (2014). They show how a simple regression model trying to determine how frequently NS and NNS use *may* and *can* indicates that NS use *may* a bit more often than NNS. However, they proceed to show that this overall difference/effect is misleading because NS and NNS use the two modal verbs very differently depending on the aspect of, and the presence/absence of negation in, the verb phrase. Thus and more generally, an observed difference of frequencies of (co-)occurrence can have many reasons: if (i) the presence of negation leads to a preference of *can* over *may* in NS data and (ii) NNS use *can* more than NS, then either the NNS overuse *can* (for reasons having to do with their non-native proficiency) or the NNS overuse *negation* and at the same time use *can* just like NS would if they also used negation more, namely more often. It is therefore necessary to recognize that overall frequencies of occurrence of some linguistic expression *e* that do not involve a detailed analysis of *e*'s contexts are potentially useless and risky because they do not allow the analyst to determine which of the two mentioned explanations (or many other competing ones) is correct or at least more likely.

The solution to this problem is to adopt an approach that is variationist in nature (i.e., is compatible with the work done for a long time in variationist sociolinguistics) and requires what is often referred to in statistics as the case-by-variable format: typically, every occurrence in the corpus to be studied—each case—is annotated (in a spreadsheet) for a variety of variables or predictors that are likely to affect the linguistic choice under investigation (in the 'Match' column), as represented in Table 7.1.

Note that it is often useful to also add a column, which might be called "Alternate", that indicates for each case whether each of the alternants would have been possible or not because, depending on one's goals, subsequent statistical analyses may be run either on all instances of the competing linguistic choices or only on those that could alternate. Either way, the next step is often a statistical analysis to determine which of the many annotated predictors (and, ideally, their interactions) are correlated with the linguistic choice and how so. Interestingly, for many of the syntactic alternations whose studies dominate the literature such as those listed earlier in (2), the linguistic factors that govern them in English at least are similar (and often related):

- *information-structural factors* having to do with the givenness, or degree of discourse activation, of the referents of noun phrases such that, usually, given/inferable elements precede new referents;
- *weight-related factors* having to do with the length/weight/complexity of the phrases whose ordering is studied such that, usually, short elements precede long elements;
- *animacy-related factors* having to do with what degree of animacy the referents of various noun phrases (NPs) in the relevant verb phrases have;

Table 7.1 A partially schematic concordance display of future choice in the case-by-variable format

Case	*Preceding*	*Match*	*Subsequent*	*Predictor 1*	*Predictor 2*	*Predictor 3*
1	Worf	will	kill the Romulan	...	...	...
...	...	...	...	...	...	...

- various other *semantic factors* having to do with aspects, aktionsart, general semantic categories, case roles, and many other phenomenon-specific ones;
- *processing-related factors* having to do with the distribution of the information provided by upcoming linguistic material (often measured in information-theoretic terms);
- *phonological factors* having to do with how much competing constituent orders violate near-universal preferences, such as rhythmic alternation or preferred syllable structure.

On the basis of fine-grained annotation of the aforementioned kind, multifactorial statistical analyses—currently these are frequently regression models—can be applied to see which of these factors are correlated with, and thus likely causes of, the relevant alternation. This kind of analysis is hugely superior to overall frequencies of (co-)occurrence because it allows one to distinguish many different potential causes for what may seem like over-/underuse of a particular expression in some groups of speakers (e.g., learners of different L1s, speakers of different dialects, speakers using language in different registers).

In much recent work, the aforementioned approach was already implemented and has yielded results that improve considerably upon the more traditional approach of the preceding section. In the remainder of this paper, I want to draw attention to a small set of additional factors whose inclusion would benefit corpus-based research on alternative linguistic choices.

Case Studies

In this section, I will discuss how the study of the to-be-explained variability in the data can benefit from taking more into consideration than the usual linguistic determinants discussed earlier, namely, by exploring effects that, in the language of statistics, could be characterized as

- *random effects*, i.e., the role of factors whose levels in the current corpus sample do not exhaust the range of possible levels in the population ('out there in the language'); these include speaker-specific variation (because typically a corpus does not contain all speakers of the language) and lexically specific variation (because typically a corpus does not contain all, say, verbs, that can occur with, say, a particular tense);
- *autocorrelation*, i.e., the fact that earlier linguistic behavior co-determines later linguistic behavior (by the same speaker or others) as when, by virtue of a process often referred to as *structural priming*, the use of a passive structure by a speaker makes it more likely that that speaker will use a passive again in the near future (see Schenkein 1980; Weiner & Labov 1983; Estival 1985 for the earliest observational studies).

The linguistic choice I will use to exemplify the large amount of variability covered by such factors is future choice as shown in (2b). Such an alternation is an interesting question for the aforementioned kinds of effects because not only are there a variety of linguistic factors governing future choices, but there are also a range of studies that have revealed sometimes marked differences in alternation behaviors/preferences of specific lexical items but also between native and indigenized varieties of English (see Mukherjee & Hoffmann 2006; Mukherjee & Gries 2009).That, in turn, makes a corpus that includes different (kinds of) varieties and topics, which may give rise to different kinds of verbs, a prime test case. Thus I used R to retrieve candidates of future choices from the Q+A corpus using the regular expression shown in (3):

(3) (((wi|sha)ll|wo)_vm|going_vvgk·to_to)·([^_]+_[^v][^]+·){0,2}[^_]+_v[^]+

This retrieved 2,329 matches of

- *will* or *shall* or *wo* (for *won't*).[1] Followed by the tag *vm* OR *going* followed, by the tag *vvgk*, followed by *to* tagged as *to*, followed by;
- between zero and two tagged 'things' that are not tagged as verbs (each followed by a space);
- followed by something tagged as a verb;
- within one line.

This (then slightly cleaned and homogenized) concordance constitutes the data on which the following sections are based. One traditional kind of approach discussed earlier would consist of providing overall frequencies of, say, *will* and *going to* in the corpus as a whole or in variety-/register-/topically restricted parts of the corpora. Table 7.2 is an example of the kind of overall frequency data that much work (especially in learner corpus research) has provided but that, given its neglect of context, cannot really reveal that much.

Another frequent instantiation of the traditional approach would be to annotate the concordance lines with regard to some features likely to affect future choice and then study each feature (often done in isolation using

Table 7.2 Frequencies of *will* and *going to* across varieties and variety types in the Q+A corpus

Type	*Variety*	going to	will	*Total per variety*	will *per type*
Indigenized	IN	38	561 (93.7%)	599	92.6%
	PH	43	529 (92.5%)	572	
Native	UK	72	354 (83.1%)	426	83.1%
	US	81	554 (87.2%)	635	

Table 7.3 Frequencies of future choices depending on negation in the Q+A corpus

Future	*Affirmative*	*Negative*	*Total*
going to	194	40	234
shall	75	22	97
will	1731	267	1998
Total	2000	329	2329

cross-tabulation). For instance, future choice is said to be affected by the presence of negation (see Szmrecsanyi 2005, 2006 for an excellent analysis). A quick classification of whether the future verb phrase (VP) is negated or not in the whole corpus yields Table 7.3, which, if tested with a χ^2-test, as many would do (not that one should, see the following section), returns a significant p value (χ^2-test = 8.509, df = 2, p = 0.014) of a rather weak effect (V=0.06) such that, with negated VPs, the proportion of *going to* and *shall* are higher for than for *will*.

One major shortcoming of such analyses is that they are not multifactorial because each such predictor is studied in isolation, which by definition already leads to an incomplete picture. However, the next few sections will show how such analyses also miss a lot of variability by neglecting sources of variability other than the 'regular' linguistic predictors discussed earlier.

Speaker-Specific Variation

The first kind of random effect that distorts all overall frequencies but is usually readily available from the fully annotated, case-by-variable format is speaker-/file-specific variation. This refers to the fact that speakers may differ considerably and systematically in terms of their future choices, which rules out the aforementioned χ^2-test. The fact that the overall percentages mask a considerable amount of speaker-specific variation is represented in Figure 7.1. Both panels represent the percentage of uses of *will* (as opposed to *going to*, *shall* has been omitted here because of its low overall frequency) on the x-axis, the variety (left panel), and the topic (right panel) are on the y-axis, and every gray point indicates one speaker's overall preference of *will* with darker grays reflecting overplotting and short vertical lines indicating group medians.

Several observations are immediately obvious: (i) there is a large amount of variability between speakers; (ii) this is true even if the notable differences of the variety-specific medians suggest that, on the whole, the native varieties use *will* less than the indigenized varieties (see the following section for more discussion); (iii) the topic-specific medians differ much less from each other than the variety-specific medians; and (iv) there are many speakers (124 in fact, nearly half of all speakers) who invariably use *will* and a few speakers (5) who invariably use *going to*, which means that these speakers'

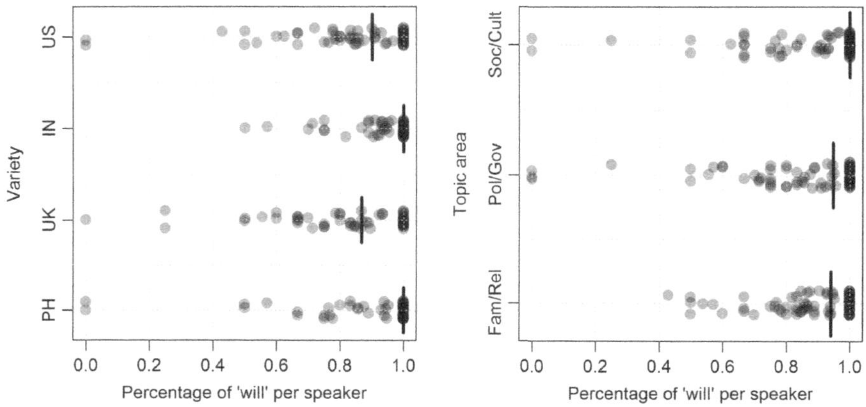

Figure 7.1 Percentages of use of *will* per file/speaker by variety (left) and by topic (right)

behavior, if not controlled for, can potentially distort the analysis of any factor affecting future choice simply because these speakers might weaken any factor's impact (since that factor would potentially not explain any variation in those speakers' choices).

For instance, if a foreign language learner of English does not know the *going-to* future yet, then he is not going to use it even when negation is present, thereby seemingly weakening the statistical effect that negation has on *going to* when the real reason is that the speaker does not even know he has a choice in the first place. In fact, if one tries to predict every future choice in the corpus and does so just by choosing the construction that each speaker prefers in general and chooses *will* when a speaker uses both futures equally often (because *will* is generally so much more frequent), then one can predict $^{2009}/_{2232}$ = 90% of all instances of *will* and *going to* correctly on the basis of speaker-specific effects alone and *will*'s general predominance.

It is for this reason that corpus-linguistic analyses should always explore speaker-/file-specific effects of the aforementioned kind.[2] In fact, an even better kind of analysis would also take into consideration the fact that speakers/files are nested into varieties (because each speaker is only attested in one variety), which are in turn nested into variety types (because each variety in this corpus is either native or indigenized), and variability in future choice can be manifested at each of these levels of resolution.

Lexically Specific Variation

The second kind of random effect that distorts overall frequencies but is readily available from concordance data is how grammatical constructions can exhibit preferences to particular lexical items; this may often be due to the lexical items' semantics (and, thus, their correlations with semantic factors discussed earlier). In corpus linguistics, this notion has been captured under the notion of *colligation* and also during the last ten-plus years under that of *collostruction*, a blend of *collocation* and *construction* (see Stefanowitsch & Gries 2003). The family of methods called *collostructional analysis* includes the method of distinctive collexeme analysis, a straightforward application of association measures from collocation research to co-occurrence of a word *w* and two constructions c_1 and c_2; the analyst creates tables of the kind of Table 7.4 for every word occurring at least once in either c_1 or c_2 and computes an association measure from that table such as Mutual Information *MI*, *t*, log-likelihood, or $p_{\text{Fisher-Yates exact test}}$.

Gries and Stefanowitsch (2004) applied this method to contrast *will-* and *going-to* futures in the ICE-GB and found that many verbs attracted to the *will-* future are characterized by relative non-agentivity and low dynamicity, including perception/cognition events and states whereas the opposite is found for verbs attracted to the *going-to* future.

An extension of this method, multiple distinctive collexeme analysis, can compare how much a word *w* is attracted to, or repelled by, more than two constructions such as the three future choices *will*, *going to*, and *shall*.[3] Given the strong predominance of *will* in the present corpus, the results will be less revealing semantically because so few verbs occur significantly more frequently with *will* than the overall high baseline already leads one to expect. However, the point is, as before, to show that much variability that can easily and prematurely be attributed to linguistic factors, learners' lack of proficiency, etc., may in fact consist (in part) just of lexical preferences (and whatever these 'operationalize' semantically).

If such a multiple distinctive collexeme analysis is applied to all 422 verb lemmas occurring with at least one future choice once in the corpus as a whole, then only a few lemmas, 32, reach significant levels of attraction; however, these 32 lemmas account for nearly half the data, namely, 1,030 future choices. Consider Figure 7.2 for a visual representation of verbs' constructional preferences.

As is obvious, many of these verb lemmas have quite distinct preferences. The three future choices are symbolized by the three differently colored segments, the sizes of which represent the percentage of times the relevant

Table 7.4 Schematic co-occurrence table for measuring the association between a word lemma *w* and each of two constructions c_1 and c_2 in some corpus

	Construction c_1	*Construction c_2*	*Total*
word lemma *w*	*a*	*b*	*a + b*
other word lemmas	*c*	*d*	*c + d*
Total	*a + c*	*b + d*	*a + b + c + d*

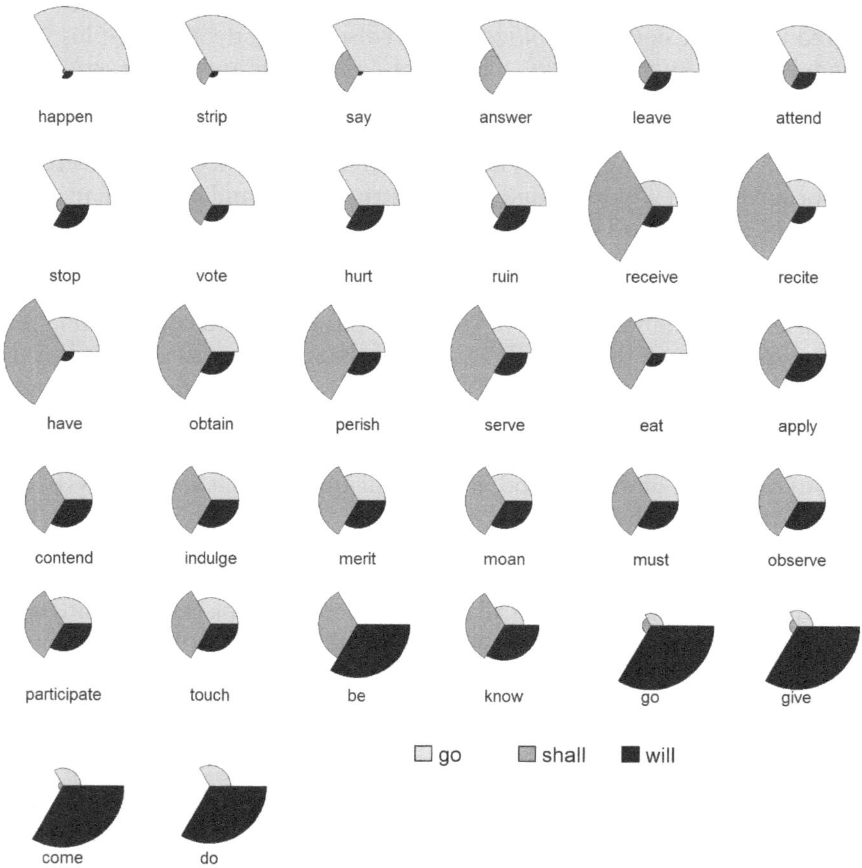

Figure 7.2 The degrees of attraction of significantly attracted verbs to futures

verb occurs with that future choice. For instance, *happen* is most strongly attracted to the *going-to* future, whereas *come* and *do* are most strongly attracted to *will*. While the dataset is too small to make meaningful comparisons between varieties or topics, it is reassuring to see that several of the earlier findings of Gries and Stefanowitsch are supported even in this more specialized corpus: *going to* is used more with rare but more specific verbs (in particular verbs of communication), whereas *will*'s default status emerges from the general high-frequency verbs it prefers; the verbs preferring *shall* are mostly rare verbs.

For the present purposes, it is most central to again point out the predictive power of these verb-specific preferences: as before with speaker-specific preferences, if one tries to predict every future choice in the corpus and does so just by choosing the construction that each verb prefers most, then one can predict $^{2042}/_{2329}$ = 87.7% of all futures correctly just on the basis of verb-specific effects. That in turn means that, if a researcher finds differences in future use between varieties or topics, he can only be confident that these are in fact due to variety- or topic-specific effects if the more general confound of lexically specific effects is not responsible for the future choices.

Persistence/Priming

After two random-effect factors, the final important source of variability to be discussed here is different in nature. In the previous two sections, the idea was to discuss annotated factors that characterize a constructional choice in the data to see how, if at all, they were related to the constructional choice. In the language of spreadsheets, this means the column of some factor or independent variable/predictor was correlated with the column that represents the dependent variable/response, here the constructional choice. In the current section, we deal with the case where what might affect a constructional choice at time t_x is in the same column; namely, a previous choice at time $t_{y < x}$. In other words, the dependent variable is potentially correlated with (an earlier value of) itself, hence the term in statistics for this is *autocorrelation*.

As mentioned earlier, this phenomenon is referred to as structural priming and has been observed in a huge number of studies from production to production, from comprehension to production, in various experimental tasks (picture description, sentence completion, dialog tasks, etc.), in observational/corpus data, in many languages, and between languages. Overwhelmingly, a certain structural choice at some point of time increases the probability that the same speaker or another speaker who heard the previous structural choice will use the same construction the next time he makes a choice from the same set of alternants. That of course means that structural priming can often be orthogonal to other linguistic factors and, therefore, make it harder to determine how much of the variability in the data can be attributed to linguistic predictors describing the utterance currently under investigation and how much is just due to something that happened a minute ago and is, correspondingly, far away from the current concordance line.

Observational studies of structural priming have become quite sophisticated in the past few years (see Gries 2015a for an overview), but exploring priming can also be achieved more simply by, for instance, switch-rate plots proposed by Sankoff and Laberge (1978). Such plots plot the rates of switches from one of the alternants to the other against the relative frequency of the latter alternant per speaker; low switch rates are compatible with priming. Consider Figure 7.3, which represents the frequencies of *will*-futures on the x-axis, the switch rate toward *will* on the y-axis, and every letter is one speaker (with letters representing varieties: *N* for IN, *H* for PH, *K* for UK, and *S* for US). The dashed line is the null hypothesis that the

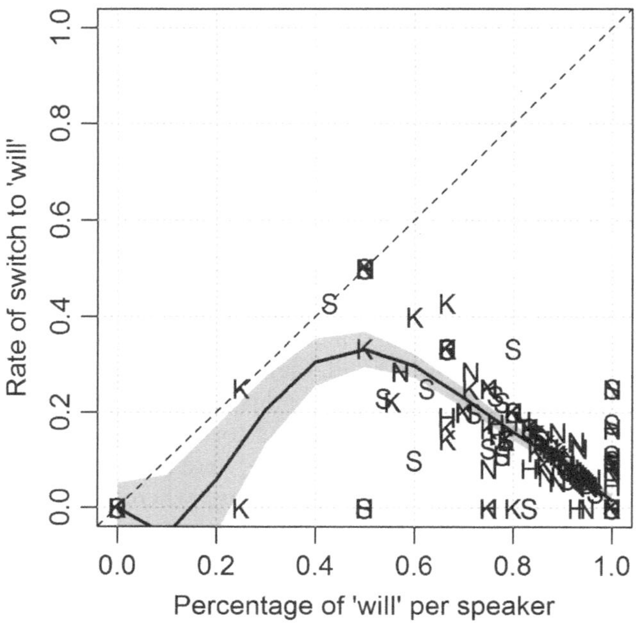

Figure 7.3 Switch-rate plot for *will*- futures

switch rate toward *will* is proportional to *will*'s frequency and the line with the confidence interval summarizes the points.

The result is very straightforward: switch rates to *will* are overwhelmingly lower than the frequency of *will* would lead one to expect. Speakers switch less, i.e., repeat more, i.e., exhibit priming effects. However, the overplotting makes it very difficult to explore the results in more detail (e.g., by variety or by topic), which is what Figure 7.3 allows one to do, which represents for each speaker the subtraction from the *x*-axis value in Figure 7.4 from the corresponding *y*-axis value: the smaller a plotted value, the more different the switch rate to *will* is from the frequency of *will* for that speaker and the more the results are compatible with priming effects.

The results are again quite clear but now come with the finer resolution of varieties and topics. The left panel shows that priming exists (given that so many values are much smaller than zero) and that it affects the speakers of the native varieties (UK and US) less than the speakers of the indigenized varieties (IN and PH): the difference between observed and expected switch rate is closer to zero for the former than for the latter, a finding that researchers may try to integrate with regard to different degrees of evolution of different varieties (as in Schneider's 2007 model) or with regard to different susceptibilities toward priming of varieties differently entrenched

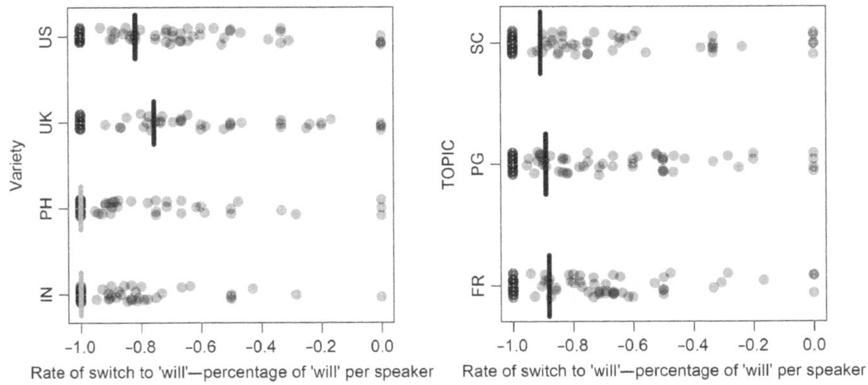

Figure 7.4 Switch rates to *will* minus percentages of use of *will* per file/speaker by variety (left) and by topic (right)

in speakers' minds.[4] However, and as might be expected, the right panel suggests strongly that the three topic areas exhibit priming effects, too, but do not differ from each other at all.[5] Also, the findings show that the Q+A corpus seems to be more similar to spoken than to written registers, given the high overall degree of priming even in the native varieties since priming has been found to be weaker in writing.

As before, let us briefly consider how predictive priming is on its own: if one tries to predict every future choice in the corpus and does so just by choosing the construction that the speakers used last time and chooses *will* for a speaker's first future (because *will* is generally so much more frequent), then one can predict $^{1884}/_{2329}$ = 80.9% of all instances of *will*, *shall*, and *going to* correctly just on the basis of what the speaker did the last time around, a finding that should again be a strong incentive to always explore priming effects.

Concluding Remarks

As mentioned initially, corpora and the frequency data that they offer to corpus linguists have become an ever-more important tool for theoretical and applied linguistics alike and various kinds of frequency information have provided immensely useful information. However, I hope to have shown (i) that overall frequencies of occurrence—absolute or relative—such as in Table 7.2, while useful in the context of surveys and overall reference works, are from my point of view most useful for exploratory purposes because such frequencies are typically both decontextualized and zero-/monofactorial in nature, whereas linguistic choices are not. Ignoring—i.e., not annotating and statistically analyzing—contextual and other features of a phenomenon of interest means the researcher cannot, *by definition*, distinguish between different explanations for whatever over- or underuse frequencies he found and reported, which in turn virtually guarantees that monofactorial results will over- or underestimate the actual trends in the data.

I also hope to have shown (ii) that even if linguistic features from the context of a linguistic choice are included—information-structural, weight-related, animacy, and other semantic factors, etc.—there are also other sources of variation that commonly remain underanalyzed: variation due to (a) speakers and (b) lexical items (and not discussed in great detail), variation due to (c) the hierarchical structure of most corpora, as well as (d) priming/autocorrelation effects, each of which has considerable predictive power on its own. That in turn means that studies ignoring such effects run the risk of (i) misidentifying the reasons for linguistic choices—the reason for a particular choice may not have been information-structural or weight-related but simply that speaker's preferred choice—and/or (ii) failing to find an explanation for what appear to be inexplicable linguistic choices—maybe the explanation for a speaker's inexplicable choice of a construction is nothing that can be seen in the current (concordance) context but is quite obvious from the previous one. Ideally, of course, all four effects discussed earlier would be included at the same time as the contextual features with, for instance, mixed-effects/multi-level modeling (see Gries 2015b for recent explanation in a corpus-linguistic context). If a multi-level model involving all four aforementioned effects is applied to the present data to determine whether the weak but significant correlation between negation and future choice apparent from Table 7.3, the risks associated with the cross-tabulation of frequencies becomes apparent: a model with all random effects and priming as a predictor is hugely more preferable (evidence $\text{ratio}_{AICc} > 10^{15}$) than a model that also involves negation—thus the simple cross-tabulation leads one to believe in an effect that better analysis shows to be non-existent.

While the exposition here could only scratch the surface, I hope that the empirical issues and methodological strategies discussed in this chapter to tackle these kinds of problems will stimulate researchers to pay closer attention to these important factors: studies of different varieties need to look beyond the immediate context to more widespread preferences of people and words, as well as previous contexts to avoid potentially misinterpreting results.

Postscript

To me, this experiment was a very interesting experience for mainly two reasons. On the one hand, I was (positively) surprised by the whole range of areas that were explored, many of which are outside my areas of expertise and thus exposed me to research that I had not known (well) before; in that connection, I have to admit I was struck by a feeling that my chapter didn't fit the rest of the volume as well as I had hoped to be able to achieve because (i) most other chapters focused on lexical items/bundles as well as (e.g., semantic) characteristics of theirs and their distributions across varieties and topics and (ii) how the papers were located on a (simplistic) continuum from mostly/exclusively qualitative to mostly/exclusively quantitative work. My own submission was narrower in scope than many others in how it focused on one small and lexicogrammatical alternation—future choice of *will* versus *going to* (vs. *shall*)—as opposed to a larger range of (lexical) expressions, and my submission was more on the (less populated) quantitative side of the spectrum (together with, say, Friginal & Biber's or Egberts' chapters).

On the other hand, and this is *not* to criticize any other submission(s) given their relevance for valuable exploratory purposes, many other submissions also reaffirmed my aforementioned views on (i) the importance, if not (often) indispensability, of context annotation of current or previous instances for the study of any frequency data (or statistics derived from them such as keywords or co-occurrence strengths) and (ii) the subsequent statistical analysis of the degree to which such annotated characteristics affect, or at least correlate with, the phenomenon of interest, and I am not implying I myself have always done this to the extent that I now consider essential! It is hard to see which, if any, of the case studies in this volume would not be affected by at least one of the three factors discussed here: any frequency can be affected by dispersion (e.g., speaker- or, here, thread-specific variation), and many frequencies of occurrences of lexicogrammatical choices will also be affected by autocorrelation/priming, which makes it ever-more important to control for such factors (using good sampling, controlling for contexts, and/or appropriate statistics). To mention but one example, do keyword statistics change if particular parts of the reference corpora are omitted, where 'parts' can be defined on any level of granularity, thread, variety, topic, etc.?

Thus, while my chapter's contribution to the identification and understanding of differences between varieties and topics in the Q+A corpus is perhaps more limited than that of many other chapters, I hope that it is still worthwhile as a perhaps cautionary but certainly complementary follow-up to the many discoveries my co-contributors have made.

Notes

1 Given the inconsistent use of apostrophized forms, for the sake of simplicity, no forms such as *I'll*, *he'll*, etc., were explored; this has no effect on the overall argument.

2 There are already some studies that adopt an approach similar to the aforementioned by computing, for instance, normalized frequencies per file (as in Figure 7.1) and then compute means, standard deviations, or more complex statistics based on all by-file normalized frequencies. This indeed addresses the role of speaker-specific variation but still usually faces problems. First, the role of context is still unclear, which means that essentially no, even only potentially causal, claims can

be made; second, the usual kinds of parametric statistics (such as means, standard deviations, etc.) must not actually be applied to such data because they are typically not normally distributed. In the present data, the seven by-speaker percentages of *will-* futures across varieties and topics are all non-normal (all seven Shapiro-Wilk test $p < 10–6$). Third, this approach cannot easily accommodate multiple kinds of random effects at the same time.

3 This extension uses exact binomial tests to test for each lexical item whether its occurrences with each of the constructions are more or less frequent than expected from the constructions' frequencies in the corpus and is implemented in Gries (2014), see <http://tinyurl.com/collostructions> for details and examples.

4 A Kolmogorov–Smirnov test comparing the plotted differences for the native speakers to those of the indigenized speakers returns a significant result ($D = 0.249$, $p < 0.001$).

5 Kolmogorov–Smirnov tests comparing the three topics to each other return only non-significant results (all $D < 0.1$, all p adjusted for three tests > 0.9).

References

Biber, D., Johansson, S., Leech, G., Conrad, S. & Finegan, E. (1999). *Longman Grammar of Spoken and Written English*. Harlow: Longman.

Estival, D. (1985). Syntactic priming of the passive in English. *Text*, 5(1–2), 7–21.

Gries, S. (2014). Coll.analysis 3.5. A script for R to compute perform collostructional analyses (major update to handle larger corpora/frequencies). Accessed online at: http://tinyurl.com/collostructions

Gries, S. (2015a). Структурный прайминг: корпусное исследование и узуальные/экземплярные подходы/'Structural priming: A perspective from observational data and usage-/exemplar-based approaches'. In Andrej A. Kibrik, Alexey D. Koshelev, Aexander V. Kravchenko, Julia V. Mazurova & Olga V. Fedorova (Eds.), *Язык и мысль: Современная когнитивная лингвистика/'Language and Thought: Contemporary Cognitive Linguistics'* (pp. 721–754). Moscow: Languages of Slavic Culture.

Gries, S. (2015b). The most underused statistical method in corpus linguistics: Multi-level (and mixed-effects) models. *Corpora*, 10(1), 95–125.

Gries, S. & Deshors, S. (2014). Using regressions to explore deviations between corpus data and a standard/target: two suggestions. *Corpora*, 9(1), 109–136.

Gries, S. & Stefanowitsch, A. (2004). Extending collostructional analysis: A corpus-based perspective on 'alternations'. *International Journal of Corpus Linguistics*, 9(1), 97–129.

Hasselgård, H. & Johansson, S. (2012). Learner corpora and contrastive interlanguage analysis. In Fanny Meunier, Sylvie De Cock, Gaëtanelle Gilquin & Magali Paquot (Eds.), *A Taste for Corpora: In Honour of Sylviane Granger* (pp. 33–61). Amsterdam & Philadelphia: John Benjamins.

Hyland, K. & Milton, J. (1997). Qualification and certainty in L1 and L2 students' writing. *Journal of Second Language Writing*, 6(2), 183–205.

Laufer, B. & Waldman, T. (2011). Verb-noun collocations in second language writing: A corpus analysis of learners' English. *Language Learning*, 61(2), 6478–6672.

Mukherjee, J. & Gries, S. (2009). Collostructional nativisation in New Englishes. *English World-Wide*, 30(1), 27–51.

Mukherjee, J. & Hoffmann, S. (2006). Describing verb-complementational profiles of New Englishes: A pilot study of Indian Englishes. *English World-Wide*, 27(2), 147–173.

Sankoff, D., & Laberge, S. (1978). Statistical dependence among successive occurrences of a variable in discourse. *Linguistic Variation: Methods and Models*, 119–126.

Schenkein, J. (1980). A taxonomy for repeating action sequences in natural conversation. In Brian Butterworth (Ed.), *Language Production* (Vol. 1, pp. 21–47). London & New York: Academic Press.

Schneider, E. (2007). *Postcolonial Englishes: Varieties Around the World*. Cambridge: Cambridge University Press.

Stefanowitsch, A. & Gries, S. (2003). Collostructions: Investigating the interaction between words and constructions. *International Journal of Corpus Linguistics*, 8(2), 209–243.

Szmrecsanyi, B. (2005). Language users as creatures of habit: A corpus-linguistic analysis of persistence in spoken English. *Corpus Linguistics and Linguistic Theory*, 1(1), 113–150.

Szmrecsanyi, B. (2006). *Morphosyntactic Persistence in Spoken English. A Corpus Study at the Intersection of Variationist Sociolinguistics, Psycholinguistics, and Discourse Analysis*. Berlin & New York: Mouton de Gruyter.

Weiner, E. & Labov, W. (1983). Constraints on the agentless passive. *Journal of Linguistics*, 19(1), 29–58.

8 Pragmatics

Jonathan Culpeper and Claire Hardaker

Introduction

As a field, pragmatics deals with the construction and understanding of meanings in social interaction. This includes implied and inferred meanings, intentional and unintentional meanings, the dynamic and the emergent—in short, with phenomena that leave little overt trace in the text or are even entirely 'invisible'. At first glance, then, pragmatics would seem like a non-starter for a corpus-based approach, since corpus methods and corpus searches, traditionally at least, rely on stable linguistic forms that can be consistently found and readily counted. Despite this apparent problem, the pursuit of 'corpus pragmatics' seems to be gaining momentum, as can be seen with the publication of major volumes and overview papers (e.g. Jucker, Schreier, & Hundt, 2009; Romero-Trillo 2008; Jucker 2013; Taavitsainen et al. 2014).

In this chapter, we show how pragmatic aspects *can* be captured through various corpus methods. Moreover, through this work we produce a preliminary characterisation of the pragmatics of our target data. Although we will comment on variation according to topic, we are particularly interested in highlighting pragmatic variation according to English variety, whether UK English, US English, Indian English, or Philippine English. This focus echoes trends within the field of pragmatics. Since the late 1970s, studies have focused on cross-cultural pragmatics, revealing how pragmatic aspects differ according to culture. Often, cultures were treated as monolithic blocks that correlated with languages. Thus 'German culture' might be compared with 'English culture'. More recently, work has focused on cultural variation within communities constituted by speakers of a particular language, leading to studies of varieties of English or of Spanish, German, and so on. This area has been dubbed 'variational pragmatics' (Schneider & Barron 2008).

In the next section, we briefly overview corpus approaches to pragmatic phenomena. We then structure the remainder of this chapter around three sections focussing on very different types of pragmatic phenomena and, moreover, types that present different problems and solutions for the corpus method: (1) forms conventionally enriched with pragmatic meanings,

(2) metapragmatic comments and labels, and (3) speech acts and speech-act sequences. Each section will begin with brief notes on the pragmatic phenomenon in hand and will then describe the methodological approach before moving on to the analysis.

Corpus Pragmatics: Approaches

Whilst it is true that the bulk of pragmatic meaning is 'invisible', some formal linguistic items are conventionally associated with particular pragmatic meanings. These include

- speech-act verbs (e.g., 'I **order** you to be quiet')
- hedges (e.g., '**Perhaps** you **might** be quiet')
- discourse markers (e.g., '**Well**, you might be quiet')
- politeness markers (e.g., '**Please** be quiet')
- referring expressions (e.g., 'Be quiet please, **darling**')

As can be seen, these are generally lexical expressions or grammatical phenomena, though they need not be restricted to this. For example, a rising intonation is conventionally associated with questioning speech acts (this is discussed further in the analysis section below) and a tentative interpersonal posture. Nevertheless, the association with particular lexicogrammatical phenomena offers a way forward to the corpus linguist. One can search for particular forms and then study their functions and contexts of use, as well as compare the frequencies of particular forms and functions. The leading exponent of this approach is Karin Aijmer, who pursued it in her book on conversational routines in English (1996). There is a danger, however, as not many forms are fully conventionalised for a particular pragmatic function. For example, *could-you* and *can-you* requests are, according to Aijmer (1996), amongst the most frequent means of achieving (typically polite) indirect requests in British English. But a simple search for 'can you X' would be flawed, as many instances are simply genuine questions about ability and thus not pragmatic. The solution is to search for the item and then screen out non-pragmatic cases. What one is left with is a list of forms plus an interpretation of how they are pragmatic.

Metapragmatic comments and labels—comments on and labels for the pragmatics of other people's discourse—can provide insights into people's understandings of pragmatics. Note here that labels are embedded in metapragmatic comments. Thus, *rude*, the label, might be embedded in the comment 'That waiter's a bit rude'. Speech-act verb labels include *[I] order, apologise, warn*, and *suggest*; inferential activities include *imply, infer, hint, innuendo, irony*, and *sarcasm*; and evaluations include *polite, impolite, rude, friendly*, and *considerate*. The basic mechanism for investigating these labels is straightforward: search for the label and then consider aspects of the context. However, how those aspects of context are considered can be made more sophisticated, notably, through the deployment of corpus methods, such as collocations, collocational networks and prosody, keyness, and so on. For example, Culpeper (2011: Chapter 3) combined grammar and collocations, using the program *Sketch Engine*, to explore impoliteness. He addressed the question of 'who is considered rude?' by retrieving the collocates that tend to fill the subject-complement slot in sentences such as the example given earlier in this paragraph. This revealed that public service staff are typically evaluated as rude.

One feature that the two types of pragmatic phenomena introduced earlier have in common is that there is no given list of conventionally pragmatic forms or metapragmatic labels to search on. Typically, researchers conduct qualitative analyses, draw on published accounts, or rely on intuition to devise a list with which to commence. In our analyses, we will suggest some more innovative techniques, drawing on corpus methods.

The final type of pragmatic phenomenon pursued by corpus linguists is perhaps the most challenging, as it is based on function. For example, researchers have pursued speech acts such as requests, threats, promises, and so on (Austin 1962; Searle 1969). Though speech acts may have formal correlates, they are not tied to them, as they are forms of action that encapsulate speaker intentions—they are what the speaker is trying to do. Thus a declarative statement such as 'I'm thirsty' could be performing a request in an appropriate situation (e.g., said to somebody else who is making a cup of tea). Furthermore, researchers are not merely interested in studying speech acts in isolation. They also seek to identify interactional meaning played out in the interaction between utterances (e.g., a request inviting compliance, a question inviting an answer) (cf. the Sinclair and Coulthard 1975 approach to discourse analysis). This involves a further challenge for the corpus linguist, as speech acts need to be aligned over different turns and can be complicated by the fact that linkages between speech acts are not always in consecutive turns. It is not surprising then that corpus approaches here have tended to involve manual annotation, i.e., reading the text, identifying the act, and supplying an appropriate code. Example annotation schemes and discussion of them can be found in, for example, Stiles (1992), Carletta, Dahlbäck, Reithinger, and Walker (1997), Core and Allen (1997), and Leech, Weisser, Wilson, and Grice (1998). The search for automated or semi-automated annotation of speech acts need not, however, be totally abandoned. Martin Weisser and Geoffrey Leech developed SPAACy, a tool that allowed human analysts to annotate speech acts semi-automatically (see Weisser 2003). However, the distinct advantage they had is that they developed it to analyse speech acts in data comprising telephone dialogues between customers purchasing train tickets and operators selling them. In other words, in more fixed registers, speech acts and how they are realized are more predictable.

Analysis

Pragmatically Enriched Forms

As mentioned earlier, the starting point for analysis of conventionalised pragmatic forms is a list of those forms. Rather than derive such a list through preliminary qualitative analyses, as other researchers have done, we decided to proceed by deploying automatic semantic annotation and then examining the contents of the relevant category. Developed at Lancaster University, the UCREL (University Centre for Computer Corpus Research on Language) Semantic Analysis System ('USAS') tool is a semantic annotation program designed for automatic dictionary-based content analysis (see at http://ucrel.lancs.ac.uk/usas/). Not surprisingly, given the complexities, semantic tagging does not achieve a perfect result. It is claimed to achieve an accuracy rate of 91% with present-day English (Rayson 2004). USAS constitutes one of the final stages of processing, once a text is uploaded to the program Wmatrix.

Our first step was to create a file containing all of the Q+A data. We uploaded this into Wmatrix, where it was processed. We then examined the major category 'Language and communication' (Q). Within this category, by far the most densely populated subcategory was 'Speech acts' (Q2.2) with 4,405 occurrences; the next most densely populated subcategory was 'Speech: Communicative' (Q2.1) with 2,970 occurrences. Table 8.1 displays

Table 8.1 Metapragmatic labels in all the Q+A data, as revealed in the USAS category Q2.2

Metapragmatic label	*Frequency*
tell (624), telling (55), tells (36)	715
ask (376), asked (86), askes (1), asking (71), asks (15)	549
question (368), questioned (5), questioning (5), questions (100)	465
answer (273), answered (33), answerer (1), answering (9), answers (102)	418
call (154), called (116), calling (35), calls (16)	321
name (92), named (12), names (16)	120
blame (76), blamed (1), blames (4), blaming (14)	95
advice (60), advices (2), advise (14), advised (5), advises (1)	82
claim (41), claimed (11), claiming (7), claims (21)	80
explain (51), explained (10), explaining (7), explains (5)	73
apologise (15), apologised (1), apologises (3), apologize (36), apologized (1), apologizes (3), apologizing (1)	60
invite (24), invited (18), invites (1), inviting (3)	46
applied (8), applies (6), apply (23), applying (5)	42
suggest (39), suggested (6), suggesting (5), suggests (4)	41
report (22), reported (4), reporting (5), reports (6)	37
complain (22), complained (4), complaining (8), complains (2)	36
demand (18), demanding (5), demands (12)	35
admit (22), admits (2), admitted (7), admitting (3)	34
refuse (14), refused (9), refuses (6), refusing (5)	34
curse (20), cursed (4), cursing (5)	29

the top-20 most frequent items that comprise the category 'Speech acts' in rank order.

In scrutinising the constituents of the category 'speech acts', we need to keep in mind the fact that it is determined by the decisions of previous researchers that particular words are labels for particular speech acts. It is possible that there are some that they missed and, conversely, some that are included but not actually speech acts. Cases in point for the latter are *name*, which in almost all cases is a noun rather than a speech-act verb, and *call*, which is split between the speech act of nomination and the act of making communication with someone (e.g., calling somebody on the telephone). Further, users may employ a verb spelling for a noun, or vice versa (consider *advice* vs. *advise*), or misspell a word (e.g., *apologies* instead of *apologise*). Individually, such instances may be infrequent, but taken as a collective whole, spelling variations and mistakes, autocorrect interference, and so forth can have an important effect on tagging success rates.

Given that our data is characterised by questions and answers, it is not at all a surprise to see speech acts relating to asking questions (*question, ask*) and answering (*answer, tell, advice*) them amongst the most frequent items in Table 3.1. Within our space constraints, we will examine two speech acts that are both reasonably frequent and especially interpersonally sensitive. Ostensibly, *blame*, to use Brown and Levinson's (1987) terminology, is a face-threatening act involving the positive face of the other; *apologise* is a face-threatening act involving the positive face of the self. We say this ostensibly here because the mere usage of a speech-act label does not guarantee a particular speech-act value, although some correlation might reasonably be expected. For example, *apologise* as an imperative is likely to be a directive speech act in the immediate discourse, not an apology, though of course the topic of apologising is raised. Their distribution across the data is displayed in Table 8.2.

It seems from the overall totals in Table 8.2 that blaming (87 occurrences) takes place more often than apologising (54 occurrences). In fact, the gap is much wider than these totals suggest. The figure of 41 for UK_FR apologising is far from well dispersed, since 40 occur in one file, due to a user specifically asking about the act of apologising:

> [UK_FR_10] If you and your husband or wife or partner have been arguing and sniping all day, **who should apologise first?**

If this outlier is excluded, the frequency of apologies drops to 14, and across these, the common theme is that of users directing others to apologise:

> [IN_FR_19] **Apologize to your fiance** and tell him to please wait a while.
> [US_FR_09] yes i would say your a jerk but your buddy would be a bigger jerk to tell her and hurt her **id apologize.**

Table 8.2 Two speech-act verbs: *blame* and *apologize/ise*

	blame	*apologize/ise*
IN_FR	1	2
IN_PG	20	1
IN_SC	3	0
IN Subtotal	**24**	**3**
PH_FR	0	0
PH_PG	7	0
PH_SC	2	0
PH Subtotal	**9**	**0**
UK_FR	4	41
UK_PG	8	3
UK_SC	3	0
UK Subtotal	**15**	**44**
US_FR	4	7
US_PG	5	0
US_SC	30	0
US Subtotal	**39**	**7**
OVERALL TOTAL	87	54

Blaming is a more general activity in the whole dataset. Although the highest subcategory figure of 30 is not well dispersed, as 29 occur in one file, they are represented in every subcategory, except one, namely, PH_FR. In addition, another observation about blaming is that the second highest subcategory number of 20 for IN_PG is reasonably well dispersed: they are spread over nine files. Interestingly, when we look across these 20 examples, we find that a quarter of them (five) involve users talking about *not* assigning blame:

> [IN_PG_12] i **don't blame** them, they have no other source of information.
> [IN_PG_21] We **can't blame** others specially any religion for our national disintegration.
> [IN_PG_23] **i don't want blame** our own people.

Overall, however, the sheer frequency of these kinds of discussions may hint at a tendency amongst the Indian Yahoo! Q+A community to construct the topic of Politics & Government with a greater emphasis on acts of blaming.

Metapragmatic Comments and Labels

In this section, we will focus on items that can be considered 'pragmatic noise', a category that overlaps with the notion of 'primary interjection' and also 'insert'. Culpeper and Kytö (2010) proposed this notion of pragmatic noise to capture items which are pragmatically meaningful noises. More precisely, such items 'do not have related words which are homonyms in other word classes, do not participate in traditional sentence construction, are morphologically simple and have less arbitrary meanings compared with most words' (2010: 199). Culpeper and Kytö (2010) studied elements such as *ah*, *ay*, *alas*, *ha*, *oh*, *um*, *huh*, and *hum*, analysing their functional profiles and how they changed over time. One reason for examining this specific group of pragmatic markers is that they have an obvious connection with speech-like discourse, as indeed does our dialogic Q+A data.

Our methodology for generating a list of pragmatic noise items to examine is similar to that outlined for conventionalised pragmatic forms, except that the relevant USAS category is 'Discourse Bin' (Z4). We scrutinised the contents of this category and selected any items that fit the criteria mentioned in the earlier paragraph. We were careful not to include spelling variants of normal words (e.g., *nah* for *no*), reduced forms (e.g., *gee* for *Jesus*), or parts of longer expressions (e.g., *bah* for 'bah humbug'). The resulting list of pragmatic noise elements in our data is displayed in Table 8.3. Note that we have combined close spelling variants (i.e., they differ by no more than one letter type) when they are also functionally similar.

It should be remembered that the figures in Table 8.3 are raw frequencies; they have not been normalised to take account of the slight differences in quantities of data across the Englishes. Nevertheless, the high number of both tokens and types for the UK data is striking. Clearly, the UK participants construct a more speech-like register. The presence of the *oh* group as the most frequent in Table 8.3 is not surprising. Biber et al. (1999: 1096) and Aijmer (1987) provide evidence for its high frequency in British conversation, the former identifying it as the most frequent 'insert' and the latter as the most frequent interjection. Its strong presence in our data confirms its speech-like qualities. Much the same can be said for the presence of the *um* group in second position (cf. Biber et al. (1999: 1096). *Ha* is a reduplicative form (e.g., 'ha ha ha'), usually representing laughter, and thus does not occur as frequently as the table suggests. Out of these results, we will examine *hey* (47) and *wow* (35) in more detail, both because they are less obvious candidates to be ranked so highly, and because they occur with some frequency, allowing distribution across the Englishes of our data to be glimpsed. Their distribution across the data is displayed in Table 8.4.

Both *hey* and *wow* appear in every subcategory, except one, suggesting that they play a role in the construction of this register as speech-like. *Hey* occurs slightly more frequently in the UK data and is fairly well dispersed in UK_PG (the 11 occurrences being spread over 7 files), but, of course, nothing solid can be drawn from such low numbers. Functionally, however, there may be a difference. The dominant context in the UK data was highly aggressive, as illustrated by these two answers to the same question:

> [UK_PG_07] Hi paul nice to know there is sm1 like you out there stay in touch **hey**? P***k! lol . . .

Table 8.3 Pragmatic noise elements in all the Q+A data, as revealed in the USAS category Z4

Category	*Pragmatic noise element*				*Total frequency (by type)*
	IN	*PH*	*UK*	*US*	
Realisation, surprise, challenge, etc.	oh (13) ooh (1) wow (3)	oh (18) ohh (1) ooh (1) wow (12)	ah (5) aha (1) ahh (3) oh (37) ooh (1) oo (1) wow (11)	ah (1) ahh (1) oh (24) ohh (2) oooh (1) wow (9)	146
Uncertainty, hesitation, mild dissatisfaction, etc.	ahmm (1) emm (1) er (1) eh (2) hm (1) hmm (2) huh (4) umm (2) ummm (1)	hm (1) hmm (4) hmmm (1) huh (2) mmm (1) umm (1) ummm (3) um (2)	hm (1) hmmm (2) huh (2) hum (1) mmm (1) uh (1) um (8) umm (3) ummm (2)	eh (1) er (2) hmm (2) hmmm (3) huh (1) mmmmmm (1) uh (2) uhh (1) um (2) umm (1) ummm (1)	68
Attention seeker, greeting, etc.	hey (11)	hey (7)	hey (16)	hey (13)	47
Laughter, amusement, joy, etc.	ha (4) hah (1) hee (2)	ha (1) hurrah (1)	ha (12) hah (4) hee (4) hoo (2)	ha (8)	39
Disgust, scorn, acknowledgement of slips, expression of pain, etc.	oops (1) pfft (1) sh (1)	blah (6) shucks (1) tch (1) ugh (1) yo (2)	blah (7) boo (1) heck (6) ow (2) ouch (2) sh (3) shucks (1) tch (1) yuck (1)	blah (1) heck (2) ugh (4) whoops (1) yo (1)	47
Total frequency (by language variety)	54	67	146	86	**Grand total: 353**

[UK_PG_07] **HEY** IM AN ENGLISH MAN IM NOT ANGRY OR IGNORANT I KNOW MY PLEASES AND THANK YOUS IT SEEMS THAT YOU HAVE BEEN SPEAKING TO THE WRONG PEOPLE SO FAR WHAT CAN I SAY I CAN ONLY APPOLIGISE FOR THE MISS LEAD ONES THAT HAVE LET US ALL DOWN.

Table 8.4 Two pragmatic noise elements: *hey* and *wow*

	hey	*wow*
IN_FR	7	0
IN_PG	3	2
IN_SC	1	1
IN Subtotal	**11**	**3**
PH_FR	2	5
PH_PG	2	3
PH_SC	3	4
PH Subtotal	**7**	**12**
UK_FR	3	7
UK_PG	11	1
UK_SC	3	3
UK Subtotal	**16**	**11**
US_FR	7	3
US_PG	3	3
US_SC	3	3
US Subtotal	**12**	**9**
OVERALL TOTAL	**46**	**35**

In the next most frequent subcategory, the US data, this kind of context was very rare. Similarly, we find that *wow* is generally infrequent, and whilst it is typically used to indicate a pleasant form of surprise, it is also used across the data to serve an aggressive, sarcastic, or critical function:

> [IN_PG_13] **Wow**, you have incredible mastery of the English language. And to think, such a highly educated question. . . .
> [PH_PG_16] **Wow**. I understand how personal this is to you, but this doesn't show even an attempt at respect for your girlfriend's—your child's mother's—situation, much less objectivity.
> [UK_FR_5] **wow** if you are freaking out over this than you are gonna hate the real harsh world.
> [US_PG_21] **wow!** you're a moron!

One might note that this feature is particularly rare in the Indian data (a mere three occurrences). It would be interesting to see if this were a general feature of Indian English.

The Q+A Speech-Act Sequence

Within speech-act theory (hereon, SAT) (Austin 1962; Searle 1969), questions fall into the category that Leech (1983) termed 'rogatives'. Searle sees them as 'attempts by S [speaker, writer] to get H [hearer, reader] to answer, i.e. to perform a speech act' (1976: 22). In practice, this definition is fairly problematic both theoretically and empirically. In theoretical terms, it is difficult to see how this definition distinguishes questions from other speech acts, such as greetings, invitations, and offers (all of which also are attempts by S to get H to respond). And empirically, this definition is difficult to operationalise, since not all questions seek a speech act in response (consider rhetorical questions or questions used to perform indirect requests). Moreover, the challenge for the corpus linguist is increased by the fact that questions are realised by a fairly wide range of forms, including intonation (consider declarative questions such as 'It's cold today?', said with rising intonation). This does not mean, however, that anything goes. There are typical formal patterns with typical functions. An important issue we will articulate in this section is that the particular mapping between forms and functions both constructs and is constructed by the context of which it is a part.

As a preliminary, let us note the main functional categories of questions. In her corpus-based work on historical courtroom interaction, Archer (2005) identifies three major functions. These included the canonical **question**, which seeks a missing variable, opinion, hypothetical response, etc., as illustrated by the following examples from our data:

> [IN_FR_15] How close you are to your brother/sister? we were 4 . . ., were some close.
> [UK_PG_21] Is Alex Salmond a racist?
> [US_SC_15] If you found $10,000 inside a bag while strolling through the park, would you keep it?

The second is the **request**, which tries to get an action or event to happen, e.g., 'Could you give me this week's pay?' said by an employee to her manager. And the third is the **require**, e.g., 'Can you walk the dog?' said by a parent to his child. Note that the examples for both the latter categories are formally marked as questions, but at a higher, implied level are performing the speech acts of request or requirement. Thus a response to the first example such as 'Yes I could', would answer the literal question, but not in itself constitute compliance with the request. Such indirect request forms are often performed for reasons of politeness. The distinction between requests and requires largely rests on the power relations between the speaker and hearer.

According to Aijmer's (1996) corpus-based work, in British English, the most frequent requestive forms are, in order of frequency, *could you*, *can you*, *would you*, and *will you*, all of which, of course, are literally questions. Throughout our Q+A corpus, we find a few examples of such questions:

> [IN_FR_11] Can you forgive someone who has betrayed you?
> [UK_SC_7] Would you share a lollipop with someone?

However, these examples are clearly not functioning as requests or requires, since these types of pragmatic acts need a context in which (a) H is able to perform the action and (b) there is a *specific* target or targets for that action. In the contexts that accompany these 'questions', the implied speech acts are more like strong assertions (e.g. 'Obviously not').

In addition to Archer's (2005) three general functions, we identified two further functions that characterised our data. The first is **support**, where S seeks comfort, advice, consolation, reassurance, and so forth:

> [IN_FR_5] Hi I want marry my boyfriend. but he already married.?

The second and arguably most interesting from the perspective of this chapter, is **criticism**, where S utilises the question to convey mockery, insult, satire, denigration, and so forth. These questions fall along a cline from fully rhetorical, where they simply utilise the question form to state an opinion, fact, observation, criticism, and so forth (see the following example) through to partly rhetorical, where the user does seem to seek some form of discussion:

> [UK_SC_2] Do you realize that Christmas is the biggest load of sh!t?

When we look across the 265 questions (defined according to Yahoo!) presented in the corpus, approximately 13% (34) are critical. The greatest majority (65%, 22) of these occur in the Politics & Government (PG) category:

> [IN_PG_18] Are majority of Americans fools?
> [PH_PG_4] Why are Republicans such Hypocrites?
> [UK_PG_2] Why do Americans try take all the credit for WW2?
> [US_PG_15] Does Obama laugh himself to sleep thinking about the stupidity of his average supporter?

Meanwhile the Family & Relationships (FR) and Society & Cultures (SC) forums account for 9% (3) and 26% (9) of critical questions, respectively. Indeed, despite Yahoo! Answers being a forum designed for individuals to pose questions and receive answers, around 13% of all questions in the Q+A corpus (34 in total) are not clearly seeking information as their primary goal. When we consider how these 34 critical questions distribute across language varieties, we find that the Philippine subcorpus accounts for the fewest (26%, 9), the Indian and US subcorpora account for a quarter (26%, 9) each, and the UK subcorpus contains a marginal majority of a third (32%, 11). However, it should be emphasised that these numbers are far too small and the datasets too restricted to use as a basis for any serious extrapolations across whole cultures!

Given the presence of this range of non-canonical questions, it is worth considering the types of responses they receive. According to work by Archer (2005), Harris (1984: 14), and Woodbury (1984: 204–205), certain (syntactic) question forms incorporate more or less control (or are conducive towards) certain types of response. For reasons of space, let us consider one question type in one language variety: the grammatical yes/no question in an instance from Philippine English:

> [PH_SC_13] Do you believe that banning certain books from public and school libraries is justified?

This question, which is structured for a 'yes' or 'no' response, receives 13 replies, and whilst they are roughly split between agreement (8) and disagreement (5), no respondent simply writes 'yes' or 'no' and nothing more. Instead, two incorporate *if*-conditionals, three contain *but/however* provisos, three imply their answer (e.g., *I don't think it is good*), and even the five that explicitly provide some form of 'yes' or 'no' (e.g., *yeah*; *absolutely not*) also elaborate their answer far more fully. In reality, whilst the question may be structured to partner with a simple 'yes' or 'no', this type of answer would be largely uninformative to the recipient. Therefore, whilst question *forms* may encourage particular answer forms, the question *function* in this context is to encourage much more, whether in the shape of opinions, anecdotes, debate, humour, and so on.

Conclusion

Superficially, the pursuit of pragmatic phenomena via corpus methods does not seem an auspicious enterprise. We hope to have demonstrated, however, that much can be done. Corpus methods can help us investigate patterns conventionalised for particular pragmatic use, metapragmatic labels, or constellations of pragmatic function and form mappings in particular contexts.

Our Yahoo! Q+A data and its subcategories have specific pragmatic characteristics. We identified the speech act of blaming as a general characteristic of the data. Furthermore, blaming seemed to be especially characteristic of the Indian construction of the subcategory Politics & Government. Pragmatic noise items, especially the *oh* group and the *um* group, were frequent in all subcategories of the data, contributing to the speech-like feel of the register. However, the items *hey* and *wow* displayed notable variation patterns. In the UK data alone, *hey* typically occurred in aggressive contexts. We also noted that *wow* is virtually absent from the Indian data. As far as our analysis of questions is concerned, we suggested that different patterns of form and function mappings would shape and be shaped by the context. In our data, a notable mapping for many syntactically interrogative question types was the expression of critical comment. Such mapping seemed to be particularly characteristic of the Politics & Government subcategory and was characteristic of all regional subcategories, except that of the Philippines.

A general limitation on our analyses is low frequencies. This is partly a consequence of the kinds of units in accounting but also the size of the Q+A data. Nevertheless, we hope to have highlighted tendencies and characteristics that are worthy of further investigation.

References

Aijmer, K. (1987). Oh and ah in English conversation. In W. Meijs (Ed.), *Corpus Linguistics and Beyond. Proceedings of the Seventh International Conference on English Language Research on Computerized Corpora* (pp. 61–86). Amsterdam: Rodopi.

Aijmer, K. (1996). *Conversational Routines in English: Convention and Creativity.* London: Longman.

Archer, D. (2005). *Questions and Answers in the English Courtroom (1640–1760): A Sociopragmatic Analysis.* Amsterdam: John Benjamins.

Austin, J. L. (1962). *How to Do Things with Words.* Oxford: Oxford University Press.

Biber, D., Johansson, S., Leech, G., Conrad, S., & Finegan, E. (1999). *Longman grammar of spoken and written English.* Harlow, UK: Pearson Education.

Biber, D., Johansson, S., Leech, G., Conrad, S. & Finegan, E. (Eds.) (1999). *Longman Grammar of Spoken and Written English.* London: Longman.

Brown, P. & Levinson, S (1987). *Politeness: Some Universals in Language Usage.* Cambridge: Cambridge University Press.

Carletta, J., Dahlbäck, N., Reithinger, N. & Walker, M. (1997). Standards for dialogue coding in natural language processing. *Dagstuhl Seminars.* Technical Report no. 167 (Report from Dagstuhl Seminar Number 9706).

Core, M. & Allen, J. J. B. (1997). Coding dialogs with the DAMSL annotation scheme. *Working Notes of the AAAI Fall Symposium on Communicative Action in Humans and Machines.* Cambridge, MA (November): pp. 28–35.

Culpeper, J. (2011). *Impoliteness: Using Language to Cause Offence.* Cambridge: Cambridge University Press.

Culpeper, J. & Kytö, M. (2010). *Early Modern English Dialogues: Spoken Interaction as Writing.* Cambridge: Cambridge University Press.

Harris, S. (1984). Questions as a mode of control in magistrates' courts. *International Journal of the Sociology of Language,* 49, 5–27.

Jucker, A. H. (2013). Corpus pragmatics. In J.-O. Östman & J. Verschueren (Eds.), *Handbook of Pragmatics* (pp. 1–17). Amsterdam: Benjamins.

Jucker, A. H., Schreier, D. & Hundt, M. (Eds.) (2009). *Corpora: Pragmatics and Discourse.* Papers from the 29th International Conference on English Language Research on Computerized Corpora (ICAME 29). (Language and Computers: Studies in Practical Linguistics 68). Ascona, Switzerland (pp. 14–18). Amsterdam: Rodopi.

Leech, G. N. (1983). *Principles of Pragmatics.* London: Longman.

Leech, G. N., Weisser, M., Wilson, A. & Grice, M. (1998). 'LE-EAGLES-WP4–4. Integrated resources working group. Survey and guidelines for the representation and annotation of dialogue'.

Rayson, P. (2004) *Key domains and MWE extraction using Wmatrix.* Talk at Aston Corpus Summer School 28th July 2009. Aston University, Birmingham.

Romero-Trillo, J. (Ed.) (2008). *Pragmatics and Corpus Linguistics.* Berlin: Mouton de Gruyter.

Schneider, K. P. & Barron, A. (Eds.) (2008). *Variational Pragmatics.* Amsterdam: John Benjamins.

Searle, J. R. (1969). *Speech Acts. An Essay in the Philosophy of Language*. Cambridge: Cambridge University Press.

Searle, J. R. (1976). The classification of illocutionary acts. *Language in Society*, 5, 1–24.

Sinclair, J. M. & Coulthard, M. (1975). *Towards an Analysis of Discourse*. Oxford: Oxford University Press.

Stiles, W. B. (1992). *Describing Talk: A Taxonomy of Verbal Response Modes*. Beverly Hills: Sage.

Taavitsainen, I., Jucker, A. H. & Tuominen, J. (Eds.) (2014). *Diachronic Corpus Pragmatics, Pragmatics & Beyond New Series 243*. Amsterdam: John Benjamins.

Weisser, M. (2003). SPAACy: A Semi-automated tool for annotating dialogue acts. *International Journal of Corpus Linguistics*, 8(1), 63–74.

Woodbury, H. (1984). The strategic use of questions in court. *Semiotica*, 48(3/4), 197–228.

9 Gendered Discourses

Paul Baker

Introduction

Unlike many of the other chapters in this collection, the focus of this chapter was decided in advance of any interaction with the corpus and took the form of a discourse or socially aware analysis rather than linguistics per se. The methodological approach was largely qualitative, mainly involving analysis of (expanded) concordance lines. I was interested in identifying gendered discourses across the four subcorpora and examining whether there were any differences or similarities, although there was no pre-existing hypothesis that I wished to test.

I use a meaning of *discourse* as a 'system of statements which constructs an object' (Parker 1992: 5) or 'ways of seeing the world, often with reference to relations of power' (Sunderland 2004: 6). A gendered discourse is ostensibly a way of seeing the world as it relates to gender. Discourses are not usually stated explicitly but need to be inferred through the ways that particular social groups are represented or through the generalisations and assumptions that are embedded in statements. The following example from file AN7 (an excerpt from fiction) in the British National Corpus indicates a fairly easy to spot gendered discourse:

> 'Is John looking after Margaret and Rose?' John was Laura's husband, Margaret and Rose their two-year-old twins.
>
> 'He offered. But he's so useless with them, typical man! I thought it best I leave them with a neighbour. She'll keep them till I get back'.

The generalising use of 'typical man' indicates that the speaker views all or most men as usually bad at providing childcare. Such a position might imply that women are good at childcare and the stretch of text (which does not appear to be criticised by the narrative voice or any of the other characters in it) references an overarching 'gender differences' discourse where men and women are viewed as being fundamentally different from one another. While gendered discourses can simply be identified in a text, politically committed analysts might want to reflect on the extent that certain discourses are (dis)empowering to particular groups.

I have argued that corpus linguistics is ideally situated for the identification of discourses due to the reliance on large amounts of text which allow the opportunity to make generalisations and identify discourses which are frequently repeated (and thus likely to be powerful, particularly if they go uncontested) and also show cases of less frequent 'minority', 'alternative', or 'resistant' discourses which might not appear in smaller datasets (Baker 2006). In this chapter, I first discuss how the frequencies of various words could contribute towards gendered discourses, leading to a description of how I determined a list of candidate words to subject to concordance searches. This is followed by a description of the 'sets' of gendered discourses uncovered by the analysis while, finally, the discussion attempts to explain and critically evaluate my findings.

Comparing Frequencies

As an initial approach, it was decided to examine frequencies of gendered words in the four subcorpora. This was for two reasons: first to narrow the focus of the study to a smaller set of words to carry out more detailed qualitative analysis on and second to consider whether the frequencies themselves indicated some form of gender-based bias in any of the subcorpora or overall. Potentially, the amount of times that a group is referred to may hint at its relative importance in society, and for many binary pairs, it is often the 'preferred' concept that receives more attention, with the less important/attractive concept being 'backgrounded'. However, this is not always the case, and sometimes a concept may attract more focus because it is problematized in some way, compared to what is seen as a norm. Clearly then, gender frequencies only indicate the beginning of the analysis, which will need to be supplemented with more qualitative approaches.

A number of candidate words which referred to gender were collected via a combination of introspection and reading samples of texts. These words included singular and plural gendered nouns and adjectives (e.g., *woman*, *women, male, males*) as well as gender-marked pronouns (*he*, *his*, *him*) and titles (*Mr*, *Mrs*, *Miss*). The list is not absolute, and one missing category is male and female names. These would have been difficult to automatically identify and count as each name would need to be considered individually.[1] An aim of this chapter was to carry out an economical yet productive analysis which did not reproduce the experience of reading substantial swathes of the corpus. Tables 9.1 and 9.2 indicate the frequencies of the gendered search terms (gathered via WordSmith 5, which was the tool used for the analysis in this chapter).

Using log-likelihood tests to compare the overall frequencies of male versus female terms searched on in the four subcorpora, it was found that there were statistically significant differences for all four subcorpora ($p < 0.0001$). For the India, Philippines, and UK subcorpora, this difference indicated a higher frequency of male terms, but for the US subcorpus, the difference

Table 9.1 Frequencies of gendered terms in the subcorpora

Search term	*India*	*Philippines*	*UK*	*US*	*Total*
man/men	178	136	145	153	612
woman/women	124	100	68	129	421
boy(s)	39	23	28	26	116
girl(s)	83	39	85	134	341
lady/ladies	10	9	20	13	52
gentleman/gentlemen	2	4	11	0	17
husband(s)	51	25	42	25	143
wife/wives	48	15	27	26	116
boyfriend(s)	26	32	19	31	108
girlfriend(s)	5	16	16	30	67
male(s)	13	5	5	26	49
female(s)	7	11	5	15	38
he	512	872	696	499	2579
she	129	294	232	472	1127
his	256	434	208	223	1121
him(self)	434	501	420	289	1644
her(self)	179	513	276	704	1672
hers	2	1	0	2	5
Mr	10	13	4	6	33
Mrs	1	1	2	0	4
Miss	1	1	1	8	11
Ms	0	2	0	0	2

Table 9.2 Summary of frequencies of gendered terms in the subcorpora

Search term	*India*	*Philippines*	*UK*	*US*	*Total*
Female terms	589	1002	732	1533	3856
Male terms	1521	2045	1578	1278	6422

indicated a higher frequency for female terms. Overall, the entire corpus showed a statistically significant difference for more male terms, even taking into account the US subcorpus. Looking back to Table 9.1, the difference in the US subcorpus is mainly due to the much higher frequency of *her(self)*, compared to *him(self)*, as well as higher usage of *she* and lower usage of *he* compared to the other subcorpora. Generally, across the whole corpus, the male terms were more frequent than the female terms, with exceptions being for the pairs *boy/girl* and *lady/gentleman*. Closer inspection of *girl* via concordances indicated that this was due to a higher frequency of cases where *girl* was used to refer to an adult female. This could be interpreted as a form of sexism, although focus group research by Schwarz (2006) has indicated that women sometimes view *girl-as-adult* as positive, suggesting a 'young inside' discourse. The term *lady* has been viewed as 'trivialising' or 'pseudo-polite' (Holmes, Sigley, & Terraschke, 2002: 195), so the notably higher frequencies of these two female terms (*girl* and *lady*) suggest ways in which women may be positioned in potentially patronising ways, rather than suggesting that women are discussed more in the corpus.

In terms of frequency then, there is some evidence for 'male bias', at least in three of the subcorpora. Similar patterns have been found in analysis of larger reference corpora (e.g., Holmes, Sigley, & Terraschke, 2002), as well as in studies of speech e.g., Coates (2002: 121–122) has noted that women tend to be absent from male narratives which 'do important ideological work, maintaining a discourse position where men are all-important and women are invisible'. However, frequencies may indicate some form of male bias, but they do not tell us much more than that. As suggested earlier, males may be discussed more because they are seen as problematic in some way. The following section thus focusses on a more qualitative approach based on concordance line analysis to find gendered discourses.

Identifying Gendered Discourses

While searching for the frequencies in Table 9.1, it was noted that sometimes the search terms appeared within the questions and subsequently there were some sections of the corpus data which contained more narrowly dispersed references to gender. A question which was about some aspect of gender often referenced at least one gendered discourse and then would prompt others to respond, either by strengthening the discourse through repetition or by providing a counter-discourse. For this reason, it is worth noting the questions which contained one or more references to the search terms in Table 9.1. This was achieved by searching on the terms again but specifying in the tags option in WordSmith that any stretches of text marked as occurring within an answer tag, from <a> to </a> should be ignored. As the pronouns resulted in numerous questions which were not usually related to gender issues, they were not included in this search. The list of questions elicited is shown in Table 9.3.

Many of these questions tend to refer to problems involving heterosexual relationships, and, indeed, when gender was discussed in the corpora, it was often within this context, with gendered discourses often being referenced as a way of explaining a problem or providing an answer to it. Some of the questions themselves could be interpreted as containing gendered discourses. For example, in the US subcorpus, the question 'Why do women blame the whole male species, when THEY keep choosing the wrong men?' contains several assumptions: that women choose men, that women choose the wrong men, and that women blame men when they get it wrong. The question could be interpreted as accessing a somewhat negative discourse that women are poor judges of character and assign blame unfairly for their own mistakes. On the other hand, a question like 'Girls don't approach me, does it mean i'm ugly?' could imply a gendered discourse based on the assumption that girls are only interested in physically attractive men.

Table 9.3 Questions containing noun and adjective search terms

India	Why do small children have to be victims of horrible crimes commited by men? I simply cannot find a answer? Are the Americans found of raping there women coz they keep raping all the woman which ever country? Why do some men hide their true feelings from girls? Why do girls got more attracted to bad boys than good guys? What should a wife do when she comes to know that her husband chats with a woman every night on internet? Whats important for a woman—beauty or brains? Hw can one know what's in the mind of girl and hw to get them.? My wife has gone to her mothers, what should I be doing alone? How do I tell my boyfriend we should move up a step? My husband abuses me and beats me up and then acts innocent and apologises at times also threatens divorce? Hi I want marry my boyfriend. but he already married.?
Philippines	Could the virginity of a none virgin girl be back if she have no sex contact in a couple of months? Been with a girl for so long and then u feel . . .? Is it ok for a man to hit you? Why is it hard to find a good man? My girlfriend is pregnant and wants an abortion what should I do? What should I do about my boyfriend's debt? Is my husband cheating on me??? My boyfriend's parents don't like me because of my background.? Is it ok to break up with my boyfriend by SMS? How Do I Forgive my Husband for a Six Month Affair with a Prostitute?
UK	Is it true that guys look at personality more than physical features in a girl? Why don't girls talk to me? I know women complain that men dont listen to them, but do you really know why that is??? Ladies, would you be happy? for a gent to open a door for you, or would you be offended? Boyfriend just smashed up chair!!! scared :(? I am a 30yr old mother of two and I am dating a 20yr old male is it wrong?
US	Why do women blame the whole male species, when THEY keep choosing the wrong men? Im a Taurus woman who likes leo men. Is this a bad match? Girls don't approach me, does it mean i'm ugly? My parents hate white girls? (I'm 14)? Guys i really don't know how to make a girl like me seriously im a loser.? How do I tell a girl I like her? What would you do if your husband lies about going to strip clubs?

However, this is a more specific case based around the experiences of a single person, so the 'warrant' for identifying a gendered discourse may be weaker. Finally, a similar question 'Why don't girls talk to me?' appears less likely to contain a gendered discourse as it is both based around the experiences of a single person and unspecific in terms of assumptions about gender. However, even questions like the latter one are potentially rich sources for eliciting gendered discourses as they often require a relevant answer to relate to gendered relationships in some way.

It is notable that several of the questions in Table 9.3 reference men who are violent or are involved in sexual infidelities, while another set involve people who want to get into relationships with the opposite sex (usually men wanting to attract women). Cumulatively, these question sets might also reference discourses which construct men more actively (as violent or as pursuers of women). Bearing in mind that these questions may help to set a particular tone and influence responses, it was decided to examine gendered discourses across all the text (not just the questions) in the four subcorpora.

Having examined concordance lines of different search terms, it was found that the most 'productive' search terms for identifying gendered discourses were plural gendered nouns. These terms were reasonably frequent and produced fewer unwanted concordance lines. Plural nouns were often used when making generalising statements which tended to translate to observable gendered discourses. As a result of having conducted numerous concordance searches, another term, a new term, *guys*, emerged as potentially useful. Sometimes *guys* referred to people in general or even inanimate objects, e.g., 'There is a lot that is hidden from the consumer by way of changing the names of certain "bad guys" in our diets', but there were other cases where *guys* referred to males, so this term was added to the list. Ultimately the following terms were searched on: *men*, *women*, *girls*, *boys*, *guys*, *gentlemen*, and *ladies*. Table 9.4 shows their frequencies across the four subcorpora.

For each subcorpus, separate concordance searches were carried out for the seven search terms and lines were analysed to identify those which referenced gendered discourses. In almost all cases, concordance lines needed to be expanded to examine at least entire paragraphs of text. Instances where the same answer used multiple search terms to refer to a single gendered discourse were considered as a single case. The following example contains both *men* and *women*, so they are considered as working in tandem: 'I know

Table 9.4 Frequencies of search terms used to identify gendered discourses

Search term	*India*	*Philippines*	*UK*	*US*	*Total*
men	71	27	57	71	226
women	70	34	41	72	217
boys	20	7	9	5	41
girls	28	11	23	56	118
guys	19	41	51	44	155
ladies	4	1	11	4	20
gentlemen	1	1	5	0	7
Total	213	122	197	252	784

women complain that men dont listen to them, but do you really know why that is???' Cases which referenced two or more gendered discourses were categorised as such.

Cases were saved in a separate file, and those which referenced similar or related discourses were grouped together. Broadly speaking, four 'sets' of gendered discourses (with accompanying resistant discourses in some cases) were uncovered through the concordance analysis. I refer to these as 'sets' because within each one a range of stances can be taken up along a continuum. The sets were labelled as follows: Mars and Venus, Male Chivalry, Sexual Standards, and Women's Equality. The first three discourses referenced an overarching Gender Differences discourse in different ways, while a fifth discourse which was resistant to Gender Differences (Gender Similarities/Diversity) was also found. These are described in more detail in the following sections.

Mars and Venus

This discourse set is named after the popular relationship advice book *Men Are from Mars, Women Are from Venus* by John Gray (1992). It purports that the sexes possess different qualities. More specifically, men are viewed as the stronger sex being physically and emotionally tough, dominant, controlling, and action oriented. This can result in them appearing unemotional or inexpressive (1). As an extreme realisation of this discourse, they can be constructed as violent (2). On the other hand, women are viewed as softer (3), they are more emotionally expressive and talkative, which can be viewed as excessive (4). Also, they are constructed as somewhat irrational, making bad or inconsistent decisions (5).

There were resistant discourses to Mars and Venus, whereby it was claimed that men are soft underneath (6) but society pressurises then to be macho (7) and 'real' men are not violent (8).

1) Men aren't into the whole "This is how I feel inside" stuff. And they do express it, just differently. (India)
2) Humans are generally violent people as a whole- or at least men are. (India)
3) i think this is because women are more delicate and feminine and they need to live their life to the full . . . (Philippines)
4) Women need to have a gossip line, 1–800–2GOSSIP, so they can just call that telephone number and tell them about all the bullshi.t that I don't give a fuc.k about. (UK)
5) Some 'women' do this and they are the ones that need to wakeup and stop making the same mistakes and accept that they are at fault. (US)
6) a little unknown fact, that these bad boys that act all tough on the streets and in front of their friends once they are at home with their women they are teddy bears (India)

7) allot of them just think its not macho 2be all lovey dovey with a girl . . . (India)
8) REAL men do NOT put their hands on a woman like this (India)

Male Chivalry

Related to Mars and Venus, this discourse set addresses the issue of whether men should treat women in a 'chivalrous' manner, such as buying them dinner or presents, holding doors open for them, or flattering them. This discourse holds that Male Chivalry is good and that women enjoy this sort of male attention (9–11). There is an 'instructional' aspect to this discourse as shown in examples (9) and (11) where answerers advise male questioners on how to behave in order to attract a woman.

One aspect of this discourse was that men are not as chivalrous as they used to be (12), which is seen as a shame. No 'resistant' discourses to Male Chivalry were found in the corpora.

9) If she is cold or something wrap it around her shoulders or if you guys are outside or walking somewhere wrap it around her before she puts her jacket on. (Philippines)
10) I think it's absurd that some women find it patronizing and offensive, because it's really just demonstrating the guy's respect and politeness toward her. (UK)
11) Next learn to flatter girls. Girls love flattery. (US)
12) In a world where the cliché "chivalry is dead" is pretty much true, it's so nice and usually catches a woman off guard to find a man who still believes in doing the little things like that to show he's a gentleman. Opening doors, car doors, etc. seem to be things men dont often think or care about anymore. (UK)

Sexual Standards

This discourse set presents different and somewhat hypocritical standards of behaviour for men and women, viewing men as having a strong sexual drive (13–14). As a complement, women are viewed as not being 'sex driven' (14–15), while descriptions of female sexuality sometimes appear to be more strongly 'policed' in the corpora. For example, in (16) a girl being overly friendly results in her getting 'herself a stalker'. Use of the reflexive pronoun *herself* appears to assign agency and thus blame to the hypothetical girl rather than this being the fault of male misinterpretation. In (17), a woman who gives her telephone number to men is exaggeratedly labelled a *whore*. This discourse was challenged in a range of ways: for example, in (18) the questioner seems to imply that sexual attraction is important to girls, indicating a less clear-cut division between the sexes. A further realisation of this discourse constructs men as sexually misbehaving but judges them negatively

(19). Even though this case does not appear to 'excuse' male behaviour as natural in the same way that cases (13) and (14) do, it still constructs *all* men as unfaithful. Similarly, (20) explicitly addresses the male double standard, although the use of the generalising term *men* with no qualifiers or exceptions implies that it is all men who hold the double standard.

13) men love to look at naked woman, just one of the bad things men have to bear the burden of, we love naked woman, and the beautiful bodies that god gave them. (US)
14) For men everything is sex. For women, it is their life. (India)
15) The thing is you have to realise; most girls aren't sex driven! (UK)
16) Of course there are some people that can take it too far to the point where it can get out of hand, feelings are hurt & some guys feel if the girl is being so overly friendly she gets herself a stalker. (Philippines)
17) and what kind of whores are handing out their # to guys they dont even know?! (US)
18) Must it mean I am bad looking if girls don't approach. (US)
19) They are all the same cheating bas*****. (US)
20) men think they can kiss other girls and it doesn't count as cheating, but if their girl kisses another man it is very much considered cheating. (US)

Women's Equality

This discourse set views women's equality movements or developments in societies that are designed to empower or give choices to women as a desirable state of affairs (21). The discourse also points to cases where women still do not have equality, or have not had it in the past, for example, citing the Bible (22) or the 1800s (23). Examples were sometimes given to indicate that the situation is improving for women and moving towards a more extreme realisation of the discourse some writers appeared to assert that equality was now achieved (24–25). A counter-discourse, however, indicated that men are now victims in society (26) and that feminism is actually a belief in female superiority (27), indicating a potential backlash against gender equality movements (although (27) also states that male 'chauvanism' exists).

21) Women should have the right to choose. (US)
22) You mean like the laws prohibiting women from voting, which were also backed up with the Bible? (Philippines)
23) it is never okay were in 2009 where abuse is not tolerated, not the 1800s where men can get drunk and slap their family around. (Philippines)
24) They are not yet very aware of the social conditions which show how much women have progressed. They are no longer inferior or say less significant compared to men. (India)

25) I dont think gender discrimination is the same as before. Most females nowadays earn the same as men do for similar positions in India. (India)
26) Women are given more concessions in ITax compared to Men. (India)
27) It's feminista dogma talking. Perhaps if more women believed in equality as opposed to feminist superiority (just as more men need to get away from male chauvanism), then we wouldn't have these problems. (US)

Gender Similarity/Diversity

While the first three discourses all access a higher-order 'gender differences' discourse, there were traces of a resistant discourse where people implied or argued more explicitly that male and female behaviour (28), attraction (29), or preferences (30) are similar. Both (29) and (30) realise this discourse by using the phrase *the same* when making comparisons between the sexes.

As a related aspect of this discourse, people claimed that there were differences among women (31). I have included (32) as a weaker manifestation of this discourse due to the claim that there are 'two types of men' as opposed to statements which imply men are all the same.

28) It isn't just men who commit these acts of abuse. (India)
29) Most guys are attracted to good looks until they get to know a girl. Then personality, character, and intelligence become more important. I assume it's the same for most girls whether they are conscious of it or not. (UK)
30) Girls like the same things guys like. (US)
31) you cant really know whats in the 'mind' of a girl mainly because all girls are different. (India)
32) Two kinds of men and he's not the one you want. (Philippines)

Discussion

Before discussing the results, I draw attention to an unexpected finding that emerged from the analysis; that is, the way that users of the forum indicated awareness of potential for offence or censorship of taboo language and how 'orthographic workarounds' were utilised to avoid this. Example (4) puts a period inside the words *bullshit* and *fuck*, while (26) replaces the last five letters of *bastards* with asterisks. While this practice does not indicate much directly about gendered discourses, it does show how a qualitative analysis can help to highlight less frequent practices, and it would be interesting to see if this phenomenon was discussed in any other chapters.

Moving on, Table 9.5 shows the frequencies of each discourse set (and their counter-discourse where relevant) across each subcorpus.

Overall, the most frequently cited discourse is Mars and Venus (89 times), and while there are 11 cases where it is countered, this never happens in the

Table 9.5 Frequencies of gendered discourses across the four subcorpora

Discourse	*India*	*Philippines*	*UK*	*US*	*Total*
Mars and Venus	20	13	24	32	89
Mars and Venus (counter)	5	0	6	0	11
Male Chivalry	0	3	15	5	23
Sexual Standards	9	3	15	14	41
Sexual Standards (counter)	1	0	0	1	2
Women's Equality	13	9	0	5	27
Women's Equality (counter)	4	0	0	2	6
Gender Similarity/Diversity	8	1	4	10	23

Philippine and US data. The discourse around Male Chivalry is never countered and is most common in the UK data (although this could be a result of this discourse being seeded by a specific question). The Sexual Standards discourse is found in all four subcorpora, and it is rarely countered. The discourse of Women's Equality was not found in the UK data at all. Finally, the overarching counter-discourse relating to Gender Similarity/Diversity is most common in the US and India.

How can these results be explained? First, the frequencies are relatively low, so caution must be taken in assuming we can generalise, particularly as discourses seem to have been influenced by specific questions asked. An outstanding feature of Table 9.5 is the lack of reference to Gender Equality discourses in the UK subcorpus or the Chivalry discourse in the Indian subcorpus. The Global Gender Gap index (Hausmann 2013) is an annual measure of the gap between men and women in terms of economic participation and opportunity, educational attainment, health and survival, and political empowerment. In its 2013 comparison of 136 countries, the four countries ranked as follows: Philippines (fifth), UK (eighteenth), US (twenty-third), and India (one hundred and first). The position of the UK does not readily explain the lack of reference to the Women's Equality discourse, and as a British native, I could postulate a weak hypothesis that perhaps the reason is due to a general assumption that in many areas, gender equality has either been 'achieved' or is at least being addressed, and it may therefore not be seen as a pressing issue by British forum contributors. However, another possible reason could be due to stigma being placed on the concept of feminism. Jaworska and Krishnamurthy (2010), who analysed representations of feminism in large British and German reference corpora, found that it was largely viewed as a thing of the past, associated with radicalism, militantism, and leftist ideology. This may suggest that some British contributors might want to avoid referencing a discourse that might mean they are labelled as 'feminists'.

India does not fare well in terms of the Gender Gap rankings, and I leave it up to readers to infer how this relates to the lack of the Chivalry discourse.

However, I would more strongly hypothesise that the distributions are due to small datasets and would not necessarily be replicated if the corpus was collected again using similar sampling techniques. I am thus reluctant to make pronouncements about discourses (or lack of them) in specific subcorpora and how this relates to the related countries or cultures.

Where I am more confident is in noting *similarities* across the four subcorpora. Mars and Venus is the most common discourse throughout, and the idea that men and women are fundamentally different does appear to be a dominant global discourse (although contributors in all four subcorpora countered it to different degrees). Men were generally constructed as powerful and privileged, and it could be argued that the Chivalry discourse indicates support of Mars and Venus, as it positions women as grateful recipients of 'gentlemanly' attention. I would suggest that the Chivalry discourse is subtly disempowering due to its adherence to unequal gender roles and also the potential to create expectations, e.g., if men are chivalrous, what should they get from women in return? Similarly, the Sexual Standards discourse also indicates a difference between the sexes, where males are seen as more driven by sex, to the point of being unfaithful in relationships. While this discourse was oriented via a wider continuum of stances (e.g., those which seemed accepting vs. those which displayed anger), little effort seems to have been made to criticise the underpinning belief that males have high sex drives that they don't seem able to control. Infidelity surveys tend to give a range of results with regard to sex differences (e.g., Blow and Hartnett (2005) Lalasz & Weigel 2011), although none of them indicate extreme sex differences in infidelity rates. It could be argued that a discourse which constructs men as having uncontrollable sex drives will create expectations about typical male behaviour and have the potential to be self-fulfilling. Additionally, the accompanying policing of female sexuality around this discourse makes it particularly problematic from a gender equality perspective.

The Women's Equality discourse and the Gender Similarities/Diversity discourses were more empowering, although less frequently expressed. Of all the discourses, Women's Equality was the one most likely to be countered, with some contributors claiming that women actually were more advantaged in society than men. The analysis thus indicates the presence of somewhat stereotyping and limiting gendered discourses—despite the appearance of more critical counter-discourses, the key way we perceive gender is still through a lens of difference.

Postscript

Having written my chapter, I wasn't expecting many of the other chapters to be very similar to it due to its relatively narrow focus on gender and also due to the qualitative way in which I carried out the analysis around a small set of terms. Despite this, although the corpus isn't large, I found it notable that the examples I quoted from it tended not to appear very often in other chapters, and I sometimes felt that when I read the other chapters that the other authors were analysing a completely different corpus.

I was interested in whether any of the corpus-driven approaches in the first few chapters would have picked up on the finding that the American subcorpus used more female pronouns than the others, something which I noted was statistically significant. Amanda Potts's chapter looked at key semantic tags (which also categorised grammatical features such as pronouns), and she noted in a table that the UK data used more pronouns, but her analysis focussed on other features such as food and impoliteness. Her US comparison did not identify any form of pronouns as key (see Table 4.5), but she only considered the five most key categories which highlighted other aspects of the corpus as being more salient. Tony McEnery's chapter had *her* as a keyword for the American data (see Table 2.1). This was reassuring, as my analysis also noted that *her(self)* was largely responsible for the high number of female terms in the US corpus, compared to the others. However, Tony did not focus on that pronoun, although he had over 100 keywords to account for and, like Amanda, chose to look at other aspects. While I had not expected to find any major differences between the four subcorpora in terms of frequency of male and female terms, I think I had a 'lucky' hit in terms of uncovering something which a corpus-driven approach identified as a keyword.

It is notable that Vaclav Brezina's analysis of collocational networks identified *love* as a particularly salient concept across all four subcorpora, and I had noted in my chapter that the type of questions set were often related to relationship problems, so this finding could be seen as complementary to Vaclav's identification of *love*. The other chapter I viewed with interest was Erez Levon's. I wondered whether a qualitative analysis of a sample of the questions would also produce something to say about gender. However, the direction that the qualitative analysis took tended to focus more on question types and thus had more in common with Jonathan Culpeper and Claire Hardaker's chapter on pragmatic aspects.

Finally, it was reassuring to see that Jesse Egbert had also noted the use of *** to mask an expletive, as my own analysis had identified something similar. This was a feature which had little bearing on my research focus, although it was rightly noted as an aspect relating to readability in Jesse's chapter.

Note

1 The grammatically tagged version of the corpus indicated that 5,986 words had been tagged as NP1 (proper noun), so all of these would need to be analysed by hand to identify male and female names.

References

Baker, P. (2006). *Using Corpora for Discourse Analysis*. London: Continuum.

Blow, A. J. & Hartnett, K. (2005). Infidelity in Committed Relationships II: A Substantive Review. *Journal of Marital and Family Therapy*, 31, 217–233.

Coates, J. (2002) *Men Talk*. Oxford: Blackwell.
Gray, J. (1992). *Men Are from Mars, Women Are from Venus: A Practical Guide for Improving Communication and Getting What You Want in Your Relationships*. New York: HarperCollins.
Hausmann, R., Tyson, L., Bekhouche, Y. & Zahidi, S. (2013). *The Global Gender Gap Report 2013*. Switzerland: World Economic Forum.
Holmes, J., Sigley, R. & Terraschke, A. (2002). From chairman to chairwoman to chairperson: Exploring the move from sexist usages to gender neutrality. In P. Peters, P. Collins & A. Smith (Eds.), *Comparative Studies in Australian and New Zealand English: Grammar and Beyond* (pp. 181–202). Amsterdam: John Benjamins.
Jaworska, S. & Krishnamurthy, R. (2010). *On the F-Word: A Corpus-Based Analysis of the Media Representation of Feminism in English and German Newspapers, 1990–2009*. Paper given at CADAAD 2010.
Lalasz, C. B. & Weigel, D. J. (2011). Understanding the relationship between gender and extradyadic relations: The mediating role of sensation seeking on intentions to engage in sexual infidelity. *Personality and Individual Differences*, 50(7), 1079–1083.
Parker, I. (1992). *Discourse Dynamics: Critical Analysis for Social and Individual Psychology*. London: Routledge.
Schwarz, J. (2006). *'Non-sexist Language' at the Beginning of the 21st Century: Interpretative Repertoires and Evaluation in the Metalinguistic Accounts of Focus Group Participants Representing Differences in Age and Academic Discipline*. PhD thesis. Lancaster University.
Sunderland, J. (2004). *Gendered Discourses*. London: Palgrave.

10 Qualitative Analysis of Stance

Erez Levon

Introduction

One of the principal findings of research on talk-in-interaction is that speakers design their utterances to perform specific social actions (Searle 1969; Atkinson & Heritage 1984; Levinson 2013). These actions, and the forms with which they are accomplished, do not arise haphazardly, but are instead sequentially organised in response to the speech of others and in keeping with the norms of particular speech events and activities (e.g., Labov 1971; Hymes 1974; Jefferson 1978; Schegloff 1982; Sacks 1987; Finegan & Biber 1994). In this chapter, I apply this basic precept to the analysis of a corpus of responses in online question-and-answer (Q+A) forums across three different topics (Family & Relationships, Politics & Government, and Society & Culture) and four world varieties of English (India, the Philippines, the UK, and the US). Like the other chapters in this volume, my central research question is how language use in these responses differs across topics and varieties. I approach this question through a close qualitative analysis of a small subset of the Q+A response corpus. The subset consists of 12 'texts'—one per topic for each of the four varieties—made up of the initial question posed and all of the responses provided. The texts themselves were automatically extracted from a larger corpus using ProtAnt, a tool that identifies the most (lexically) 'typical' text in a corpus by identifying texts that contain the most keywords when compared to a reference corpus[1] (Anthony & Baker 2015). Table 10.1 lists the files that were identified as most typical in this way. Thus while the subcorpus I analyse in the following section is admittedly rather small (a total of 15,140 words with a mean value of 1,261.7 words per text), it is in a sense representative of the larger corpus from which it is drawn. The benefit of focusing on a smaller subcorpus is that doing so enables a detailed examination of certain aspects of linguistic form and content that would be difficult to explore in a larger sample. That said, it is nevertheless important to highlight that the findings to be discussed are based on a restricted empirical set, and it is therefore necessary to exercise caution when attempting to generalise from any patterns identified.

Table 10.1 Files identified as most typical using ProtAnt

	Family & Relationships	*Politics & Government*	*Society & Culture*
India	06	06	07
Philippines	17	06	05
UK	14	17	13
US	12	01	03

I begin in the next section with a brief introduction to my theoretical and methodological approach, which draws on insights gleaned both from the literature on questions (and responses) in conversation analysis (Enfield, Stivers, & Levinson 2010; Stivers & Enfield 2010) and from work on propositional and interactional stance-taking in discourse (Agha 2007; Lempert 2008, 2009; Damari 2010). While research in these areas has focused primarily on spoken interaction, I follow Jaworski and Thurlow (2009) in arguing that the ideas developed there are equally applicable to the study of written discourse (see also Baker & Levon 2015, 2016), particularly for interactive genres such as online Q+A forums. I then turn in the next section to a consideration of the responses observed in the subcorpus across topic categories before concluding with a very brief discussion of more general patterns that emerge across varieties.

Responses as Social Actions

The first step in analysing any pattern of variation in language use is to identify the specific type of language in question (e.g., Goffman 1974, 1981). In the current study, we are dealing with a form of computer-mediated communication that appears in a public forum (i.e., produced for an audience personally unknown to participants) and written in a generally informal style. Each of these characteristics—mode, genre, audience, register, style—could be a subject of enquiry in and of itself. In this chapter, however, I focus on the type of speech *activity* shared by all of the texts in the corpus: namely, that of question-response sequences.

Questions are a ubiquitous form of speech activity (Steensig & Drew 2008; Enfield, Stivers & Levinson 2010). From a functional perspective, the prototypical goal of a question is the elicitation of information unknown to a speaker from a knowing respondent (Konig & Siemund 2007). So when a speaker asks 'What time is it?' or 'Have you ever been to Paris?', the illocutionary force of the question is a request for information and the conversationally preferred response is an answer (i.e., the provision of the requested information; Schegloff 1968; Stivers & Robinson 2006). Yet research has demonstrated that in informal interaction, information-seeking questions make up only a minority of the total questions observed (e.g., Stivers 2010).

Other question types identified include other initiations of repair (e.g., *Wasn't it Cambridge, not Oxford?*), assessments (e.g., *Isn't it a beautiful day?*), and rhetorical questions (e.g., *How many times do we have to go through this?*) (see Enfield, Stivers, & Levinson 2010; Stivers & Enfield 2010; Sicoli, Stivers, Enfield, & Levinson 2015 and references cited there). Though all of these examples can be formally coded as 'questions' by virtue of their lexical, morphosyntactic, and/or prosodic content, their primary function is not to seek the provision of new information. Instead, they are used to seek agreement with the relevant propositional content and/or inter-subjective alignment between the questioner and the respondent.

We can simplify this more articulated taxonomy into two broad question-type categories: questions that seek information (what Stivers & Enfield 2010 call 'real' questions) and those that seek agreement and/or alignment (what Sicoli et al. 2015 call 'evaluative' questions). Each of these question types is associated with a distinct preferred response. As already noted, answers are the preferred response to information questions (e.g., Stivers & Robinson 2006), whereas agreement is the preferred response to evaluative questions (e.g., Pomerantz 1984; Sacks 1987). Moreover, there exists a general preference (at least in American English) for agreement to be structurally aligned with the question, such that negative polarity questions, for example, prefer negative responses (Enfield, Stivers & Levinson 2010). Despite these general patterns, it is nevertheless important to note that it is rare for questions to serve a single and unique function. An evaluative question such as 'It's a beautiful day, isn't it?' seeks propositional agreement and/or inter-subjective alignment via a request for information about a respondent's state of mind. Similarly, as Steensig and Drew 2008 note, requests for information often also present respondents with an opportunity to evaluate (and thus position themselves in relation to) propositional content (e.g., Q: *What time is it?* R: *It's already 8 o'clock. We should go*). What this means is that while certain question types more strongly favour evaluative responses than others, all questions offer respondents a potential site for stance-taking. An analysis of variation in question-response sequences therefore also requires a theory of stance.

Du Bois (2007: 163) defines stance as

> a public act by a social actor, achieved dialogically through overt communicative means, of simultaneously evaluating objects, positioning subjects (self and others), and aligning with other objects, with respect to any salient dimension of the sociocultural field.

There are two aspects of Du Bois's definition that are crucial to our discussion here. The first is that stance-taking is an inherently *dialogic* phenomenon. Stances are taken in response to other stances. These prior stances can occur within the same interactional context (e.g., S1: *I don't like apples.* S2:

I don't either; see Du Bois 2007: 159). They can, however, also occur interdiscursively (Lempert 2008), such that a stance taken at a given moment can respond to a stance from an earlier interactional context (e.g., Lempert 2009; Damari 2010) or to a more general calcified stance that circulates in society (e.g., Agha 2007; Bucholtz 2009). The second important aspect of Du Bois's definition is that all acts of stance-taking operate on two interrelated dimensions—what Du Bois calls the *evaluative* dimension and the *alignment* dimension. Evaluations are object focussed. They provide a stance-taker's assessment of a stance object and, hence, communicate the stance-taker's relative orientation to that object. Alignments, in contrast, are subject focussed. They indicate a stance-taker's relative positioning with respect either to other subjects in the current interaction or to those who exist in the sociocultural field more generally. The strength of Du Bois's framework lies in its insistence that the evaluative and alignment dimensions are inextricable. As Du Bois (2007: 163) puts it, 'I evaluate something, and thereby position myself, and thereby align with you'. Returning to the earlier example, when S2 states that she does not like apples either, not only is she orienting herself negatively away from apples (the stance object) or positioning herself as an 'apple hater'. She is also aligning herself with S1 via dialogic stance-taking.

This example illustrates how inter-subjective alignment (what Agha 2007 labels *interactional stance*) can arise from evaluative agreement at the level of propositional content (Agha's *propositional stance*). In other words, the taking of a propositional stance that agrees with the proposition of another simultaneously enacts interactional alignment between the two stance-takers. Content agreement is not, however, the only method available for bridging propositional and interactional stance. Rather, the literature has also highlighted the ability of formal or poetic structure (Jakobson 1960) to fulfil this function. When S2 responds *I don't either* to S1's earlier statement, we have an instance of agreement at the level of propositional content. Yet at the same time, we also find in S2's response a certain amount of lexical overlap and text-metrical parallelism (Silverstein 2004; Lempert 2008) with S1's initial statement. It is argued that the degree of structural *resonance* between stances (what Agha 2007 calls their *fractional congruence*) can also be taken as a measure of emergent alignment/disalignment between the stance-takers themselves. In short, both the content and form of propositional stance participate in the enactment of interactional stance in discourse.

The point about the relationship between propositional and interactional stance is important for the current study because it bears directly on the ways in which language use may vary in question-response sequences. As we saw earlier, information questions generally prefer answers. Yet in providing these answers, respondents also have the opportunity to evaluate the question (and their response), and in so doing, to position themselves in relation to the questioner. Similarly, respondents are able to go beyond the simple (propositional) agreement preferred by evaluative questions and take a variety of propositional and interactional stances in their responses. Question-response sequences of the kind examined here thus offer an ideal setting for examining the interaction between the preference structures associated with particular types of questions and the acts of dialogic stance-taking performed by respondents.

With these analytical tools in hand, the specific research questions of this chapter are

(1) a To what extent do respondents (across topics and varieties) provide preferred responses to the questions posed (i.e., answers for information questions and agreement for evaluative questions)?
b To what extent do respondents (across topics and varieties) use their responses as an opportunity for stance-taking (both propositional and interactional)?

Because the data in question arise from written texts, I operationalise the presence/absence of stance-taking in terms of both message content and certain formal properties of the responses. The first of the formal properties I consider is the use of **overt politeness mechanisms**, particularly tokens of positive politeness and mitigators of (negative) face threats. I examine these as one of the most common (and explicit) means for indicating propositional and interactional stance (e.g., Brown & Levinson 1987). Second, I consider whatever **structural resonance** may exist between responses and questions. As described earlier, patterns of text-metrical parallelism provide respondents with a means to pivot between propositional and interactional stances (Agha 2007; Du Bois 2007; Lempert 2008) and so are crucial to the research questions posed in (1). Interestingly, work in conversation analysis has also argued that structural resonance is a *dispreferred* response to questions and that their use indicates a greater amount of agency on the part of the respondent (Raymond 2003; Stivers & Hayashi 2010). Investigating the prevalence of resonance thus provides a clear mechanism for identifying instances where the desire for stance-taking overrides more general preference structures. Finally, I also consider the use of *inter-textuality* in responses since research on stance-taking (e.g., Lempert 2009; Damari 2010) has shown that it can be used as a means to assert a shared or solidary common ground and so adopt a particular interactional stance (see also Brown & Levinson 1987; Britain 1992).

Variation in Responses by Topic

I begin by examining variation in responses across the three topic categories in the corpus: Family & Relationships, Politics & Government, and Society & Culture. When examining the questions posed in these topic categories in the subcorpus, it emerges that they roughly correspond to the different question types described earlier. The four questions (one for each variety) categorised as Society & Culture, for example, are all predominantly information questions: they seek an answer that provides new, presumably unknown informational content. The Politics & Government questions, in contrast, are more clearly evaluative. They take a stance with respect to a particular political issue and seek responses to the stance taken. Lastly, the Family & Relationships questions fall somewhere in between these two poles. While they all request information, they also have a strong evaluative component and appear to request both information and intersubjective alignment. I cannot comment on whether this correspondence between question-type and topic category holds for the entire corpus from which these data are drawn. Given that the subcorpus under consideration here is arguably representative of 'typical' texts in the larger corpus, this is certainly a possibility and one worth exploring in subsequent research. For our present purposes, however, the distribution of different question types across topic categories allows us to operationalise our examination of variation by topic and to set it within the theory of question-response sequences and stance-taking outlined earlier.

Society & Culture

The four Society & Culture questions in the subcorpus are listed in (2):

(2) a *India*: If tsunamis & earthquakes r by Stan, and God is unable to control Satan—don't u think S is poweful than G?
b *Philippines*: What can God not do? If God is all-powerful or omnipotent, is there a thing that He can not do?
c *US*: What is the "trinity" in the cathlic faith?
d *UK*: Do you wash the handles of your forks? or is washing the pointy bit enough for you?

We see in (2) that of the four questions posed, three relate to religion, and more particularly to Christianity, while the question from the UK forum relates to individual practice in dishwashing. Moreover, the questions from the Indian and Philippine forums not only relate to Christianity, but they assume it to be the shared explanatory framework (or coherence system; Linde 1993) of forum participants. Despite these small differences in specific topic (and as already noted), all four questions primarily seek the provision of new information. As such, the preferred (i.e., 'unmarked') response to these questions would be an answer in a format that structurally agrees with the way the question was posed, though without extensive structural (i.e., text-metrical) overlap (e.g., Stivers & Robinson 2006).

To a greater or lesser degree, this is what we find in the responses of the Philippine and US forums. Philippine responses, in particular, are preferentially 'conforming' in the sense that they are mostly restricted to single-word responses that provide the information requested, as in (3a–b):

(3) a sin.
b Lie.
c Yes, he can not lie.
d He can't lie or break any covenant He makes and he can't sin.

Some responses go beyond this most unmarked form and include certain elements of structural resonance. The response in (3c), for instance, shows a perfect repetition of the questioner's *can not* formulation. Interestingly, the response in (3c) is also the only one in the dataset to first respond to the polar interrogative form of the original question before going on to provide the relevant information. Finally, responses such as (3d), while not perfect replications of lexicogrammatical structure, display a certain amount of resonance with the question and, hence, a relative interactional orientation to the question/questioner (e.g., Agha 2007). This orientation, in both Philippine and US responses, is, however, minimal, and the responses in these varieties are principally characterised by their conformity to normative preference structures.

This is not the case for responses in either the Indian or UK forums. To illustrate, let us first consider the response selected as the 'best answer' in the Indian forum, which is reproduced in (4):

(4) Emm, !!

Where do people get concepts like that from ?!?!
let me answer u with a coupla question :

- Why do u think GOD made Satan ??
- Why did Adam and Eve decend to Earth all the way from heaven ??

chk ur story dude !!
Source(s):
The holy books ! ;)

The response in (4) never explicitly answers the questions posed (*don't you think* S[atan] *is* [more] *powe*[r]*ful than* G[od]*?*). This is not to say that an answer is not provided. It is clear from the response in (4) that the respondent clearly does not think that Satan is more powerful than God. However, the respondent also berates the questioner for having posed the question in the first place. What this means is that while the response conforms to the requirement that information questions receive answers, it is also heavily evaluative and contains elements of both propositional and interactional stance.

The propositional stance expressed is a strongly negative evaluation of the question itself. This stance is encoded in the response via a series of three rhetorical questions (*where do people get concepts like that from ?!?! Why do u think GOD made Satan ?? Why did Adam and Eve de*[s]*cend to Earth all the way from heaven ??*) and a strongly emphatic statement (*chk ur story dude !!*). Rhetorical questions are an effective means for evaluative stance-taking since by not requiring (or even preferring) an answer, they serve to posit the evaluation embedded in the questions as the most common-sense, logical, and 'correct' attitude to adopt. Normally, a negative evaluation of the propositional content of a question (as in (4)) would also imply a negative evaluation of the questioner and hence an inter-subjective disalignment between questioner and respondent. It is therefore interesting to remark how in (4) the respondent goes to some length to mitigate the extent of interpersonal evaluation and so minimises inter-subjective disalignment. We see this, for example, in the use of the direct vocatives 'Emm' (an abbreviation of the questioner's username) and 'dude'. The use of vocatives in this context functions as a solidarity marker, a positive politeness mechanism (e.g., McCarthy & O'Keeffe 2003) that serves to indicate shared group membership between questioner and respondent despite their propositional disagreement. A similar function is performed by the respondent's use of inter-textual references. Even though the response's rhetorical questions negatively evaluate the original question posed, they rely on an assumption of shared background knowledge between respondent and questioner, i.e., a belief that they both are familiar with 'The holy books' and the stories contained therein. Like vocatives, these inter-textual references to shared background knowledge help to highlight the inter-subjective closeness of the questioner and the respondent, in spite of the respondent's negative evaluation of the question.

The response in (4) is typical of the responses in the Indian forum, which are characterised by strong (and mostly negative) propositional evaluations combined with mitigation of any interactional disalignment. Responses in the UK forum, in contrast, tend to emphasise the inter-subjective element and evaluate questioners in addition to the questions themselves. Some representative examples of UK responses are provided in (5):

(5) a The whole thing goes into the sink to wash. Do you lick the plates clean?
b I always wash the whole thing pointy bits and the handle. You mean that there are some people that don't?
c I wash the whole fork! I also wash the bottoms of plates and the outsides of cups.
d No, I let the dog lick them clean.

We can observe quite readily in (5) the extent to which respondents negatively evaluate the questioner just for having asked the question. The responses have a largely sarcastic and/or derisive tone and make assumptions about the overall cleanliness and, by extension, character of the questioner (e.g., *you mean that there are some people that don't?*). This is true despite the fact that the questioner never revealed her/his own practice (i.e., whether s/he washes fork handles in addition to the *pointy bit*). Respondents nevertheless assume the worst about the questioner and demonstrate little to no restraint in uttering explicitly evaluative statements and bald-faced threats (e.g., *do you lick the plates clean?*). Interestingly, many of the UK responses show a high degree of structural resonance, with respondents adopting the same basic lexico-syntactic structure in their responses as appears in the question. This seems to confirm the assertion made by Stivers and Hayashi 2010, mentioned earlier, that text-metrical parallelism allows respondents to assert agency over the questioner. In the case of UK responses, this agency appears to be deployed in the service of (negative) interactional evaluation.

Politics & Government

For Society & Culture questions, I argue that responses in the US and Philippine forums tend to correspond to the preference structure for information questions, while responses in the Indian forum included an additional dimension of propositional stance-taking and in the UK forum one of interactional stance-taking. A roughly similar pattern can be observed in responses to the Politics & Government questions, which were reproduced in (6):

(6) a *India*: Why do the Israelites and Palestines fight?? Why do the Israelites and Palestines fight and for what??

b *Philippines*: Why do you think most Obama and Clinton supporters are so polarized? I don't believe it is as simple as race or gender. I personally believe it's as simple as going with the status quo or choosing not to. I am curious where the bitterness is coming from within the party lines. Do you think this can only hurt the party in the long run?

c *US*: Which Republican presidential nomination candidate benefits from Fred Thompson's drop from the race [additional detail omitted]?

d *UK*: Greggs forced to rename it's Cornish pasties thanks to another EU farce? Because they contain carrots and peas they must be renamed according to the EU as Cornish pasties contain neither says the EU [additional details omitted].

In (6), the questions from the Indian forum and the US forum are primarily information questions (seeking respondents' opinions on the topic), and so I will not deal with them in detail here. Suffice it to say that US responses largely conform to preference structures by providing individuals' views of the matter, while responses in the Indian forums provide both the relevant information and propositional evaluations of the Israeli–Palestinian conflict (e.g., *I think that the whole world is getting weary of their childishness. I know I am*).

The questions posed in the Philippine and UK forums, in contrast, are primarily evaluative in nature—they do not seek information per se, but rather invite respondents to (dis)align themselves with the view presented by the questioner. The questioner in the Philippine forum, for instance, solicits agreement with the assertion that the *bitterness* between Obama and Clinton supporters arises from a desire to 'go with the status quo or choosing not to'. Clearly, none of the respondents can provide a true 'answer' to the question. All they can do is provide responses that position themselves in relation to the original statement and thus align/disalign with the questioner's views. Interestingly, respondents in the Philippine forum largely refuse to engage with this solicitation for propositional and/or interactional alignment. The responses all adopt a fairly neutral tone and tend to express respondents' own political preferences (e.g., *Personally, Bill's time in the whitehouse did it for me. I didn't like Hillary then, and since, she's become even more manipulative and tricky*) rather than a view about the animosity between Obama and Clinton supporters. In other words, respondents in the Philippine forum are generally nonconforming with respect to the preference structures of evaluative questions, choosing instead to simply position themselves in relation to the figures of Hillary Clinton and Barack Obama and not in relation to the actual question asked or the opinions of the questioner.

This is not at all the case for responses in the UK forum (see (6d)). Here the question posed is really not a question at all. It is an evaluative statement characterising a recent European Union ruling as a 'farce'. From the way the question is phrased, it clearly invites agreement with the questioner's evaluation. Responses are pretty much evenly split between agreement and disagreement with the initial evaluation, but what is notable is the extent to which they also embed interactional stance-taking with respect to the question. The following is a selection of responses provided in (7):

(7) a I don't understand why the UK doesn't thumb it's nose at the endless stream of useless EU nonsense.

b [initial statement omitted] Thank God the EU is standing up to crooks who try to sell us fake food—while our government and our Food Standards Agency do nothing about it.

c We Cornish do not think it is a farce [additional statements omitted].

d First World Problems. . .

e Sweat Pea . . . Are "Hamburgers" only made in Hamburg ? Enough said. All the best to you and keep licking your fingers, before they ban that too.

Responses (7a) and (7e) agree with the original question's evaluation of the situation. While (7a) restricts itself to propositional stance-taking on the matter, (7e) goes further and explicitly aligns with 'Sweat Pea' (the questioner's username). The alignment itself is encoded via both the conventional salutation 'all the best to you' and the initial vocative, which, as described earlier, serve to mark in-group membership and solidarity between the respondent and the questioner. Responses (7b–d), in contrast, disagree with the initial sentiment. In (7d), this is accomplished via a quick dismissal of the issue as not worthy of consideration and, by extension, of the questioner as someone who is needlessly troubled by such trivial matters. The responses in (7b–c) do not dismiss the issue as unimportant. Instead, they adopt precisely the opposite viewpoint to that expressed in the original question and label those who hold the questioner's viewpoint as 'crooks'. In (7c), moreover, the respondent adopts the voice of the Cornish community (and a resonant lexeme) to explicitly reject the questioner's assertion of a 'farce'.

Family & Relationships

While the Society & Culture and Politics & Government topics roughly correspond to information and evaluative questions, respectively, Family & Relationship questions (as in (8)) seem to contain properties of both.

(8) a India: what if time comes that u have to choose.. ur life or ur life's happiness?.. 4 example . . . u find out that ur love one doesnt love u anymore.. but u don't want to loose him/her . . . wat will u do to let him/her stay with u?????

b Philippines: I'm in love . . . help? i'm in love with him and he loves me back. but everyone's against our little fairytale . . . should i keep this relationship?? or let it go because of the people around us??

c US: My parents hate white girls? (I'm 14)? [sentences omitted about the questioner's parents' dislike of interracial relationships] 1) Is it possible for me to ask her out on Friday? 2) If she says yes, can I date her with my parents knowing that she's white?

d *UK*: Im agnostic, where do I get married? So my fiance and I are getting married in about 2 years from now (September 2010) and we are both Agnostic-but our families are religious and want the traditional church wedding. Where could we have our wedding so that its very elegant and simple but not at a church.

All of the questions in (8) seek information in the form of advice. They also all, to varying degrees, seek inter-subjective alignment and validation from the questioner. The single exception to this is the question in the UK forum (8d), where the questioner really only appears to be seeking suggestions about possible non-religious venues for a wedding. It is therefore notable, then, that responses to this question contain explicit markers of interactional stance. One response, for example, provides a list of possible ideas for the ceremony and then closes with 'Congrats on your upcoming wedding and I wish you both much happiness and love'. Similarly, though with the opposite valence, another states (in full) 'You're pretty much sh*t out of luck then. Unless you can find a nice building in your area and rent it'. Thus participants in the UK forum insert interactional stance markers in their responses, even though the question itself does not seek them.

The opposite pattern is found in the Philippine forum, where, as before, respondents refrain from effecting interpersonal alignment even though the initial question (8b) seems to seek it out. Instead, they tend to seek further information from the questioner. Responses include statements such as 'Well if people are objecting for a good reason and But why everyone's against our little fairytale you must tell clearly'. In making these statements, respondents are in a sense refusing to content themselves with glib or facile reassurances (though readers may get the impression that that is precisely what the questioner was after) and instead adopt a rational or 'common-sense' approach to the situation. In this way, respondents appear to be more oriented to the information-seeking function of the question, as opposed to its more affective component. The pattern is somewhat the same in responses in the Indian forum, though there is at times an additional layering of an (generally negative) interactional stance. While most respondents offer their own views of whether it is possible/desirable to stay with a partner who no longer wants to be with you, some also make threatening bald-face statements that demean the questioner's stated positioning, including 'Have some self respect! and pfft. say byebyee to girl/boy'. These comments are in keeping with a generally more evaluative tone of responses in the Indian forum and demonstrate a willingness on the part of respondents to engage with both the informational and affective aspects of the question. Responses in the US forum, finally, are also both heavily information-laden and strongly affective. A number of responses make use of explicit solidarity markers, such as 'bro' and 'pal', to encode alignment with the questioner. We also find explicit (propositional and interactional) disalignment (e.g., *You are too young to have a girlfriend, and should be going on group dates ONLY*). What is important, though, is that, as in the Indian forum, US respondents are willing to attend to both the informational and the affective dimensions of the question.

Discussion

Though brief, the preceding discussion provides a flavour of the types of variation we find in question-response sequences across four varieties of English. I focus on the extent to which respondents conform to the normative preference structures for questions and whether they use their responses as an opportunity for propositional and/or interactional stance-taking. On the whole, it is interesting to note that the responses observed are largely in line with predictions drawn from the conversation analysis literature—information questions generally receive answers and evaluative questions generally receive agreement/alignment. What's more, though these patterns have been previously identified primarily on the basis of US and UK English, they also do seem to hold for the other varieties (India and the Philippines) under consideration. That said, however, certain potentially interesting differences, nevertheless, do emerge in the sample. For one, UK respondents are shown to be highly evaluative and to make use of non-mitigated face-threatening statements, even when the questions do not require any evaluative responses at all. This finding contrasts with the commonly accepted claim that the UK is a normatively negative-politeness society (e.g., Jucker 2008) and may perhaps be due to the online mode of communication investigated here, which may perhaps engender a different set of politeness norms than those that exist in face-to-face communication in the UK. Similarly, responses in the Indian forum also contain more (primarily negative) evaluations that we would normally expect, though these are more heavily weighted towards evaluating propositional content (where in the UK forum, evaluations tend to be interactional in nature). The US and Philippine forums, in contrast, tend to adhere most closely to relevant preference structures, though respondents in the Philippine forum show a greater reticence than their US counterparts to engage in evaluative stance-taking at all.

Taken together, these results, therefore, seem to point towards a cultural divide of sorts, with the UK and India displaying the highest degrees of interpersonal evaluation and interpersonal disalignment, while the US and the Philippines are more preferentially conforming in their responses and, when evaluation is called for, tend to be more positive and focused on alignment. Whether this binary division between the UK and India, on one hand, and the US and the Philippines, on the other, is due to shared sociolinguistic history or broader cultural norms would need to be investigated in a larger and more diverse sample of texts. Nevertheless, the results presented here provide evidence of an indicative pattern that may be worthy of further research. Yet whether or not this pattern is ultimately shown to be robust, I hope to have illustrated in this chapter how concepts such as preference structure and stance-taking can help us to undertake comparative qualitative examinations of variation in language use. While in the current example I apply these tools to the study of online question-response sequences, they are clearly available for use on a wide variety of texts and can help us to pinpoint how conventional norms of language use interact with individuals' desires to position both self and others in discourse.

Note

1 The reference corpus was created by using a matched set of files in each case. For example, the Indian Family & Relationships files were compared against a reference corpus consisting of all the F&R files from the other three countries.

References

Agha, A. (2007). *Language and Social Relations.* Cambridge: Cambridge University Press.

Anthony, L. & Baker, P. (2015). ProtAnt: A tool for analysing the prototypicality of texts. *International Journal of Corpus Linguistics*, 20, 273–293.

Atkinson, J. M. & Heritage, J. (Eds.) (1984). *Structures of Social Action.* Cambridge: Cambridge University Press.

Baker, P. & Levon, E. (2015). Picking the right cherries? A comparison of corpus and qualitative analyses of news articles about masculinity. *Discourse & Communication*, 19, 221–236.

Baker, P. & Levon, E. (2016). 'That's what I call a man': Representations of racialized and classed masculinities in the UK print media. *Gender & Language*, 10(1): 106–139.

Bois, J. Du. (2007). The stance triangle. In R. Englebretson (Ed.), *Stancetaking in Discourse* (pp. 139–182). Amsterdam: John Benjamins.

Britain, D. (1992). Linguistic change in intonation: The use of High Rising Terminals in New Zealand English. *Language Variation and Change*, 4, 77–104.

Brown, P. & Levinson, S. (1987). *Politeness: Some Universals in Language Use.* Cambridge: Cambridge University Press.

Bucholtz, M. (2009). From stance to style: Gender, interaction and indexicality in Mexican immigrant youth slang. In Alexandra Jaffe (Ed.), *Stance: Sociolinguistic Perspectives* (pp. 146–170). Oxford: Oxford University Press.

Damari, R. (2010). Intertextual stancetaking and the local negotiation of cultural identities by a binational couple. *Journal of Sociolinguistics*, 14, 609–629.

Enfield, N. J., Stivers, T. & Levinson, S. (2010). Question-response sequences in conversation across ten language: An introduction. *Journal of Pragmatics*, 42, 2615–2619.

Finegan, E. & Biber, D. (1994). Register and social dialect variation: An integrated approach. In Douglas Biber & Edward Finegan (Eds.), *Sociolinguistic Perspectives on Register* (pp. 314–347). Oxford: Oxford University Press.

Goffman, E. (1974). *Frame Analysis.* Cambridge, MA: Harper and Row.

Goffman, E. (1981). *Forms of Talk.* Philadelphia: University of Pennsylvania Press.

Hymes, D. (1974). Ways of speaking. In Richard Bauman & Joel Sherzer (Eds.), *Explorations in the Ethnography of Speaking* (pp. 433–452). Cambridge: Cambridge University Press.

Jakobson, R. (1960). Closing statement: Linguistics and poetics. In Thomas Seboek (Ed.), *Style in Language* (pp. 350–377). Cambridge, MA: MIT Press.

Jaworski, A. & Thurlow, C. (2009). Taking an elitist stance: Ideology and the discursive production of social distinction. In Alexandra Jaffe (Ed.), *Stance: Sociolinguistic Perspectives* (pp. 195–226). Oxford: Oxford University Press.

Jefferson, G. (1978). Sequential aspects of storytelling in conversation. In J. Schenkein (Ed.), *Studies in the Organization of Conversational Interaction* (pp. 219–248). New York: Academic Press.

Jucker, A. (2008). Politeness in the history of English. In Richard Dury, Maurizio Gotti & Marina Dossena (Eds.), *English Historical Linguistics 2006. Volume II: Lexical and Semantic Change* (pp. 3–29). Amsterdam: John Benjamins.

Konig, E. & Siemund, P. (2007). Speech act distinctions in grammar. In T. Shopen (Ed.), *Language Typology and Syntactic Description* (pp. 276–324). Cambridge: Cambridge University Press.

Labov, W. (1971). Some principles of linguistic methodology. *Language in Society*, 1, 97–120.

Lempert, M. (2008). The poetics of stance: Text-metricality, epistemicity, interaction. *Language in Society*, 37, 569–592.

Lempert, M. (2009). On 'flip-flopping': Branded stance-taking in US electoral politics. *Journal of Sociolinguistics*, 13, 223–248.
Levinson, S. (2013). Action formation and ascription. In Tanya Stivers & Jack Sidnell (Eds.), *The Handbook of Conversation Analysis* (pp. 103–130). Oxford: Wiley-Blackwell.
Linde, C. (1993). *Life Stories: The Creation of Coherence*. Oxford: Oxford University Press.
McCarthy, M. & O'Keeffe, A. (2003). 'What's in a name?': Vocatives in casual conversations and radio phone-in calls. *Language and Computers*, 46, 153–185.
Pomerantz, A. (1984). Agreeing and disagreeing with assessments: Some features of preferred/dispreffered turn shapes. In J. Maxwell Atkinson & John Heritage (Eds.), *Structures of Social Action* (pp. 57–101). Cambridge: Cambridge University Press.
Raymond, G. (2003). Grammar and social organization: Yes/no interrogatives and the structure of responding. *American Sociological Review*, 68, 939–967.
Sacks, H. (1987). On the preferences for agreement and contiguity in sequences in conversation. In G. Button & J. R. E. Lee (Eds.), *Talk and Social Organisation* (pp. 54–69). Clevedon: Mutlilingual Matters.
Schegloff, E. (1968). Sequencing in conversational openings. *American Anthropologist*, 70, 1075–1095.
Schegloff, E. (1982). Discourse as an interactional achievement. In Deborah Tannen (Ed.), *Analyzing Discourse* (pp. 71–93). Washington, DC: Georgetown University Press.
Searle, J. (1969). *Speech Acts: An Essay in the Philosophy of Language*. Cambridge: Cambridge University Press.
Sicoli, M., Stivers, T., Enfield, N. J. & Levinson, S. (2015). Marked initial pitch in questions signals marked communicative function. *Language and Speech*, 58, 204–223.
Silverstein, M. (2004). 'Cultural' concepts and the language-culture nexus. *Current Anthropology*, 45, 621–652.
Steensig, J. & Drew, P. (2008). Questioning. *Discourse Studies*, 10, 5–133.
Stivers, T. (2010). An overview of the question-response system in American English conversation. *Journal of Pragmatics*, 42, 2772–2781.
Stivers, T. & Enfield, N. J. (2010). A coding scheme for question-response sequences in conversation. *Journal of Pragmatics*, 42, 2620–2626.
Stivers, T. & Hayashi, M. (2010). Transformative answers: One way to resist a question's constraints. *Language in Society*, 39, 1–38.
Stivers, T. & Robinson, J. D. (2006). A preference for progressivity in interaction. *Language in Society*, 35, 367–392.

11 Stylistic Perception

Jesse Egbert

Introduction

Stylistic Perception (SP) analysis is a new method of investigating linguistic variation from the perspective of audience perceptions. As such, SP analysis gives researchers an additional lens through which to analyze and interpret corpus-linguistic data. Recent work in this area has revealed substantial and systematic variability in the perceptions lay readers have of published writing. Egbert (2014a) used SP analysis and Biber's multidimensional (MD) analysis to show that certain aspects of author style (e.g., use of noun-noun sequences, nominalizations, and formulaic language) can predict reader perceptions of university textbook comprehensibility and effectiveness. Egbert (2014b) also used SP analysis and MD analysis to investigate relationships between linguistic variation and lay reader perceptions of published academic writing. This study showed moderate and statistically significant relationships between reader perceptions of writing style and linguistic variation within and across three publication types (journal articles, university textbooks, and popular academic books) in two disciplines (biology and history).

To date, SP research has been limited in that it has been applied only to academic writing. However, the usefulness of SP analysis in those studies suggests that this method could be effectively used to analyze and interpret reader perceptions in other registers. In particular, this approach seems to be particularly appropriate for the register of Q+A forums. Q+A forums are widely used as a source of information and advice. However, answers to questions in these forums differ widely across individual responses, countries, and topics. Based on the SP analyses in academic registers, we might hypothesize that these variables will predict reader perceptions of answer quality. However, this is an empirical question.

The purpose of this study is to quantitatively and qualitatively investigate variation in reader perceptions of Q+A forum answers across four varieties of English (India, Philippines, UK, and US). Variability within these four varieties due to topic or individual answer will also be explored.

Method

Corpus

This study is based on a sub-sample of the Q+A corpus. The entire Q+A corpus contains a total of 265 questions and 7,188 answers. Because collecting reader perceptions on over 7,000 answers was simply not practical, I constructed a representative subcorpus by collecting a random, stratified sample of the Q+A corpus. The design of this subcorpus is stratified according to two of the key variables of this study: country and topic. I randomly sampled five questions from each topic within each country (5 questions x 3 topics x 4 countries = 60 questions). For each of those questions, I then sampled five answers: the 'best' answer (as selected by the requester) and a random sample of four 'other' answers (60 questions x 5 answers = 300 answers). Table 11.1 displays the design of the corpus, along with total word counts for the answers.

Perceptual Differential Items

The next step in this analysis was to construct a simple instrument composed of perceptual differential items, which is the term I use for semantic differential items used for the purpose of eliciting reader perceptions. Semantic differential items consist of a scale with points lying between two bipolar adjectives (see Osgood, Suci, & Tannenbaum, 1957). Participants are asked to indicate their attitude toward a subject by choosing a position between the two adjectives. In this study, I use five of the perceptual differential items developed by Egbert (2014b). Each of these items is on a six-point scale. The five items are

Unreadable (1) _ : _ : _ : _ : _ : _ (6) Readable
Unbiased (1) _ : _ : _ : _ : _ : _ (6) Biased
Ineffective (1) _ : _ : _ : _ : _ : _ (6) Effective
Irrelevant (1) _ : _ : _ : _ : _ : _ (6) Relevant
Not informative (1) _ : _ : _ : _ : _ : _ (6) Informative

These five items were selected because it was determined that they are particularly relevant and interesting for the variation of interest in this study. Another reason these were chosen is because they each represent distinct parameters of stylistic perception. The full 38-item stylistic perception survey from which these items were selected contains many items that overlap in terms of the perceptions they represent (e.g., readable/unreadable and comprehensible/incomprehensible). Egbert (2014b) showed very high correlations between items that represented similar perceptual parameters. Therefore, it was determined that one item per

Table 11.1 Descriptive information for the Q+A subcorpus used in this study, including number of questions, answers, and words

	Family & Relationships			*Politics & Government*			*Society & Culture*			*Total*		
	Q	*A*	*W*	*Q*	*A*	*W*	*Q*	*A*	*W*	*Q*	*A*	*W*
IN	5	25	396.2	5	25	413.4	5	25	415.8	15	75	1225.4
PH	5	25	310.4	5	25	414.2	5	25	447.0	15	75	1171.5
UK	5	25	370.0	5	25	423.0	5	25	301.0	15	75	1094.0
US	5	25	438.2	5	25	529.6	5	25	250.4	15	75	1218.2
Total	20	100	1514.8	20	100	1780.2	20	100	1414.2	60	300	4709.1

Q: number of questions; A: number of answers; W: total number of words in the answers

parameter of interest is sufficient to capture reader perceptions along that parameter.

Data Collection

The items introduced in the previous section formed the basis of a survey instrument that was developed in Google Forms. This instrument contained the title, 'Yahoo! Answers Perceptions', brief instructions, and text boxes for participants to enter their unique Worker ID and the ID number for the question they were given. The survey contained five pages, one for each answer, which included the same five perceptual differential items introduced earlier.

Mechanical Turk was used as a tool to recruit, correspond with, and pay participants. Mechanical Turk (MTurk) is an Amazon crowdsourcing company designed to facilitate the creation of simple Human Interaction Tasks (HITs) by Requesters and the completion of these tasks by participants, or Workers. Although MTurk was originally developed for human computation tasks, it has been used extensively in recent years for research in the social sciences, including linguistics (Mason & Suri 2012). After creating a Requester profile on MTurk, I created a separate HIT for each of the 60 questions in the corpus.

Five independent participants completed a survey for the five answers for each of the 60 questions. All participants were residing in the US at the time the survey was administered. Participants were also required to have a minimum MTurk HIT approval rate of 95% or above in order to participate. Participants were allowed to complete surveys for multiple questions. However, a setting was used in MTurk that limited them to completing only one survey per question. Participants were paid 30 cents for each HIT they completed. Participants were instructed to read the Yahoo! Answers question they were given, along with each of the five answers to that question. The participants were not told which of the five answers was originally rated by the Yahoo! Answers requester as the 'best' answer.

Data Analysis

The completed survey data were downloaded from Google Forms in spreadsheet form. Information was added to the spreadsheet regarding country, topic, and whether or not the answer was a 'best' answer or an 'other' answer. Mean scores for the five participants were calculated for each of the perceptual differential items on each answer to the 300 questions. This reduced a total of 7,500 participant responses down to 1,500 mean perceptual scores (300 answers x 5 perceptual differential items).

The first statistical analysis I performed was a series of bivariate correlations between each pair of perceptual items. Correlations were performed to determine the extent to which the five perceptual items are related in the minds of participants.

A series of independent t-tests was then performed to measure for statistical differences between the 'best' answers and the 'other' answers on each of the five perceptual items. This was done in order to determine whether independent readers perceive differences between 'other' answers and the answers designated as 'best' answers by Yahoo! Answers requesters.

A multivariate analysis of variance (MANOVA) was then performed in order to test for significant differences across countries in US readers' perceptions of answer readability, bias, effectiveness, relevance, and informativeness. Individual factorial ANOVAs and pairwise Tukey HSD tests were subsequently used to investigate statistical differences for each of the different groups on each of the five perceptual items.

Finally, I qualitatively investigated the perceptual patterns that emerge from the dataset. Comparisons were made between answers from different countries to investigate text-linguistic differences between them. Textual excerpts are used in the following section to illustrate these differences.

Results

Correlations

The correlation matrix in Table 11.2 displays the correlations between each pair of perceptual differential items in the survey. The correlations

Table 11.2 Matrix of correlations between readers' responses to the five perceptual differential items

	Readable	*Biased*	*Effective*	*Relevant*	*Informative*
Readable	1				
Biased	−0.28**	1			
Effective	0.50**	−0.65**	1		
Relevant	0.45**	−0.54**	0.87**	1	
Informative	0.48**	−0.57**	0.92**	0.84**	1

**Correlation is significant at the 0.01 level.

were statistically significant between all of the item pairs. However, the correlations varied widely in their strength and directionality. The strongest correlations occurred between the following three item pairs: Relevant/Informative (r = 0.84), Relevant\Effective (r = 0.87), and Effective/Informative (r = 0.92). These correlations are high, which suggests that they are measuring distinct, yet closely related parameters of reader perceptions of Q+A forum answers. Answers that are perceived as effective are also perceived as being relevant and informative.

The amount of perceived bias in Q+A forum answers correlates quite strongly in the negative direction with reader perceptions of answer effectiveness (r = –0.65), informativeness (r = –0.57), and relevance (r = –0.54). This suggests that answers perceived as being strongly biased are typically perceived as being less effective, relevant, and informative than answers that are seen as more objective.

Finally, there were moderate positive correlations between perceived answer readability and reader perceptions of answer effectiveness (r = 0.50), informativeness (r = 0.48), and relevance (r = 0.45). This suggests that more readable answers tend to be perceived as effective, informative, and relevant.

These correlations are meaningful in that they demonstrate the varied relationships between different perceptual parameters. Although the remaining sections of this chapter will focus on measuring differences between answers in various groups, it is important to recognize that these perceptual items are not entirely independent of each other. In fact, they are quite closely related in a few cases.

Answer Status

A series of independent samples t-tests were performed to measure for significant differences between the 'best' answers—as selected by Yahoo! Answers requesters—and the 'other' answers. The results of these t-tests can be seen in Table 11.3. No statistical differences were found between the 'best' answers and the 'other' answers on any of the five perceptual items. This suggests that independent readers in the US do not perceive any differences in readability, bias, effectiveness, relevance, and informativeness between answers selected by Q+A requesters as the 'best' answer and other answers to the same questions.

Table 11.3 Results of t-test comparisons between 'best' and 'other' answers for the five perceptual differential items

Item	*df*	*t*	*p*	*Cohen's* d
Readable	298	–0.46	0.65	–0.06
Biased	298	–0.93	0.35	–0.13
Effective	298	–0.22	0.83	–0.03
Relevant	298	0.13	0.89	0.02
Informative	298	–0.45	0.65	–0.07

There are at least two possible explanations for these findings: Yahoo! Answers requesters (a) do not determine the 'best' answer based on any of the five perceptions measured in this study or (b) do not assess an answer's readability, bias, effectiveness, relevance, and informativeness in the same way as the US raters. Regardless of the reason for these findings, these results offer no evidence that 'best' answers and 'other' answers are perceived differently by readers. Therefore, the remainder of the analyses in this study will disregard this variable and treat all five answers to each question as a homogeneous group.

Country

A one-way MANOVA was performed to determine whether there are significant differences in reader perceptions of readability, bias, effectiveness, relevance, and informativeness across countries and topics. Using the Wilks' Lambda criterion, the results revealed no significant interaction between country and topic. However, the combined perceptual variables were significantly affected by country, $F(5, 292) = 4.73$, $p < 0.001$, $R^2 = 0.08$. The results reveal modest effects of country across the combined perceptual variables. The results in Figures 11.1–11.4 display the perceptual data for each item across the four countries.

Individual one-way ANOVAs were also performed in order to investigate the effect of country on each of the five perceptual variables. Using a Bonferroni-corrected alpha criterion of 0.01 (0.05 / 5), the results showed a significant effect of country on the variables of readability and bias and a marginally significant effect on relevance. The results of these analyses can be seen in Table 11.4.

Tukey's HSD post hoc tests were used to test for statistically significant pairwise differences. The results of these tests are displayed in Table 11.5. In this table, the results of the Tukey HSD are reported to the left of the country labels in the form of groupings using letters (e.g., A, AB). Within the Tukey HSD groupings, pairwise differences are statistical in cases where two countries do not have the same letter next to them.

Table 11.5 shows that the answers from India were perceived as being significantly less readable than those from the Philippines and the UK.

Table 11.4 Results of one-way ANOVAs for country across the five perceptual items

Independent variable	*Dependent variable*	*df*	*F*	*p*	R^2
Country	Readable	3	4.63	0.004	0.05
	Biased	3	8.04	< 0.001	0.08
	Effective	3	1.33	0.26	0.01
	Relevant	3	3.64	0.01	0.04
	Informative	3	0.65	0.58	0.01

Table 11.5 Tukey HSD groupings for countries in perceptual items of readability, bias, and relevance

Readability		
Mean	*Group*	
4.68	A	India
4.93	AB	US
5.02	B	Philippines
5.11	B	UK
Bias		
Mean	*Group*	
3.35	A	US
3.59	AB	India
3.78	BC	UK
4.05	C	Philippines
Relevance		
Mean	*Group*	
4.28	A	India
4.37	AB	Philippines
4.65	AB	US
4.69	B	UK

However, there was not a significant difference between the perceived readability of answers from India and those from the US. These results are visually displayed in the boxplots in Figure 11.1. The top and bottom of the boxes represent the upper and lower quartiles, respectively. The overall group mean is displayed by the square point in each box. Finally, because it was hypothesized that at least some of the variability in perceptual scores could be due to topic variation, the mean perceptual rating for each of the three topics (Family & Relationships, Politics & Government, and Society & Culture) is plotted using abbreviations for the topics.

It is somewhat surprising here to observe that answers from within the US were perceived by US readers as being less readable than those from the Philippines and the UK, although not significantly so. It should be noted that all of the country means were much closer to the highest score of six ('Readable') than to the lowest score of one ('Unreadable'). This shows, unsurprisingly, that Yahoo! Answers responses are relatively easy to read for US readers. Table 11.6 contains a side-by-side comparison of two question-answer pairs that received very different mean perceived readability scores. It should be noted that the answers in this section are numbered according to the order in which I reference them in this chapter, not their order in the

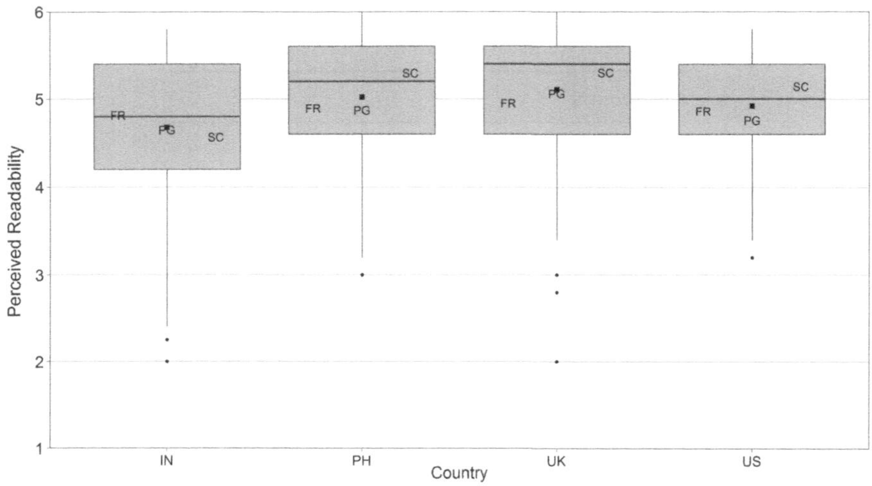

Figure 11.1 Boxplots displaying results for perceived readability by country (Note: The means for each topic group are reported using abbreviated labels: FR: Family & Relationships; PG: Politics & Government; SC: Society & Culture)

Table 11.6 Comparison between two question-answer pairs in terms of their perceived readability

Question: IN_PG_11 American cant find anything of mass distruction in Iraq stills he is trying same with Iran Why ?	**Question: UK_FR_11 (21/179 words)** Im meant to be getting married on June 16th 2007 but my mum has just said she isnt paying for anything!!?
Answer 1 Y coz he has som selfish needs.As u can c with Iraq,there's somthin valuble in Iran dat US wants,lik Oil in Iraq,& construction of a pipline in Iraq from da mediteranian 2 US 2 deliver natural gas. All dis is 4 fulfilling da selfish needs of US	**Answer 2 (113/213 words)** If you're old enough to get married you're old enough to fund it. Despite many misconceptions to the contrary, the parents of the happy couple aren't obligated to fund anything. There is certainly a tradition, but it's not something you're entitled to. I'm sorry your mother reneged on her promise to fund this. Blame is irrelevant anyway; let's get to fixing this. You don't have to cancel your wedding. You do have to scale it back to something within your own means. Keep in mind that the wedding day is just that: a day. All that fairy princess queen-for-a-day stuff is flogged by a bridal industry with a HUGE profit margin. If you lose deposits, you lose deposits.
Mean Readability Score: 2	**Mean Readability Score: 6**

Q+A thread. Answer 1, from India, received a mean readability score of two, which is the lowest score in the dataset. In contrast, answer 2, from the UK, received the maximum possible mean score of six, meaning all five raters assigned a six to this answer.

A qualitative comparison of these two answers reveals some clear differences between them. Answer 1 contains several cases of using either abbreviated forms (e.g., Y, coz, u, c, 2) or missing letters (e.g., som, lik) and missing articles (e.g., '2 US', 'needs of US'). Forms such as these do not occur in Answer 2. Answer 1 also uses many non-standard forms (e.g., dat, dis, da). Answer 2 uses only full word forms. Answer 1 contains many misspelled words (e.g., mediteranian, pipline) and instances of missing spaces after punctuation (e.g., 'Iraq,there's', 'wants,lik'), whereas Answer 2 contains none. These differences are likely to have played a role in the differences between the perceived readability of these two answers.

Reader perceptions of answer bias also varied significantly across country groups. Answers from the US were perceived as significantly less biased than those from the UK and the Philippines. Answers from the Philippines were perceived as being significantly more biased than those from India and the US. These results can be seen in Figure 11.2.

Table 11.7 contains a side-by-side comparison of two answers that received perceived bias ratings on opposite ends of the scale. Answer 3, from the US, received a mean score of 1.4, the lowest in the dataset. Answer 4, on the other hand, was from the Philippines and received a score of 5.8, the

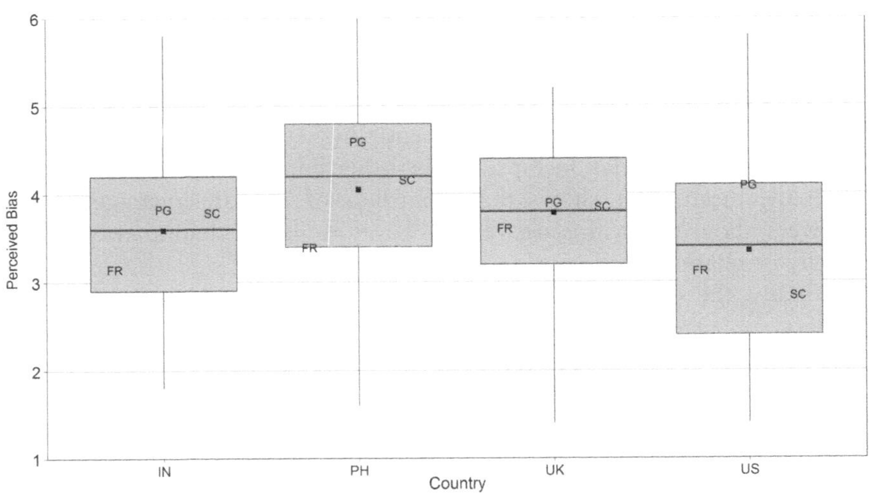

Figure 11.2 Boxplots displaying results for perceived bias by country (Note: The means for each topic group are reported using abbreviated labels: FR: Family & Relationships; PG: Politics & Government; SC: Society & Culture)

Table 11.7 Comparison between two question-answer pairs in terms of their perceived bias

Question: US_SC-13 Should Homeless people be sent to jail? **Answer 3** No, being poor is not a crime. It would cost less to develop drop in centers where they could sleep, get food, clean themselves up and maybe look for work.	**Question: PH_FR_02** Why is it hard to find a good man? **Answer 4** Because . . . There are very few men like me.
Mean Bias Score: 1.4	**Mean Bias Score: 5.8**

second highest in the dataset. Answer 4 makes only one statement, which is entirely focused on the author. The author of this question essentially states that it is 'hard to find a good man' because he is one of 'very few men' who qualifies. It is possible that this author is being facetious or sarcastic here. Regardless, it comes as no surprise that this answer was perceived as being biased. In contrast, the author of Answer 4 writes in general terms and makes a logical argument based on cost effectiveness. The author to Answer 4 also refrains from any personal references to him/herself and to the reader. These differences likely played a role in the perceptual ratings these answers received.

Marginal statistical differences were found across countries in the level of perceived answer relevance. The only statistical pairwise differences found along this perceptual item were between the countries of India and the UK, where the answers from India were perceived as being significantly less relevant. It is worth noting here that there seems to be systematic patterns in topic variation across the four country groups. Answers within the Politics & Government strand are consistently higher than the mean. Answers within Family & Relationships, on the other hand, are consistently lower than the mean. This shows that regardless of English language variety, answers about political issues tend to be more biased than answers about family or relationship issues.

Finally, the statistical results revealed a marginally significant effect of country on reader perceptions of answer relevance. The post hoc results showed that answers from the UK were rated as being the most relevant and that they were significantly more relevant than those from India. It is interesting to note that for every country, answers to questions on Politics & Government are lower than the mean and Society & Culture answers are above the mean. These results are displayed in Figure 11.3.

Table 11.8 contains examples of a low-scoring answer (Answer 5) and a high-scoring answer (Answer 6) in perceived relevance. Answer 5 comes from India, the country with the lowest mean relevance score. In response to a question that asks who is to blame for the situation in the Middle East, the

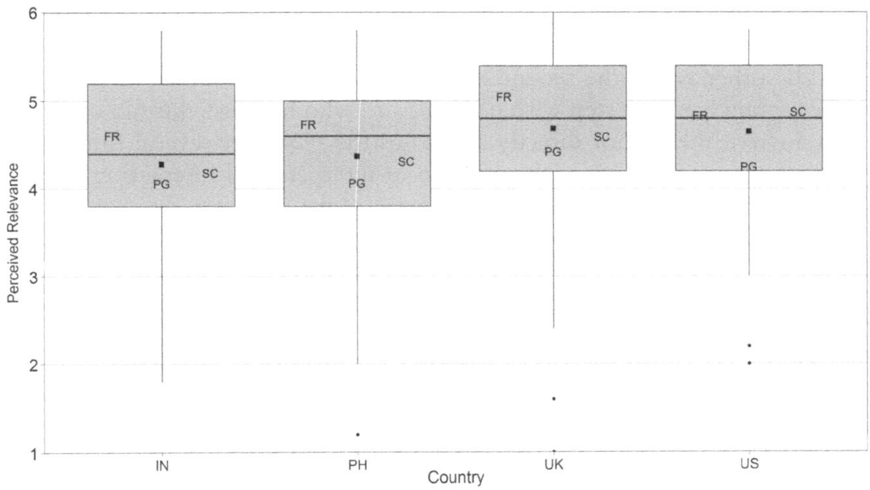

Figure 11.3 Boxplots displaying results for perceived relevance by country (Note: The means for each topic group are reported using abbreviated labels: FR: Family & Relationships; PG: Politics & Government; SC: Society & Culture)

Table 11.8 Comparison between two question-answer pairs in terms of their perceived relevance

Question IN_PG_15: Who do you think is responsible for the current situation in the Middle East? There are many fingers going many ways who is yours' pointed at?	**Question UK_FR_15:** How to survive to the end of a long lasting relationship? We were together for 5 years, he was my first love, my first man, and he is the father of my 20 months old baby. I gave him everything from me . . . . I just found out two weeks ago the he had cheated on me with his ex . . . He says He doesn't love her of feel anything for her anymore. I already broke up with him . . . but this is too hard to do . . . does anyone have advice? Or something to share that could help me? Do I forgive him?
Answer 5 the map of middle east should change,it is one of zionism protocols in the world. their ultimate goal is all the world to be a village,and they manage it all.ONE leader of zionisms for ALL the world . . .	**Answer 6** Anything worth doing is difficult. It doesn't matter if he says he doesn't love her or feel anything for her anymore . . . this is about YOU and your baby. He's proven what kind of person he is, and by breaking up with him (congratulations, by the way) . . . you've proven what kind of person YOU are. [. . .]
Mean Relevance Score: 1.8	**Mean Relevance Score: 6**

author of Answer 5 writes a vague and difficult-to-understand answer about 'zionism protocols' and the world as a single 'village' under 'ONE leader'. On the other hand, the second answer is a detailed response to a woman questioning her next step with her husband who had just cheated on her. In this answer, the author directly addresses the requester several times using second-person pronouns. This pattern of interpersonal interaction appears to be common in the UK answers. Answer 6 also contains direct references to this woman's husband, their potential breakup, their child, and the difficult nature of her decision. It seems that the level of detail and the explicit references to the content of the question are reasons that this answer was perceived as being more relevant than Answer 5.

Figure 11.4 displays the perceptual results for reader perceptions of informativeness and effectiveness by country. The lack of significance across country groups for these two perceptual variables may be due, in part, to the large amount of within country variability along these two variables. One possible explanation for this large within group variance is the large amount of variability across topic areas.

Individual Answer Variation

Up to this point in the chapter, I have focused on means-based comparisons between groups along two independent factors: country and topic. These have revealed important patterns of variation in reader perceptions of Q+A

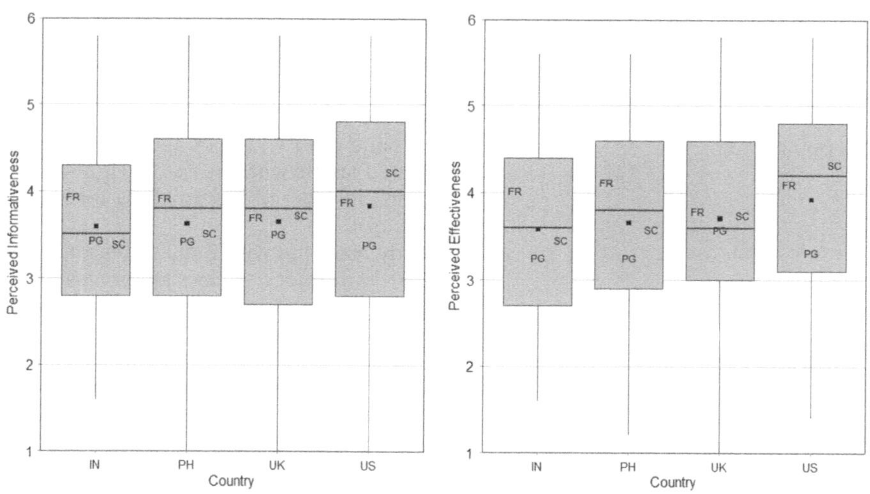

Figure 11.4 Boxplots displaying results for perceived informativeness (right) and perceived effectiveness (left) by country (Note: The means for each topic group are reported using abbreviated labels: FR: Family & Relationships; PG: Politics & Government; SC: Society & Culture)

forum answers. However, these analyses fail to fully account for variation between individual answers to individual questions. This variation is clearly displayed in Figures 11.1 and 11.2. This section disregards group differences and focuses on qualitatively investigating within-question variation. This section is organized according to perceptual item and will include comparisons of answers along each item.

Table 11.9 contains a side-by-side comparison between two answers to the same question, PH_SC_07. Answer 7 received a mean readability score of three, which was the sixth lowest score in the dataset. In contrast, Answer 8 received the maximum possible mean score of six, meaning all five raters assigned a six to this answer. A qualitative comparison of these two answers reveals some clear differences between them. Answer 7 does not use capitalization for proper nouns or sentence-initial words (e.g., jesus; i'm). In contrast, Answer 7 capitalizes all sentence-initial words. In addition, Answer 7 contains several cases of using either abbreviated forms or missing letters (e.g., yu; hi; coz). Answer 8 uses only full word forms. Finally, Answer 7 contains one expletive (motherfucker) and one set of asterisks to mask an expletive (***), whereas Answer 8 contains no expletives. These differences are likely to have played a role in the differences between the perceived readability of these two answers.

Table 11.10 compares two answers to question UK_PG_02 that received different perceived effectiveness scores. In this question, a female requester describes her physical characteristics before asking about whether men focus more on 'personality or looks'. The author of Answer 9, which received the lowest score of one from all five readers, tells the requester to disregard anything else she has heard, 'stay under 140' pounds and 'wear dresses'. This author then claims that men accept women based on their physical characteristics and their knowledge. This is in stark contrast with Answer 8, which focuses entirely on self-confidence and communication skills, rather than physical characteristics such as weight and clothing. Clearly, the readers of these answers felt that Answer 9 was ineffective in addressing the needs of the requester.

Table 11.9 Comparison between two individual answers to Question PH_SC_07 in terms of their perceived readability

Question: When you get to heaven and come face to face with the eternally existent Jesus what do you want to say to him	
Answer 7	**Answer 8**
if yu mean jesus that washes the dishes over at the taqueria, i'm gonna kick hi *** coz he owes me 2.37. and that's in euros. motherfucker.	'Thank you'. 'I love you'. 'I've got about a million questions to ask, do you have a little time?'
Mean readability score: 3	**Mean readability score: 6**

Table 11.10 Comparison between two individual answers to Question UK_PG_02 in terms of their perceived effectiveness

Question:
Is it true that guys look at personality more than physical features in a girl? I sometimes think that guys like short and skinny girls a lot more than the curvy and tall girls which makes me feel a little sad because I'm 5'9 and weigh 160 and I eat healthy everyday. Most of the weight is in the legs. I don't think that guys will find that attractive even though most of it is muscle. Will most guys pay more attention to my personality or looks?

Answer 9	**Answer 10**
Whatever you hear try to stay under 140. Wear dresses you would look better. I am not sure what is good personality but guys will accept you through your body and knowledge.	First off all guys like different things about a girl! But none of that should matter if you like yourself and love how you look of course you are going to meet guys that may focus more on your looks vs personality from what I have asked guys and my experience personality in the right guy would be the first thing they look for if your confident and can hold a convo that makes you 20 times more attractive trust me I'm 19 and for most of my time I have been insecure and not confident around guys once I realized I am beautiful and that who cares and I started to speak with confidence and me myself I saw how many guys found that attractive!!!
Mean effectiveness score: 1	**Mean effectiveness score: 5.4**

Conclusion

In this chapter, I have introduced SP analysis as a method of investigating discourse patterns from the perspective of reader perceptions. Participant readers residing in the US were asked to report their perceptions of 5 answers to 60 questions that were sampled from the Q+A corpus. Each answer was rated by five participants on five perceptual differential scales (readability, bias, effectiveness, relevance, and informativeness).

Correlations among the five items showed that the items were all related to each other, but to varying degrees and, in the case of bias, in different directions. Comparisons between the requester's 'best' answer and the 'other' answers in the corpus yielded no significant results across the five perceptual scales. However, there were significant differences among the four countries for readability, bias, and relevance. Finally, qualitative comparisons of high- and low-scoring answers revealed useful insights into factors that may affect reader perceptions of Q+A forum answer quality and style.

The analysis in this chapter employed subjective perceptions of readers to quantify perceptions of stylistic variation in Q+A forum answers. The findings reported here showed that readers' perceptions are related to variation in world English variety and the style and language of individual answers. More extensive investigations of linguistic variation across Q+A forum answers would likely reveal important relationships between readers' perceptions of answer style and the linguistic choices of answer authors.

Postscript

The method used in this chapter—Stylistic Perception analysis—is distinct from all of the other methods used in this volume in that it is the only method that accounts for reader perceptions toward the texts in the corpus. In the other methods, any manual analysis of the texts is carried out by the researcher(s). While this analysis and interpretation by expert linguists is certainly valuable, these researchers are often outside of the target audience for the texts they analyze. This necessarily limits their ability to understand fully and interpret patterns of discourse in their corpus.

Stylistic Perception, on the other hand, provides us with information about texts from the perspective of target readers. Unsurprisingly, the unique nature of this approach makes it more likely to produce findings that are not discovered by any other approach. Many of my findings were unique to this study simply because of the nature of my data. These unique findings include variation across country and topic area in perceived readability, bias, and relevance, as well as particular features of discourse that may be related to those perceptions.

However, there were a couple of findings that were found by SP analysis and at least one other method. I reported earlier that answers from the UK tend to be more oriented toward interpersonal interaction than the other countries. A similar finding was reported by Friginal and Biber and Levon. I also noted the non-standard orthography and use of acronyms in Q+A forum responses from India. This pattern was noted by both McEnery and Potts.

After reading the other chapters, it is easy to see a number of similarities between the results of other methods and patterns in my data that I simply didn't report. For example, Friginal and Biber concluded that Q+A forums use very few linguistic features related to informational discourse. The participants in my study rated the Q+A forum responses lower in the category of 'Informative' than in any other category. The means for each category can be seen in Table 11.11. It seems that readers were able to perceive that the primary purpose of Q+A forums is not informational.

Table 11.11 Mean reader perceptions for each of the five perceptual differential items

Category	*M*
Readable	4.93
Biased	3.69
Effective	3.72
Relevant	4.50
Informative	3.67

Overall, the method used in this chapter seemed to complement the other methods well. While there were not many cases of overlap in features mentioned between SP analysis and other methods, the cases that were reported on in this chapter revealed similar findings. Finally, there appears to be a great deal of potential for triangulating reader perceptions with linguistic results in order to gain greater insights into patterns of discourse.

References

Egbert, J. (2014a). Student perceptions of stylistic variation in introductory university textbooks. *Linguistics and Education*, 25, 64–77.

Egbert, J. (2014b). Reader Perceptions of Stylistic Variation in Published Academic. Writing, Doctoral Dissertation. Northern Arizona University.

Mason, W. & Suri, S. (2012). Conducting behavioral research on Amazon's Mechanical Turk. *Behavior Research Methods*, 44(1), 1–23.

Osgood, C. E., Suci, G. & Tannenbaum, P. (1957). *The Measurement of Meaning*. Urbana, IL: University of Illinois Press.

12 Research Synthesis

Jesse Egbert and Paul Baker

Introduction

In this chapter, we attempt to synthesise the findings from the previous ten analysis chapters by conducting a comparative meta-analysis in order to answer our overarching research question about the extent to which different approaches to a corpus yield the same results. First, we describe how we carried out the meta-analysis in terms of identifying and comparing findings across the ten chapters. Then we discuss how the findings related to the research questions set, noting that as a by-product of their analysis, some of the authors actually answered a question which was not given to them. We then discuss the extent to which the findings were convergent, complementary, or dissonant, focussing in most detail on those which were dissonant. This is followed by a reflection of the different methods that were used, where we revisit the chapters again, as well as consider the broad categories of corpus-driven, corpus-based, and qualitative approaches. The chapter ends with a consideration of the benefits and challenges of methodological triangulation within corpus linguistics, as well as a discussion of the limitations and implications of our study and suggestions for future research in this area.

Making Comparisons

Once we received the ten chapters, the two editors read them separately, making a list of the findings from each one. By 'finding' we mean a discovery noted in the form of a statement which contributes toward answering one or more of the research questions based on the analysis the researcher had carried out. We did not base findings on parts of tables that appeared in chapters but were not noted in the main body of the text by the analysts themselves, as that would have involved overly imposing our own interpretation on the tables. Instead, we based the findings on the authors' own interpretations. We also noted cases when authors attempted to provide an explanation for a finding.

Once we had both created a table of findings for each author, we then shared our documents, noting which findings we had both spotted, while spending more time on the ones where only one of us had noted a finding the other missed. There were a handful of cases where we disagreed on a finding, although these were easily resolved by referring back to the appropriate chapters. In other cases, we had both noted a similar finding but focussed on slightly different aspects of it, so for those cases, we used a combination of our wordings. Table 12.1 gives an example to show how we synthesised our interpretations of one chapter (Chapter 6 by Vaclav Brezina). The first column shows the summary of Vaclav's findings that were unique to Jesse's meta-analysis, the second shows Paul's, and the last column indicates cases where we noted similar points. In this last column, the parts in italics show how an initial finding noted by one of us was then supplemented with further information from the other.

We then converted this table into a document which indicated the extent to which authors had noted similar findings. This document was organised according to feature rather than author, and we classified findings within features in terms of which of the two research questions they related to: either differences across the four world English varieties or differences across topic. At this point, something interesting emerged: most of the authors had made observations about the corpus as a whole, in effect answering a question which had not been set: what are the characteristics of the Q+A corpus?

Table 12.1 Sample comparison of the meta-analysis

Jesse	*Paul*	*Noted by both*
God, love, and president occur much more frequently than expected across all of the countries (These topics are universal across these four cultures.).	Q+A corpus contains a lot of question words.	God, love, and president occur predominantly in SC, FR, and PG, respectively, *and indicate discourses.*
IN/PH–collocation networks for President are split between domestic and international politics.	The collocates of question words point to subjectifing strategies with a social function for eliciting personal response and building rapport.	*IN/PH/US*–strong connection between God and love (*related to Christian rhetoric*).
Efficient way of analyzing complex meaning relationships.	Questions tend to be opinion seeking, personal advice seeking, or fact seeking.	UK–collocates of President typically refer to American politics.
Simple way of visualizing collocational relationships.	There is an American contributor in the non-American data.	*US–uses President the least* (More common to simply refer to last names of presidents in US.)
Requires additional context in order to interpret patterns.		UK–discussions related to God and love are largely secular.
		IN–*competition* between religious and *secular associations between God and love.*

We thus organised the findings into three sections: 1) those relating to the corpus as a whole, 2) those answering the research question comparing the four varieties of English, and 3) those answering the research question about the three topic areas. We also noted the extent to which authors of chapters agreed or disagreed about the use of a feature. The following section deals with these three areas in turn.

Results

Table 12.2 shows our research synthesis for findings that relate to the corpus as a whole.

Table 12.2 Findings relating to the whole corpus

Feature	*Findings*	
Interaction/ involvement	**Bethany:** Q+A forums are highly interactional and therefore contain characteristics of spoken discourse, such as stance bundles	**Eric/Doug:** Highly interactive and involved
	Agree: Two authors mention that Q+A forums are highly interactive.	
Purpose of questions	**Vaclav:** The collocates of question words point to subjectifing strategies with a social function for eliciting personal response and building rapport. Questions tend to be opinion seeking, personal advice seeking, or fact seeking.	**Jonathan/Claire:** Thirteen percent of the questions are not seeking information as their primary goal.
Informational aspects of the corpus	**Eric/Doug:** Q+A forums use relatively low frequencies of linguistic features related to informational discourse.	**Jesse:** Answers that are perceived as informative and relevant are also perceived as effective and unbiased.
Oral vs. literate	**Bethany:** Q+A register relies on oral bundles (verb/clause) more than literate bundles (noun phrase), with the forums being similar to conversation.	**Stefan:** The Q+A corpus seems to be more similar to spoken than to written registers.
	Agree: Two authors mention that the Q+A forums have features closer to spoken registers.	
Formulaic language	**Bethany:** Lexical bundles are often multi-functional, with a single bundle carrying multiple meanings.	
Stance	**Bethany:** Q+A forums rely on stance bundles which relate to answering questions and giving advice.	

(*Continued*)

Table 12.2 (Continued)

Feature	*Findings*
Future tense	**Stefan:** All varieties prefer *will* over *going to*. Large amounts of variability due to speakers. Some speakers use one variant exclusively while others vary in their choices.
Blame	**Jonathan/Claire:** Blaming is more frequent than apologising in the whole corpus.
Gender differences	**Paul:** Gender similarity is not referred to much as a discourse.
Sexual standards	**Paul:** All four countries discuss sexual standards, and it is hardly ever countered. There is a global discourse of a sexual double standard—men are unable to control their sex drives, but women must.
Reader perceptions	**Jesse:** Independent readers in the US do not perceive any differences in readability, bias, effectiveness, relevance, and informativeness between answers selected by Q+A requesters as the 'best' answer and other answers to the same questions. Explanation: Yahoo! Answers requesters (a) do not determine the 'best' answer based on any of the five perceptions measured in this study or (b) do not assess an answer's readability, bias, effectiveness, relevance, and informativeness in the same way as the US raters.
Readability of answers	**Jesse:** More readable answers tend to be perceived as effective, informative, and relevant.
	Answers generally received relatively high readability scores.
Bias of answers	**Jesse:** Answers perceived as being strongly biased are typically perceived as being less effective, relevant, and informative than answers that are more objective.

Bethany Gray, who examined lexical bundles, is represented the most times in this table, although we are cautious in terms of assigning equal value to findings, noting that some findings are more specific and small scale than others. For this reason, we would warn against counting the number of findings made by each author and declaring the 'best' analysis to be the one which made the most findings.

We note that Bethany's approach found that there was little variation in terms of the main research question involving variation by country, so this may explain her increased focus on other questions.

However, most of the findings related to the first research question involving variation between the four world Englishes. We had expected this to be the case and had possibly primed an increased focus on this by having it as the first question. Table 12.3 shows the summary of findings relating to this question.

We note here a distinction between the corpus-driven and other approaches, in that where there are areas which were focussed on by more than one

Table 12.3 Findings relating to variation between the four world Englishes

Feature	*Findings*		
Interaction/ involvement	**Eric/Doug:** UK used most features of interaction. US also highly interactive. US/UK are less formal and more personal. IN/PH less interactive.	**Erez:** UK used most interpersonal interaction.	**Jesse:** UK answers were most interpersonal.
	Agree: Three authors mention that UK uses more features of interpersonal interaction.		
Private verbs	**Eric/Doug:** UK/US use more private verbs than the non-native varieties.		
Purpose of questions	**Jonathan/Claire:** UK uses most non-informational questions, PH uses fewest.	**Erez:** IN/US tend to use information-seeking questions. UK/PH tend to use evaluative questions.	
	Agree: Two authors mention UK uses few information-seeking questions.		
Informational	**Eric/Doug:** IN had the most informational texts (due, at least in part, to the use of information copied from informational websites). PH also more information than US/UK.	**Erez:** US responses are heavily information-laden. Information-seeking questions receive answers and evaluative questions receive agreement/alignment.	
	Disagree: One said US responses are heavily informational. The other did not find this.		
Code-switching	**Tony:** Code-switching is more common in PH.	**Eric/Doug:** The results in their study were consistent with findings about PH contexts where limited code-switching is expected.	
	Disagree: One said code-switching is common in PH responses, the other said findings suggest code-switching is limited in the PH responses.		

(*Continued*)

Table 12.3 (Continued)

Feature	*Findings*			
Social values	**Tony:** PH responses have most keywords related to conservative social values. PH/IN–use of words in *wrong* semantic field (*sin* and *evil*). (PH has a focus on moral values of individual people. IN has a focus on moral values of society and culture.).			
Politeness	**Tony:** UK English uses more politeness markers than other countries, particularly using *sorry* more than IN/US/PH, often as a precursor to disagreement.	**Amanda:** UK uses most words related to impoliteness. Interpretation: this relates to cultural policing of politeness.		**Erez:** UK respondents are highly evaluative and make use of non-mitigated face-threatening statements, even when the question does not require any evaluative response at all. Interpretation: this may be due to the nature of CMC.
Religious/ secular	**Tony:** PH/IN–use religious keywords. US/ UK do not.	**Amanda:** IN uses *god* and *religion* much more than the other varieties (IN discourse uses *god* and *religion* as an answer to many of life's difficulties. Religion is discussed in relation to societal problems.).	**Vaclav:** IN/PH/US–strong connection between *god* and *love* (related to Christian rhetoric). UK–discussions related to *god* and *love* are largely secular. IN–competition between religious and secular associations between *god* and *love*.	**Erez:** UK more secular, others more religious.
	Agree: Four mention UK is more secular than the other three. Four mention IN is more religious. Three mention PH is also religious.			
Obligation (e.g., modals)	**Tony:** IN/PH uses modals of obligation and US/UK use fewer (UK and US are moving away from using obligation modals.).			
Acronyms	**Tony:** IN uses many CMC acronyms (speed writing, e.g., *r*, *u*, *ur*).	**Amanda:** IN uses most instances of unrecognized words (Many of these are CMC acronyms.).		**Jesse:** Lower perceived readability for IN may be related to more misspelled words and abbreviations/acronyms in IN.
	Agree: Three authors mention IN uses more acronyms.			

Non-standard orthography	**Tony:** PH/IN–*lets* preferred over *let's* (apostrophe dropping).	**Paul:** Posters use punctuation or other marks to swear (Perhaps to avoid censorship/offence?).	**Jesse:** Perceived readability seems to be related to features such as capitalization, abbreviations, and expletives.
Rights	**Tony:** US/PH–use more keywords related to entitlement (*rights*).		
Hedges	**Tony:** UK uses more *just* as a minimizer.		
Advice giving	**Tony:** UK/PH have more advice giving.		
Oral vs. literate	**Bethany:** UK uses more noun phrase–based (literate) bundles than other two-structural types (oral). PH uses more verb phrase–based (oral) bundles than US/UK.		
Formulaic language	**Bethany:** No significant differences in the frequency of lexical bundles by the four countries.		
Stance	**Bethany:** PH uses more stance bundles than the other countries.		
Psychological states	**Amanda:** IN uses two semtags from psychological actions, states, and processes that are used nowhere else (IN is more preoccupied with psychological states, such as concentration, meditation, and focus.).		
Politics	**Tony:** UK–talks less about people and politics than the other three countries.	**Amanda:** PH has highest number of semtags related to government (high level of personal engagement with politics in PH; lots of discussion of the president). UK uses many words related to politics of US mostly relating to history and WWII.	**Vaclav:** UK–collocates of *President* typically refer to American politics; US–uses *President* the least (More common to simply refer to last names of presidents in US.). IN/PH–collocation networks for *President* are split between domestic and international politics.
	Agree: Two mention that when UK talks about politics, it often refers to US politics.		

(*Continued*)

Table 12.3 (Continued)

Feature	*Findings*
Education	**Amanda:** PH has highest number of education semtags (the quality of the educational system and the government's role in improving education in PH seems to be a top priority for posters; lesson used in abstract sense—life lesson).
Geographical names	**Amanda:** UK uses more geographical names (UK has a wealth of history that is widely understood by Brits.).
Priming	**Stefan:** Priming affects US/UK speakers less than IN/PH (native vs. indigenized).
Future tense	**Stefan:** IN/PH–preference for *will* is much stronger than US/UK (native vs. indigenized).
Discourse markers	**Jonathan/Claire:** The UK has more "pragmatic noise" appearing more speech-like than the other corpora, especially *oh*. UK–uses *hey* most (Uses of *hey* in the UK tended to be aggressive). US–uses *wow* most (tend to be aggressive, sarcastic, or critical). IN–wow is absent.
Blame	**Jonathan/Claire:** IN–more uses of *blame* in PG than other varieties (tendency to construct the topic of politics with a greater emphasis on blaming).
Gender pronouns	**Paul:** India, Philippines, and UK have significantly more male terms than female. The opposite is the case for the US.
Gender equality	**Paul:** All four countries discuss women's equality and gender similarities, although to a lesser extent than the other categories (Strong stereotypes of gender differences seem to prevail.). UK does not refer to the women's equality discourse—explanation—it is not seen as an 'issue'.
Gender differences	**Paul:** All countries refer to the Mars and Venus gendered discourse the most (and this is never countered in India or the US). IN/US–most references to Gender Similarity/Diversity (IN has a large Gender Gap.).
Sexual standards	**Paul:** UK/US–most references to Sexual Standards
Male chivalry	**Paul:** UK refers to Male Chivalry discourse the most—explanation—may be due to a specific thread.

Evaluation	**Erez:** UK respondents are highly evaluative, even when the question does not require any evaluative response at all (may be due to CMC nature). Cultural divide with UK and India similar (highest degrees of interpersonal evaluation and interpersonal disalignment) and US and Philippines similar (more preferentially conforming in their responses and, when evaluation is called for, tend to be more positive and focused on alignment; possibly due to shared sociolinguistic history). Indian respondents contain more (primarily negative) evaluations than we would normally expect, though these are more heavily weighted toward evaluating propositional content. Philippine forums, in contrast, tend to adhere most closely to relevant preference structures, though respondents in the Philippine forum show a greater reticence than their US counterparts to engage in evaluative stance-taking at all.
Readability of answers	**Jesse:** Not a significant difference between the perceived readability of answers from India and those from the US. Answers from within the US were perceived by US readers as being less readable than those from the Philippines and the UK, although not significantly so. IN–significantly less readable than UK and PH (possibly more misspelled words and abbreviations/acronyms in IN).
Relevance of answers	**Jesse:** IN answers were significantly less relevant than UK answers (IN answers tended to be vague and opaque, whereas UK answers were typically more direct, contextualized, and interpersonal.) and seen as the most relevant.
Bias of answers	**Jesse:** Answers from the Philippines were perceived as being significantly more biased than those from India and the US (and UK). US–significantly less biased than UK and PH (Answers seem to be more informational and logical.).

author, we tend to find at least one of those authors was taking a corpus-driven approach. The parts of the table where only one author is focussing on a feature tend to be more corpus-based or qualitative approaches (this is not always the case; e.g., the row for 'purpose of questions' contains findings by Jonathan/Claire and Erez, neither of whom took a corpus-driven approach). For the shared areas of focus, we note with interest a range of agreements and disagreements, which we will examine more carefully in a moment.

Finally, we come to the second research question, involving variation across topic. It is notable that authors had less to say about this question, and in fact Table 12.4, which addresses this question, is shorter than Table 12.2, which details the authors' responses to a question that was not set!

As well as being the shortest table, this one does not contain much in terms of shared focus, with only two of the corpus-driven chapters (Bethany Gray and Eric Friginal/Doug Biber) making a similar finding around interaction and involvement.

Table 12.4 Findings relating to variation between the three topics

Feature	*Findings*	
Interaction/ involvement	**Bethany:** FR most involved	**Eric/Doug:** FR most involved, followed by SC
	Agree: Two authors note FR is most involved	
Purpose of questions	**Erez:** SC predominately informational questions, PG uses evaluative questions, FR seeks information in the form of advice	
Informational	**Eric/Doug:** PG most informational and edited	
Oral vs. literate	**Bethany:** FR uses more dependent clause–fragment bundles (oral)	
Formulaic language	**Bethany:** More bundles in FR than PG and SC	
Stance	**Bethany:** FR uses more stance bundles (More personal advice, directives, and criticisms when people are talking about FR)	
Politics	**Amanda:** PG has key semantic domains: POLITICS (G1.2), GOVERNMENT (G1.1), WARFARE, DEFENCE AND THE ARMY; WEAPONS (G3), and LAW AND ORDER (G2.1)	
Priming	**Stefan:** Priming exists across all of the topic areas, but there are no differences across topics	
Future tense	**Stefan:** Differences between *will* and *going to* are smaller across topics than across varieties	
Relevance of answers	**Jesse:** For every country, answers to questions on Politics & Government are lower than the mean (for relevance) and Society & Culture answers are above the mean. FR are the most relevant	

Discussion of Results

Taken as a whole then, Tables 12.2–12.4 indicate a picture that is mainly complementary. The ten authors have tended to make unique discoveries that others did not find. There are a few areas of shared focus, and within that, slightly more agreement than disagreement. Table 12.5 summarises the agreements.

Again, we note the prevalence of the more corpus-driven authors in this table, which perhaps indicates that these approaches, which tend to cast a wider net, are more likely to light upon similarities than those which take a narrower but more focussed perspective, or consider a smaller set of texts.

However, within the tables, we noted two disagreements and these are worth focussing on in more detail (see Table 12.6).

The first case concerns whether US responses to questions contain information or not. Erez Levon indicates that they do. With regard to the Politics & Government question, he notes that 'responses in the US and Philippine forums tend to correspond to the preference structure for information questions'. For the Society & Culture question he notes that 'all four questions primarily seek the provision of new information' and that 'To a greater or lesser degree, this is what we find in the responses of the Philippine and US forums'. For the Family & Relationships question, he writes that 'Responses in the US forum, finally, are also both heavily information-laden and strongly affective'. We interpreted these points collectively as

Table 12.5 Agreements

Finding	*Authors*
Q+A forums are highly interactive	Bethany/Eric and Doug
Q+A forums have features closer to spoken than written registers	Bethany/Stefan
UK uses more features of interpersonal interaction	Eric and Doug/Erez/Jesse
UK uses few information-seeking questions	Erez/Jonathan and Claire
UK is more secular than other three. Four mention IN is more religious. Three mention PH is also religious	Tony/Amanda/Vaclav/Erez

Table 12.6 Disagreements

Finding 1	*Finding 2*
US responses are highly information-laden (Erez)	US responses not heavily information-laden (Eric/Doug)
Code-switching is more common in Philippines (Tony)	Limited code-switching in Philippines (Eric/Doug)

pointing to a high use of information-led responses in the US subcorpus. However, Eric Friginal and Doug Biber write 'The UK forum responses have the highest average Dimension 1 scores, with Indian texts having the lowest scores (16.849 and 10.939, respectively). The US and Philippine mean scores are quite similar (US = 15.195, Philippines = 14.517) and fall between averages from the UK and Indian subcorpora'. Here the disagreement is not a case of Eric and Doug completely disagreeing with Erez—they only note that the US mean scores for information come somewhere in the middle when the four varieties are compared. We would also note that Erez examined a smaller number of texts than Eric and Doug, and while this approach actually resulted in agreement with some of the quantitative approaches (see Table 12.5), in this case, the smaller sample size resulted in a disagreement.

In the second case of disagreement, we looked closely at what the two sets of authors claimed about code-switching in the Philippines. Tony McEnery made the point that 'code-switching is more frequent or, at the very least, more systematically related to a singly non-English language in the Philippine data'. Eric Friginal and Doug Biber wrote 'These results appear to be very similar to those Filipino researchers have also reported as characteristic features of written Philippine English, again, as Gonzalez (1998) called it, 'Philippine-American' English, namely, formal and scholarly in contexts where very limited code-switching is expected'. So while Tony argues that code-switching is most frequent in the Philippine data, Eric and Doug imply that it is very limited. Both mention code-switching but in different ways. However, this raises the question of whether 'more frequent or more systematically related' and 'very limited' are reconcilable analytical points to make. In both cases of disagreement then, the disagreement could be seen as partial rather than full.

Reflecting on the Methods—Corpus Driven, Corpus Based, and Qualitative

At this point, we might want to ask about general points we can make about the different types of approaches that the analysts used on the corpus, along with any perceived strengths and weaknesses. In this section, we focus on general methods in the three categories of corpus driven, corpus based, and qualitative, while in the following section, we take a closer look at each of the ten individual methods included in this volume.

First let us consider the approaches that we have called more corpus driven, namely, those in chapters 2–5, which considered the corpus as a whole and used techniques which largely identified statistically salient or frequent phenomena. Such approaches normally yield the largest range of findings because they take so much into account. This can result in genuinely unexpected findings but also many which simply confirm expectations, so-called 'so what' findings, in other words. The sheer amount of output in terms of lists of key or frequent items is likely to involve a process of narrowing or funnelling, which may result in the application of quite brutal cutoff points in order to reduce the results to a manageable amount. Even with cutoffs, analysts may still then focus on a smaller subset, weeding out or de-emphasizing those which are deemed 'so what'.

Obviously, this may impact on what is reported or focussed on in the individual research write-ups. So for example, one finding was that the Politics & Government forum has more words about politics. In some ways, this would perhaps be so expected that it could be dispensed with very quickly and would not require much (or even any) focus or explanation. Some analysts may have noticed it but decided not to even report it, while others may be working from a perspective that a rigorous analysis needs to tell everything, even the 'so what' findings. On the other hand, a less expected finding, such as India using more computer-mediated acronyms, might be seen as more interesting and thus valuable, requiring perhaps further work to explain why this would be the case.

This may mean that such findings may not always overlap or be congruent, as the application of a cutoff point may simply delete a potential finding completely, or the consideration of a finding as not interesting may also mean that it goes unreported. The reflective addendum by Amanda Potts thoughtfully addresses some of these points. However, with that said, we note overlaps in findings between the corpus-driven approaches. For example, both the lexical bundle and the multi-dimensional analyses noted the highly interactive aspect of the Q+A forums, with the Family & Relationships forums being most involved. Also, the keyword and key semantic categories approaches found that the UK had more focus around (im)politeness and mentions of US politics, as well as India using more acronyms. These two approaches also had similar findings relating to religion.

With the corpus-based approaches, this tended to be where we found the least amount of overlap or shared findings, perhaps because these researchers began from a position of narrowing their focus to a specific aspect of language use. These findings were often not as wide-ranging as the other approaches and the choice of what to look for became crucial. For example, Chapter 8, which considered a range of pragmatic features, used a predetermined list of words that were searched for. One word which was not included in this list was *sorry*, which emerged as an interesting keyword for the British subcorpus in Chapter 2. However, even with the corpus-based approaches, if different approaches were taken to examine the same feature, it was heartening to see agreement. For example, Chapters 6 and 8 both considered the communicative purpose of questions across the corpus. Chapter 6, which considered collocates of question words, concluded that the questions had a social function for eliciting personal response and building rapport, with many questions tending to seek opinions or personal advice rather than facts. Similarly, Chapter 8, which looked at the questions more qualitatively, found that 13% of them did not appear to be seeking information as their primary goal.

Finally, with the qualitative approaches, the issue of sampling becomes crucial. A rare feature in a small sample size risks getting blown out of proportion, although we found it interesting that there was overlap between the qualitative and corpus approaches in terms of what they found. Erez Levon who wrote Chapter 10, for example, agreed with Jonathan and Claire in Chapter 8 in noting that the UK tended to use the fewest information-seeking questions, while Erez also noted that the UK tended to be more secular in tone than other varieties, agreeing with approaches made by three other authors. Jesse Egbert who wrote Chapter 11, which involved reader perceptions of a sample of the questions, agreed with the multi-dimensional analysis in Chapter 5 that the UK used more features of interpersonal interaction. Perhaps most interestingly, the other qualitative approach (Chapter 10), also made this point. However, Chapters 5 and 10 disagreed on another point relating to the extent that American responses were informational. Sampling, even when carefully done, may not always result in a set of findings that can be widely generalized beyond itself (although we need to bear in mind that the corpus itself is a sample from a wider population).

An issue relating to all forms of analysis, and a point we signposted in Chapter 1, is that the presence of a difference tended to be viewed as more interesting (requiring greater focus and interpretation) than an absence of one. Most of the analysis in the chapters has thus foregrounded cases where there are differences. In providing a research question with two parts which allowed analysts to focus on either cultural or topic variation, it is interesting to see how most analysts responded to the question, tending to focus on cultural variation as long as it provided something interesting to say in relation to differences. When it did not, the second part of the question tended to be addressed (e.g., with Chapters 3 and 10). Similarities may not exactly be 'non-findings', but they are certainly seen as reason to find something additional to say.

Reflecting on the Individual Methods

In this section, we reflect on the various methods used in this study in terms of their strengths and limitations. This includes a summary of commentary from the authors on the methods they used, as well as our own synopsis of each method.

Keywords

In Chapter 2, Tony McEnery described keyword analysis as a useful method for comparing corpora in order to discover what makes them distinctive or similar. He emphasized the need for contextualization and interpretation—in the form of close reading of concordance lines and investigating collocations—both of which require sufficient data to support conclusions. He also noted that keyword analysis relies on accurate tools in order to reduce error. He concluded his chapter by encouraging researchers to triangulate keyword analysis with other methods.

Tony's insightful commentary on keyword analysis seems to be a fair one. The usefulness of corpus-driven methods, such as keyword analysis, depends on contextualization and interpretation from the researcher. Without this, we are left with nothing more than the product of automated computer algorithms. One of the obvious limitations of keyword analysis is that it does not typically account for variation beyond the word (e.g., phraseology, grammar, pragmatics). However, Tony demonstrated one way in which keyword findings can be used in conjunction with grammatical information in his analysis of modal verbs.

Semantic Annotation

Amanda Potts described semantic annotation as a method that is ideal for comparing small corpora. This is because analyzing individual word types gives an advantage to highly frequent words, especially in small corpora. In contrast, grouping words by meaning highlights important semantic categories that may be otherwise overlooked. Amanda emphasized that while semantic annotation is ideal for exploratory analysis, it should not be viewed as a comprehensive analytical approach. Like Tony McEnery in his description of keyword analysis, Amanda emphasized the benefits of triangulating this type of semantic analysis with other corpus research methods.

The results of Amanda's semantic field analysis speak for themselves. This method is clearly a useful approach that can reveal semantic patterns that would be otherwise difficult to identify. Her comment on the usefulness of this approach for small corpora is an interesting one. The issue of type distributions in linguistic data has perplexed corpus linguists for decades. Semantic field analysis allows the researcher to analyze aggregated word frequencies based on shared meanings. This seems to be a viable means of mitigating the effect of individual word-type frequencies.

Amanda also demonstrated how keyness can be applied to semantic domains in order to identify distinctive characteristics of a particular subcorpus. This is a great example of the benefits of triangulation. By applying a keyness approach to semantic field analysis, Amanda was able to capitalize on the strengths of both approaches.

Lexical Bundles

Bethany Gray began her chapter by describing the lexical bundles methodology as fully corpus driven. She demonstrated throughout her study that these are important and meaningful linguistic units that are typically ignored by other methods. She concluded with a discussion of lexical bundle functions and the impact of particular methodological choices she made on the results that she reported. According to Bethany, lexical bundle functions are context-dependent, and this would need to be accounted for in order to produce a more precise analysis.

Like keyword analysis and semantic annotation, the lexical bundle approach is not designed to be a comprehensive analysis at every linguistic level. However, it is somewhat surprising to witness the amount of lexical, phraseological, grammatical, and functional information that can be extracted from an analysis of frequent four-word sequences.

Multi-dimensional Analysis

Multi-dimensional analysis is perhaps unique among the ten methods included in this experiment in that the authors claim it provides an 'overall linguistic profile of corpora' in contrast with studies that 'focus largely on isolated linguistic and functional features of texts'. According to Eric Friginal and Doug Biber, the strengths of MD analysis lie in its ability to simultaneously account for many lexical, grammatical, and semantic features in order to produce a smaller set of latent linguistic dimensions.

The results of the MD analysis certainly offer support for its comprehensiveness. The functional dimension of involved versus informational production is supported by a range of linguistic features. In combination, those features seem to be strong predictors of both country and topic area. Clearly, MD analysis can offer unparalleled insights into the use of a wide range of functionally related linguistic features. However, MD analysis is not without its limitations. This method relies heavily on quantifiable variables. Linguistic questions that depend on qualitative analytical techniques (e.g., Chapters 8 and 10) are beyond the scope of the MD approach. Moreover, questions relating to relationships among words (e.g., Chapters 3 and 6) are typically outside of the scope of MD analysis.

Collocation Networks

Vaclav Brezina described collocation networks as 'effective exploratory summaries of different aspects of texts or discourses'. Throughout his chapter, he emphasized several benefits of this approach, including the visualization of complex lexical association patterns and the efficiency with which it allows researchers to analyze those patterns. He discussed the need for additional investigation of qualitative patterns in concordance lines in order to fully interpret the meaning relationship patterns.

Collocation networks are indeed an appealing approach for analyzing collocations. One of the major challenges of describing lexical associations is that they are intricate and interwoven. However, as with many of the other methods included in this volume, this method is most likely to produce meaningful results when coupled with other methods.

Variationist Analysis

Stefan Gries offered the most comprehensive methodological discussion of all of the authors. He began his chapter with a detailed comparison of two fundamentally different methods for analyzing corpus data. The first was based on frequencies of occurrence for particular linguistic features. The second, which he labels 'the variationist case-by-variable approach', was based on the identification of predictors of linguistic alternants. He argued that the former approach is not particularly useful beyond simple explorations of (de-contextualized) frequencies. He noted in his postscript that his chapter was an outlier in the sense that it was narrow in scope rather than being a broad exploratory study.

The variationist approach used by Stefan is an undoubtedly useful approach for answering a range of research questions related to linguistic alternation and the contextual factors related to it. This approach, however, cannot address other questions. The variationist approach is typically limited to a single dichotomy between two linguistic alternants. Currently, there are not established methods for analyzing alternation beyond a two-way dichotomy, although some have been proposed. Furthermore, while the variationist approach is ideal for comprehensive analyses of linguistic features, it is not ideally suited for comprehensive analyses of linguistic varieties. The findings from methods such as MD analysis and keyword analysis would not be possible from a variationist framework. One thing is clear, the variationist approach is certainly complementary to the many other methods in corpus linguistics.

Pragmatic Features

Jonathan Culpeper and Claire Hardaker began their chapter by noting the challenges inherent to corpus pragmatics. However, in this chapter, they proposed a methodology for identifying pragmatic forms that are based on Wmatrix, the same semantic annotation program used by Amanda Potts in her semantic field analysis. They demonstrated that this approach allowed them to identify conventionalized pragmatic forms for analysis. The major limitation mentioned by the authors is that the features they investigated are often low in frequency. Thus they suggest that the method they propose may be ideal for exploratory purposes.

One of the intriguing aspects of the method used in this chapter was the combination of automatic identification of pragmatic markers and manual mapping of form and function. This multi-method approach is a clear example of the benefits of methodological triangulation. Overall, this exploratory approach to identifying and interpreting pragmatic markers seems to be a promising avenue for an inherently challenging area of research.

Gendered Discourses

Chapter 9 focused on an analysis of discourse patterns related to gender. Paul Baker states that a major benefit of corpus linguistics is the opportunity to make generalizations beyond a researcher's dataset. The method in this chapter focused first on a qualitative investigation of extended concordance lines in order to identify cases of gendered discourse. These cases were then counted in order to measure the extent to which gendered discourses differed across the four varieties of English. One limitation of this approach that Paul noted was the low frequencies for some of the gendered discourse patterns. This challenge was mentioned by authors in more than one chapter. While this could certainly be related to queries of low-frequency phenomena, it was definitely related to the relatively small size of the corpus in this study.

One of the most prominent strengths of this study is the critical interaction between qualitative and quantitative data. After identifying cases of a particular gendered discourse using a qualitative approach, these cases were quantified. The quantitative results were then thoroughly interpreted and explained. Using this approach, quantitative and qualitative methods, which are often seen as competing approaches, were seamlessly interwoven in this study.

Qualitative Analysis of Stance

Erez Levon's analysis of stance markers was entirely qualitative. As such, it was beneficial to limit the size of the corpus sample for analysis. Therefore, he used ProtAnt, a new tool for measuring the degree to which a given text is (lexically) 'typical' of the corpus it was drawn from. This is an innovative approach to creating a corpus sub-sample. Erez mentions that this is beneficial since it allows for a detailed examination of all of the texts in the sample. The clear limitation is that all findings are based on the sub-sample, raising questions about generalizability.

The benefits of this wholly qualitative approach are evident in the rich, contextualized linguistic description offered in this chapter. Whereas other authors may have struggled to find space for illustrative textual examples, this analysis is entirely focused on them. There were also multiple points of overlap between Levon's findings and the results of the quantitative approaches. Obvious limitations aside, a strictly qualitative approach to corpus linguistics seems to have a great deal of insight that naturally complements other approaches.

Stylistic Perception Analysis

Jesse Egbert's approach was unique among the other chapters in this volume in that it drew on data outside of the corpus sample itself. He measured audience perceptions of texts from the corpus. Like the preceding chapter, this was done on a sub-sample of the corpus. However, instead of endeavoring to select typical texts, Egbert used random selection. While it is beyond the scope of this study, it would be interesting to compare the results of the two sampling methods to systematically compare their contents. Regardless of which sampling approach is used, both are necessarily limited by the simple fact that they are sub-samples. Egbert presents Stylistic Perception analysis as an additional perspective on corpus data that allows expert linguists insight into the perceptions and reactions of actual target audience members of the discourse they analyze.

One obvious limitation of this approach is the challenge of collecting reader perception data. In the case of this study, only US readers were sampled, thus limiting the generalizability of the results. Additionally, the reliability of audience perceptions is questionable. However, the results shown here seem to suggest that they are quite reliable. Overall, this seems to be an innovative method that naturally lends itself to triangulation with many other corpus methods.

Assessing Methodological Triangulation

In this section, we make some general observations on the use of methodological triangulation in corpus-linguistic research. After addressing several of the benefits of methodological triangulation, we present some of the challenges associated with it.

Benefits

As the previous chapters have indicated, there are a multitude of specific benefits associated with methodological triangulation. In this section, we focus on three which we have identified as most important.

First, methodological triangulation allows researchers to validate their data through cross-checking the results of two or more approaches. Corpus-linguistic researchers regularly discover findings of interest in corpora designed to represent a discourse domain of interest. When this happens, the typical assumption is that the finding is *real* and *generalizable* to the larger target population the (representative) corpus sample is drawn from. However, there is another possibility; it may be the case that a particular finding is nothing more than an artifact of the method used to discover and measure the phenomenon. In other words, if this finding is indeed *real* and *generalizable*, then we should be able to find a similar result using a different methodological approach. This use of methodological triangulation is a powerful means of cross-checking results in order to offer additional support for the validity of the finding. Throughout the chapters in this volume, this type of validation research has not been the primary focus. However, the results from the various chapters have offered insight into cases where multiple methods agreed or disagreed on particular findings. As we have seen in previous sections, however, the vast majority of the findings were unique to a single method. This relates to the next benefit.

Second, then, methodological triangulation provides a more thorough, complete picture of discourse than that which could be discovered using a single method. Human behavior, especially behavior related to language, is remarkably complex and multi-faceted. This is the reason that researchers in corpus linguistics—or any of the social sciences, for that matter—have not been able to find a single methodological approach that can tell us everything that we want to know about every feature. We began the research experiment for this volume based on that assumption. However, even we were surprised at how few of the findings were mentioned by more than one author. Based on counting the number of cells in Tables 12.2–12.4 and taking each cell as a finding (in itself an underestimate, as many cells contain multiple findings) and then noting the proportion of cells that contain shared findings, 74% of the findings were only mentioned by the researcher(s) of one methodological approach. Clearly, we are overlooking an immense amount of information about a particular discourse domain when we explore it using only one method. It seems we are only finding a few pieces of a large puzzle with each method. In order to discover more pieces, we need to approach the same data using more than one technique, and in order to have confidence that our picture is comprehensive, we will need to triangulate many methodological approaches.

A third benefit of methodological triangulation is increased collaboration in the field of corpus linguistics. Research collaboration among two or more scholars is relatively commonplace in contemporary corpus research. However, it seems that the most typical collaborative scenario involves multiple scholars who use the same research question with the same method. This type of collaborative relationship is undoubtedly beneficial. It is likely to increase the quality of the research and decrease the amount of time required to complete a given study. However, the type of collaboration we propose in this volume is based on a different scenario, one in which multiple scholars who are experts of different methods come together to triangulate the results of their methods in order to learn more about a discourse domain than they could if they each analyzed it independently. We believe there are many benefits associated with this type of collaboration. Two of the benefits are directly related to two of the challenges we discuss in the next section: time and expertise. Another benefit is that scholars from different methodological (and possibly theoretical) orientations can come together in order to achieve better answers to shared questions. This type of collaboration is likely to build bridges and produce positive synergy among corpus linguists as they recognize that their methods are not in competition, but complementary. The variety of methods in corpus-linguistic research has the potential to fragment corpus researchers into camps that compete with each other or, worse yet, that stop communicating with each other altogether. Yet this fragmentation is not inevitable. Through methodological triangulation, corpus researchers from different methodological orientations could maintain open lines of communication and synergistic collaborative relationships.

In terms of what the research synthesis can tell us about triangulation of methods around corpus linguistics, it is hopefully clear that an approach which uses more than one method is going to offer a more comprehensive picture of language variation than any single approach could on its own.

In writing this book, we were fortunate in that we were able to recruit people who were experts in their chosen method, and while all of the approaches have demonstrated different sets of strengths and weaknesses, we would argue that viewing the multiple sets of findings in combination will help to compensate for individual weaknesses. In cases where multiple approaches have found the same finding, we can be more confident of the claim that has been made. Cases of complementary findings indicate that no single approach can do everything, helping to provide a justification for triangulatory methods.

How do we view the contradictory or dissonant findings though? At the start of the book, we expressed concern at the possibility that our ten analysts would all disagree with one another. Thankfully that has not shown to be the case, although the separate analyses did indicate a couple of instances of disagreement. The fact that there were only a small number of these is in itself encouraging, and we may want to view these contradictory findings as positive outcomes, perhaps indicating that the features under examination are particularly complex and deserving of further study. Our comparison also suggests, though, that methodological perspective can result in contradictions and has a wider implication for disagreements between researchers which may be found in the field. The methodological approaches involved need to be queried and considered in terms of their ability to do justice to the questions asked.

We hope that people reading this book will take with them a more nuanced understanding of the pros and cons of the different sorts of methods they could potentially use on corpus texts, which may mean they either engage in forms of triangulation themselves, or they exercise caution in terms of the claims they make. And ultimately, we hope that the book will promote synergy rather than fragmentation. With a potentially wide range of 'doing things' within corpus linguistics, it is perhaps easy to develop or adopt a method and stick with it throughout a range of different projects, simply applying that one approach to different corpus data. A possible problem with such a mindset is that it may not acknowledge that different corpora or questions may require a new tool, or a set of tools, rather than our favorite one. Rather than arguing that one approach can do everything, corpus linguistics as a field will stand to benefit if its adherents are cognizant of the range of approaches that can be taken and know when to use or combine different elements. We thus hope to encourage analysts to experiment with a wider range of methods than the ones they normally use.

Challenges

There are, however, challenges associated with methodological triangulation. While we believe that the benefits outweigh and compensate for these challenges, we think it is important to acknowledge three of them here. The first challenge is that of time. Applying more than one method to analyze a particular discourse domain will inevitably require a greater time commitment. Researchers whose primary concern is to produce linguistic descriptions in the most efficient way possible may view the use of more than one method as a potential waste of time. We hope, however, that we have sufficiently demonstrated throughout this volume that triangulation is well worth the time commitment. Moreover, researchers who effectively collaborate on triangulation research are likely to find that they are able to save time through division of labor.

The second major challenge associated with triangulation is methodological expertise. Many researchers in corpus linguistics are most comfortable approaching data with a limited set of methods. The work and time required to develop enough expertise to apply an unfamiliar technique is understandably daunting. Another benefit of collaboration among researchers is the possibility of combining two or more different skill sets to the same data. We believe this is the ideal scenario for effectively applying methodological triangulation to a corpus. Not only does this save researchers from having to become experts in a novel research methodology, it also offers greater credibility and quality to the study.

The final challenge of methodological triangulation is the amount of space required to write the methods, results, and discussion for publication. Many journals have strict limits for the maximum page length or word count of submitted manuscripts. Meeting these requirements presents special challenges to studies that include more than one methodology. We feel that this should not deter researchers from pursuing methodological triangulation in their corpus research. However, it should be acknowledged that these researchers will need to be creative and succinct in their writing in order to accommodate all of the information. We call on editors and publishers to be sensitive to these special challenges by being flexible enough to make special space allowances for researchers who are endeavoring to apply multiple methods in a single study, and we believe the increase in study quality will more than compensate for the challenges associated with these special arrangements.

Implications and Future Research

In this section, we offer several practical implications of the findings in this volume for corpus researchers. The first implication is probably the most obvious one. Methodological triangulation is a powerful means of carrying out corpus-linguistic research. Our results showed that while contradictions are rare, incompleteness is to be expected from a single research method. Therefore, triangulation should be seriously considered by corpus-linguistic researchers as a viable means of getting answers to their questions that are more complete and valid.

A second implication of our study is that not all methods are equally well suited to every research question or language corpus. During the early stages of this research experiment, we worked hard to carefully select research questions that could be answered using any of the methods included in this volume. We also spent a great deal of time designing a corpus of Q+A forums that was amenable to analysis using each of the research methods. The compromises we made during this process necessarily resulted in challenges for each of the researchers. For example, researchers such as Amanda Potts, Jonathan Culpeper and Claire Hardaker, and Bethany Gray mentioned that they would have benefited from access to a much larger corpus of Q+A forums. On the other hand, Erez Levon and Jesse Egbert were both required to subsample from the corpus because it was impractical to analyze each text in the full corpus using their methods. These challenges illustrate two important implications of this research experiment. First, researchers should select or create a corpus that is well suited for the research question they want to answer. Second, researchers should select methods that are well suited for answering a particular research question with the corpus they have.

A third implication is that there is a need for contextualizing research findings in terms of a study's particulars. Our results have highlighted the strong relationship between choices of researchers and the results they find. When researchers write up the results of their studies, they should discuss their methodological choices in detail. This should include an overview of what method they selected and why, as well as all of the specific choices they made when carrying out the method on their corpus. Researchers should also include a discussion of any specific preferences they have when using that particular method and interpreting the results. We have seen from the chapters in this book that all of these choices impact on the results that researchers find and the way that they interpret those results. It would also be good for researchers to try to surmise and report on what their study does *not* tell us about the discourse domain under study. Our study has clearly illustrated that any single methodological approach is only giving us a fraction of the full picture.

A fourth implication of this study is that there is a need for more replication-based research. In our experiment, we have focused on what we can learn from multiple approaches to the same corpus. During our study, we also showed, however, that there is likely to be substantial variability across multiple studies that use the same method. Replication studies are quite rare in corpus linguistics. This may be due in part to our overconfidence in the results of a single study. There seems to be an assumption that as long as a corpus is large, it will not be difficult to identify important patterns of discourse using a particular method. However, our results have shown that a large amount of variability in what is found is due to methodological choice. Replication studies could be used to study the role of these choices in more detail. It would also be beneficial to replicate studies in order to cross-check the validity of results from a single study.

A fifth implication of this study is that corpus researchers would benefit from more methodological commentary in major corpus journals. Clearly there is a great deal we have yet to learn about corpus-linguistic methods in terms of the improvement of existing methods, the development of new methods, and the triangulation of multiple methods. Journals such as *International Journal of Corpus Linguistics*, *Corpora*, and *Corpus Linguistics and Linguistic Theory* encourage the submission of methodologically oriented papers. While this type of paper certainly appears in these journals, it is not nearly as common as it could be. We call on corpus researchers to contribute high-quality methodological commentary to improve corpus-linguistic methods. We also call on the editors of corpus-related journals to continue to encourage and accept high-quality methodological research.

A sixth and final implication of this study is the need for further research of the type carried out in this volume. As we discussed in Chapter 1, only a handful of studies have been carried out to investigate the potential of methodological triangulation in corpus linguistics. The current volume constitutes the most extensive study of this nature to date. However, there is still much that can be done in this area. Researchers could attempt to replicate our experiment (possibly on a much smaller scale) using a different corpus, different research questions, different methodological approaches, and/or different researchers. All of these were variables that played a role in the outcome of our study. Modifying these variables would certainly enhance our understanding of the role of these variables, specifically, and the strengths and challenges of methodological triangulation, in general.

Limitations of Our Experiment

The overarching experiment we carried out in this volume has a number of limitations. With one corpus, we must take care in generalizing our findings too much. As noted earlier, replication studies which use different corpora would shed more light on the role and benefits of triangulation within corpus linguistics. Such studies could use a similarly constructed Q+A corpus which either contains different questions or questions from different cultures or forums. Alternatively, it would be interesting to consider triangulation approaches on a completely different corpus or one which is divided into different subcorpora (or is not divided at all).

Our study has indicated that cutoffs for what is viewed as statistically significant have a huge impact in terms of making something into a 'finding' that is subjected to more detailed analysis. Cutoffs are often imposed rather arbitrarily within corpus linguistics, though, and may even be reflective of other forms of cutoffs (journal word count limits or submission deadlines), which may reflect how much analysis can be carried out. In spite of this, cutoffs impose a kind of reification and authorization onto our findings. In terms of a follow-up triangulation study, it would be interesting to ask analysts to carry out a broadly similar method (such as a keywords approach), but to apply different cutoff points and then conduct a comparison of findings.

However, we should also note the experimental nature of this study and ask whether it actually reflected the types of research projects that analysts engage in in their everyday work lives. To an extent, the analysts involved in this project were limited by our (relatively short) deadlines and word limits, whereas many research projects can take much longer and authors can be more verbose in terms of reporting findings. Also, we forced our analysts to limit themselves to a single technique, whereas, realistically, some may use a combination of techniques or may have selected a different technique than the one we asked them to use (or switched to a different one) had they been given the opportunity. The amount of freedom afforded to analysts in these kinds of comparative studies is likely to impact on the results found, in other words.

Concluding Comments

In this volume, we have attempted to evaluate the strengths and challenges of methodological triangulation in corpus linguistics. We developed a two-part research question and created a corpus designed to represent Q+A forum discourse in four world English varieties and three topic areas. Ten researchers independently applied ten different corpus-linguistic methods to our corpus in order to answer the research question we developed. Each presented their findings in a short chapter. We then synthesized and summarized their findings and compared and contrasted their research methods. Finally, we offered our assessments of the strengths and challenges of methodological triangulation in corpus linguistics and its potential to improve the quality of research in this area.

At the beginning of this book, we asked whether all corpus methods lead to Rome. To continue the metaphor, we would conclude that most of them will lead to different parts of Rome. In other words, many of the findings detailed over the ten analysis chapters in this book were not shared, but were complementary—providing different parts of an overall jigsaw puzzle which enabled a holistic view of the nature of the Q+A corpus and its subsets. There were a few cases of shared findings, but they were relatively less frequent than the complementary ones and tended to involve only between two and four of the ten analysts. We thus note that, on the whole, different techniques are most likely to produce different results and should not be viewed as simply 'interchangeable'. Ultimately, then, the message to take away from this book is that within corpus linguistics, the choice of the techniques that are to be applied to our data is hugely important, and we would be well advised to experiment with multiple approaches and to reflect on which one(s) can best answer our research questions.

While there are certainly challenges inherent to triangulation research, we believe the benefits of triangulation make efforts to overcome these challenges worthwhile. Moreover, the challenges associated with triangulation research may help motivate corpus linguists to develop synergy in their research through effective collaborative relationships with scholars from different research orientations. Ultimately, we believe we have shown that methodological triangulation is a very promising, if not necessary, direction for future corpus-linguistic research.

Contributors

Paul Baker is Professor of English Language at Lancaster University. His research involves applications of corpus linguistics and his recent books include *Using Corpora to Analyze Gender* (2014), *Discourse Analysis and Media Attitudes* (2013), and *Sociolinguistics and Corpus Linguistics* (2010). He is the commissioning editor of the journal *Corpora*.

Doug Biber is Regents' Professor of English (Applied Linguistics) at Northern Arizona University. His research efforts have focused on corpus linguistics, English grammar, and register variation (in English and cross-linguistic; synchronic and diachronic). He has written over 200 research articles, 8 edited books, and 15 authored books and monographs; these include a textbook on *Register, Genre, and Style* (Cambridge 2009), the co-authored *Longman Grammar of Spoken and Written English* (1999), and other academic books on grammatical complexity in academic English (Cambridge 2016), American university registers (Benjamins 2006), corpus-based discourse analysis (Benjamins 2007), and multi-dimensional analyses of register variation (Cambridge 1988, 1995).

Vaclav Brezina is a Senior Research Associate at the ESRC Centre for Corpus Approaches to Social Science, Lancaster University. His main research interests are in the areas of corpus methodology and design, statistics, and applied linguistics. He has also created software tools for corpus and statistical analysis.

Jonathan Culpeper is Professor of English Language and Linguistics in the Department of Linguistics and English Language at Lancaster University, UK. His work spans pragmatics, stylistics, and the history of English and is often underpinned by corpus methods. His most recent major publication was *Pragmatics and the English Language* (2014; with Michael Haugh). Until recently, he was co-editor-in-chief of the *Journal of Pragmatics*.

Jesse Egbert is Assistant Professor in the Department of Linguistics and English Language at Brigham Young University. His primary area of interest is register variation, mostly within the domains of academic writing and Internet language. He is also interested in corpus-linguistic methods such as corpus design and quantitative research designs.

Eric Friginal is an Associate Professor of Applied Linguistics at the Department of Applied Linguistics and ESL at Georgia State University (GSU), Atlanta, Georgia, US. He specializes in (applied) corpus linguistics, sociolinguistics, cross-cultural communication, distance learning, discipline-specific writing, bilingual education, and the analysis of spoken professional discourse. His recent book, *Corpus-Based Sociolinguistics: A Guide for Students* (Routledge) is co-authored with his doctoral student Jack A. Hardy.

Bethany Gray is Assistant Professor of English (Applied Linguistics and Technology program) at Iowa State University. Her research employs corpus linguistics methodologies to explore register variation in English, with a particular focus on the use of phraseological and lexicogrammatical features across registers.

Stefan Th. Gries earned his MA and PhD degrees at the University of Hamburg, Germany, in 1998 and 2000. He is a Professor of Linguistics in the Department of Linguistics at the University of California, Santa Barbara (UCSB) and Honorary Liebig-Professor of the Justus-Liebig-Universität Giessen (since September 2011). Methodologically, he is at the intersection of corpus linguistics, cognitive linguistics, and computational linguistics and uses a variety of statistical methods to explore language from a usage-based/cognitive perspective.

Claire Hardaker is a Lecturer in Forensic Corpus Linguistics at Lancaster University. Her research focuses on online deception, aggression, and manipulation. She is currently working on a European Union project investigating the role of the Internet in human trafficking, and she was Principle Investigator on the recently completed ESRC-funded project, "Twitter Rape Threats and the Discourse of Online Misogyny" (ES/L008874/1). Claire is currently writing a book entitled *The Antisocial Network*.

Erez Levon is Senior Lecturer in Linguistics at Queen Mary University of London. His work uses quantitative, qualitative, and experimental methods to examine patterns of socially meaningful variation in language. He primarily focuses on the relationship between language and gender/sexuality and particularly on how they intersect with other categories of lived experience, including race, nation, and social class.

Tony McEnery is Professor of English Language and Linguistics at Lancaster University. He is the author of many books and papers on corpus linguistics, including *Corpus Linguistics: Method, Theory and Practice* (with Andrew Hardie, CUP 2011). He is currently director of the UK ESRC's Centre for Corpus Approaches to Social Science.

Amanda Potts is a Lecturer in Public and Professional Discourse at Cardiff University. Her research interests include corpus linguistics, (critical) discourse analysis, and representations of identity with a particular emphasis on discriminatory discourses. Her specialism is in interdisciplinary (often collaborative) approaches to discourse analysis, and her most recent publications are studies on the language of health care, the media, and the law.

Index